Classics of philosophy and science series, ed. Desmond Clarke

A. Arnauld
On True and False Ideas

Classics of philosophy and science, ed. Desmond Clarke

G. W. Leibniz *Discourse on Metaphysics and related writings*
Edited and translated by R. Niall D. Martin and Stuart Brown

François Poulain de la Barre *The Equality of the Sexes*
Translated with an introduction and notes by Desmond M. Clarke

A. Arnauld
On True and False Ideas

Translated, with an
introductory essay, by
Stephen Gaukroger

Manchester University Press
Manchester and New York

Distributed exclusively in the USA and Canada by St. Martin's Press

Published by Manchester University Press
Oxford Road, Manchester M13 9PL, UK
and Room 400, 175 Fifth Avenue,
New York, NY 10010, USA

*Distributed exclusively in the USA and Canada
by* St. Martin's Press, Inc.,
175 Fifth Avenue, New York, NY 10010, USA

British Library cataloguing in publication data
Arnauld, A. (Antoine)
    On true and false ideas.—(Classics of philosophy and
science series).
    1. Man. Cognition
    I. Title   II. Series
    153.4

Library of Congress cataloging in publication data
Arnauld, Antoine. 1612–1694.
    [Des vrayes et des fausses idées. English]
    On true and false ideas/A. Arnauld: translated, with an
introductory.essay, by Stephen Gaukroger
        p. cm. — (Classics of philosophy and science)
    Translation of: Des vrayes et des fausses idées.
    Includes bibliographical references.
    ISBN 0–7190–3203–2
    1. Malebranche, Nicolas, 1638–1715. Recherche de la vérité.
2. Knowledge, Theory of.   3. Occasionalism.   4. Perception—Early
works to 1800.   5. Languages—Philosophy.   I. Gaukroger, Stephen.
II. Title.   III. Series.
B1893.R33E5   1990
121—dc20   90–30773

ISBN 0 7190 3203 2 *hardback*

Photoset in Linotron Sabon
by Northern Phototypesetting Co. Ltd., Bolton

Printed in Great Britain
by Billing and Sons Ltd., Worcester

Contents

Preface

This is the first English translation of *On True and False Ideas*. For the translation, I have used the text provided in *Oeuvres philosophiques de Antoine Arnauld*, edited by Jules Simon (Paris, 1843). I have also consulted the text provided in volume 38 of *Oeuvres de Messire Antoine Arnauld* (43 vols., Paris, 1773–83), and that provided in *Logique de Port Royal, Objections contre les Méditations de Descartes, Traité des vrais et des fausses idées, par Arnauld* edited by C. Jourdain (Paris, 1864). There are no substantial differences between the editions, so far as I have been able to discover, the most significant divergence being in paragraph breaks. On all but those few occasions in which they seemed to me especially clumsy, I have followed the paragraph breaks in the Simon edition.

I have provided references to the standard English translations for all quotations from Descartes and Malebranche, although the translations are my own. The edition of *The Search after Truth* that Arnauld uses is in fact different from the final 1712 edition which Lennon and Olscamp use for their English translation, but this has not given rise to any significant problems in supplying cross-references. The reader should, however, be warned that Arnauld hardly ever quotes exactly, preferring to paraphrase, change syntax, or omit words or passages, so that the passages I have translated, which are of course Arnauld's own versions, will often have only a rough correspondence to those in the standard editions or in the standard translations which are cited.

My aim has been to produce an accurate but readable translation into modern English, and to the extent that I have succeeded in this aim I would like to thank Helen Irving for advice, and especially Desmond Clarke, who patiently looked over the whole translation and suggested numerous improvements. I am solely responsible for the defects which remain.

Abbreviations

AT   *Oeuvres de Descartes*, ed. Charles Adam and Paul Tannery, 11 vols., Paris, 1974–86.

CSM   *The Philosophical Writings of Descartes*, trans. John Cottingham, Robert Stoothoff and Dugald Murdoch, 2 vols., Cambridge, 1984–85.

OC   *Oeuvres complètes de Malebranche*, under the direction of André Robinet, 20 vols., Paris, 1958–70.

ST   *Nicholas Malebranche, The Search after Truth* and *Elucidations of the Search after Truth*, trans. Thomas M. Lennon and Paul J. Olscamp, Columbus, Ohio, 1980.

Introduction

The background to the problem of perceptual cognition

Arnauld's treatise *On True and False Ideas* (1683) is a reply to Malebranche's *Search after Truth*, the most influential philosophical treatise of the second half of the seventeenth century, eclipsed only at the end of that century by Locke's *Essay*. *The Search after Truth* was first published in two parts in 1674 and 1675, and a set of *Elucidations* was appended to the third edition of 1677–78, designed to answer objections and queries, and to clear up misunderstandings. Malebranche espoused a number of controversial doctrines in *The Search after Truth*, but other than his doctrine of grace, which was only fully developed elsewhere (in the *Short Meditations of Humility and Penitence* of 1677 and especially in the *Treatise on Nature and Grace* of 1680), the two most contentious doctrines were his occasionalism and his doctrine of ideas. The first was not especially contentious among Cartesians (for reasons we shall look at below), but it did issue in a famous exchange with Leibniz. The second, which is our concern here, was fiercely opposed by Cartesians, although it drew its inspiration partly from doctrines to be found in Descartes himself. My aim in this introductory essay is to provide some philosophical background to the dispute between Malebranche and Arnauld on the nature and origin of ideas.

At first glance, it is tempting to see the dispute as one between a radically new account of ideas and a reasonably orthodox Cartesian account. But some degree of support for both accounts can in fact be found in Descartes, and both can be seen as developments of Cartesianism, albeit of opposing kinds. The issues revolve around the question of perceptual cognition. Descartes had established a central role for ideas in perceptual cognition but the exact nature of the role is somewhat ambiguous, and his account of the issue was so problematic that it became the central question for the Cartesian tradition, one on which it ultimately came to grief.[1] Just what is problematic about it is best illustrated by comparing it with the earlier conception of perceptual cognition which originates with Aristotle and which forms the basis for the medieval treatment of the question.

But before we look in any detail at the difference between Descartes' account and the Aristotelian one, and the subsequent debates within Cartesianism, it may be helpful if some of the principal differences between the Cartesian account and the traditional Aristotelian one are set out in summary fashion. The key issues in assessing Descartes' accounts of perception, I want to argue, are the following:

Mechanism. Although there had been a number of natural philosophies in antiquity which implied that the world must be very different from how it appears to us (Epicureanism and Neoplatonism being the most important in this respect), the Aristotelian conception of the natural world, which was the dominant one in the Middle Ages and Renaissance, was one on which the world actually has all the properties and qualities that our perceptual processes lead us to ascribe to it. On the mechanistic construal of the natural world, however, it has very few of these properties. A great gap is opened up between what we perceive the world to be like and what it really is like. This poses distinctive problems about the precise role of perceptual cognition and about the status of information gleaned perceptually which do not arise on the Aristotelian account.

Dualism. Aristotelian psychology was largely naturalistic, and the mind was conceived principally as the 'organising principle' of the body. There is no difference in kind, on Aristotle's conception, between what perceives and knows and what is perceived and known. On Descartes' account, of course, there is such a difference of kind, one so radical its seems unbridgeable. Here we have a new problem wholly alien to Aristotle's own thought, and quite different from medieval problems about the nature of the soul.

Dissolution of a comprehensive theory of vision. Aristotle's account of perceptual cognition integrated epistemology, physiology, psychology, metaphysics and natural philosophy into a broad and powerful unified theory. In the seventeenth century, perceptual cognition, which had previously been seen as a single philosophical subject, became split up into a number of disciplines – optics, physiology, psychology, epistemology – which no longer had any obvious or clear connections with one another, and which were not even always consistent with one another. The epistemology of perceptual cognition became especially problematic. Aristotle's account had involved a commitment to the most obvious and natural epistemology for a theory of vision, resemblance: what you saw resembled what was there in the world. Developments in optics and physiology, combined with a commitment to mechanism, undermined the resemblance view. But trying to put the revised pieces back together again failed to yield a coherent epistemology of vision. It is such a coherent epistemology that Malebranche and Arnauld, in their different ways, attempt to provide.

Compatibility with Christian teaching. It was an assumption of seventeenth-century philosophy, just as it was of medieval philosophy, that knowledge is a tripartite relationship involving God, His creation, and human beings. It is not just that the natural world that we seek to know has been created by God, but that our sensory/cognitive organs and faculties have been created by God also. Once it is maintained, for whatever reason, that our perceptual images of the world differ in systematic ways from how the world is in its own right, then the medieval belief that God has given us our sensory and cognitive organs and faculties so that we might know His creation (and in doing so come to know its creator, to however small an extent) is no longer sustainable. This puts an onus on seventeenth-century philosophers not only to show that God does not deliberately deceive us by providing us with sense organs which systematically mislead us, but also to provide some account of why God chose to give us these particular organs.

Among these points, the first and second have been recognised by commentators but they have sometimes been run together. It is quite wrong to do this, for even though dualism is (I believe) very dependent upon mechanism, there were plenty of mechanists in the seventeenth century – Gassendi and Hobbes for example – who were not dualists, and their adherence to mechanism gives rise to problems about the nature of the perceptual process and representation which are common to all mechanists, whether dualist or not. As we shall see, in the dispute between Malebranche and Arnauld mechanism is as much a source of problems as dualism is. This has sometimes been obscured by the mistaken view that Malebranche's occasionalism, one of the most distinctive features of his philosophy, is exclusively a response of the mind/body problem. In fact occasionalism was as crucial to his attempt to provide a coherent mechanist account of natural philosophy as it was to his attempt to establish what the nature of the relation between mind and body was.

Of the four points, the third is that which has been most seriously neglected, and with the assumption of mechanism, which is a crucial contributory factor in the dissolution of a comprehensive theory of vision, it is absolutely central to an understanding of why Cartesianism had so much difficulty trying to provide a satisfactory account of perceptual cognition and the role of ideas in it. This will be my guiding thread in what follows. I want to show what the unity of the Aristotelian account of perceptual cognition lay in; how this unity was unwittingly undermined in medieval accounts of perceptual cognition inspired by Aristotle; how it was decisively destroyed in Descartes and how he tried to reshape the understanding of perceptual cognition drawing on his work in optics, ocular anatomy and natural philosophy; and finally how conflicting strands of thought in Descartes were taken up and developed in Malebranche and Arnauld. One thing that I hope will become clear in all this is that the disagreement between Malebranche and Arnauld is not just a local dispute within Cartesianism, but one that goes to the very core of the way in which epistemology was reshaped in the seventeenth century.

The unity of the Aristotelian account of perception[2]

In the *De Anima* (428^b 17–25), Aristotle distinguishes between three different kinds of perceptual object or 'sensible' (*aisthēton*), which he calls special sensibles (*idia aisthēta*), incidental sensibles (*kata sunbebēkos aisthēta*), and common sensibles (*koina aisthēta*). Special sensibles, with a qualification I shall come to, are those sensibles that are perceived by one sense only: colour, for example, is a special sensible because it is perceived by vision alone, and not by hearing, taste, touch or smell. The principal case of incidental sensibles is that of those sensibles that are not special to any of the senses, but which we perceive incidentally when we perceive special sensibles; when I see or hear the son of Diares, for example, I am seeing or hearing special sensibles, and in virtue of this I am seeing or hearing him, but he himself is not a special sensible. Finally, common sensibles are those sensibles that are common to more than one sense: shape, for example, is as appropriate to vision as it is to touch, although when I see a shape by means of colour, or feel it by means of tactile sensations, I am in each case perceiving a different sensible. Aristotle tells us that our degree of liability to error increases in each case. It is virtually non-existent in the first case, provided certain conditions are met; it is present in the second case, however, and most prevalent in the third. The way in which Aristotle deals with perception here not only cuts across what were later separated into optical, physiological, epistemological and psychological questions, but the epistemology which provides the dominant and unifying strand in his account is often directed towards different kinds of questions from those we find in the seventeenth century. It is of paramount importance, for my interpretation, that we capture what the coherence of Aristotle's account consists in, so I want to discuss the three cases of perception in turn.

Although Aristotle allows that error may arise in the case of perception of special sensibles (428^b18), he immediately qualifies this by saying that as long as a perception genuinely occurs, it will be veridical (*alēthos*). This is in line with statements that Aristotle makes elsewhere to the effect that error never occurs in the perception of special sensibles (*de An.* 427^b18, 428^a11, 430^b29; *de Sens.* 442^b8; *Metaph.* 1010^b2) or even that error is impossible in such cases (*de An.* 418^a13). The question we must ask is why error does not arise in such cases. Aristotle seems to be claiming that when, for example, I perceive something white then, because this is the proper object of vision, the belief that it is white cannot be false. It is clear that Aristotle is not simply conflating the belief that there is something white in front of me with the belief that I am having a white sensation. For such a conflation would apply equally well to common and incidental sensibles: it would mean that I cannot be mistaken when I visually perceive something's sweetness, which is a kind of incidental sensible (a kind I shall look at below). Yet Aristotle makes it very clear that he considers the perception of incidental and common sensibles to be liable to error.

What, then, is so distinctive about special sensibles? The answer to this question is to be found in the *De Anima*, 418^a 24–5, where Aristotle remarks that the special sensibles are the really primary (*kurios*) sensibles and that the essence of each sense, or more strictly speaking sense organ, is naturally adapted to its respective special sensibles. He even tries to give this a foundation in natural philo-sophy: at the beginning of the third Book of the *De Anima*, he insists that there can only be five senses, because it can be shown that these are sufficient to respond to the four elements that everything is made from.[3] But leaving to one side this kind of justification, what Aristotle is maintaining, as Block has pointed out,[4] is that each sense is fitted to perceive one specific kind of sensible so that the natural function of these senses is activated when they are actually perceiving their respective special sensibles. When each organ functions properly it fulfills its purpose properly since otherwise nature would have made an imperfection in a fully developed organ. In the case of vision, this means that our perception of colours is accurate under normal circumstances, i.e. in circumstances which are natural to, and therefore optimum to, the functioning of the sense organ. The incorrigibility attaching to the perception of special sensibles by their respective senses is, therefore, something that depends upon Aristot-le's teleological view of the function of our sense organs.

If we accept this teleology, then we can simply argue that such perception must be incorrigible because it is the standard by which we judge veridicality. Vision under normal circumstances is the only standard we have by which to determine what colour something is. The question of incorrigibility arises because conditions are not always normal; it does not arise because there is some other standard by which to judge corrigibility in the case of normal perception. The situation is analogous to that of the standard metre rod. We can ask whether the metre rod is in fact a metre long in that we can ask whether the conditions (temperature and pressure) match those specified for the rod to be used as a standard, but once we are satisfied that these normal or specified conditions hold there is no further question as to what length the rod is. It is a metre long and incorrigibly so because it could not be otherwise. It might truly be a metre long under other conditions, e.g. at high temperatures and high pressures where these exactly complement one another, but it is no longer incorrigibly a metre long under these conditions because they are not the specified ones. Similarly, bad atmospheric condi-tions and bad eyesight may complement one another so that we see nothing but sand dunes where others see mirages or whatever; our perception here would be veridical, in that we would see what was really there to be seen and nothing else, but it could hardly be said to be incorrigible.

There are, then, two components in Aristotle's argument that the senses are incorrigible with respect to their special sensibles. The first is a reliance on teleology, on the idea that we have the sense organs we do because they naturally display to us the nature of the world we wish to understand. The second is a notion of 'normal conditions' which involves the idea that veridicality is only guaranteed when our sensory organs are functioning normally and when the various concomitants of perception – e.g. the medium in the case of distance perception – are behaving normally.

Bearing in mind these two factors, we may now ask what kinds of error Aristotle considers to arise in the case of incidental perception and common perception.[5] If I am correct in construing *De Anima*, 428[b]ff. as maintaining that the perception of special sensibles is only corrigible under conditions which are not normal, then we have no reason to consider the different degrees of corrigibility attaching to incidental and common perception as being anything other than different *degrees*: in particular, we have no reason to construe them as being different in kind. There are, I suggest, conditions under which perception of all these kinds of sensibles is incorrigible but the conditions simply become more restrictive as we go down the list, the list here being that provided at 428[b] 17ff, which begins with the perception of special sensibles, which 'is liable to falsity to the least possible extent', then mentions the perception of incidental sensibles, and finishes with the remark that 'it is most possible to be in error' about the perception of common sensibles.

Aristotle's statement about common sensibles raises the question of why the perception of common sensibles should be more liable to error than that of special sensibles, and why it should be more liable to error than that of incidental sensibles. A clue to the answer to the first of these questions is given in the *De Sensu*, 442[b]8, where Aristotle argues that it is because the common sensibles are common to more than one sense that we are more liable to error in perceiving them. As far as I can see, there can only be one explanation of the 'because' in this passage. It is that we are more liable to error in the perception of common sensibles because no one of our senses is specifically designed to perceive them. Consider what happens when we visually perceive colour. The colours overlying the surfaces of visible bodies produce disturbances in the medium, which in turn acts on the sense organ (cf. *de An.*, 418[b]32ff.) The result of this instantaneous[6] process is that the watery substance of the eye assumes the colour of the object perceived. This does not happen when we visually perceive a common sensible such as shape since here it is in virtue of perceiving something else – the special sensible, in this case colour – that we perceive the common sensible, shape. Similarly in the more complex case of perceiving shapes by touch.[7]

Now it does not follow from the fact that our perception of special sensibles is incorrigible, under the normal conditions peculiar to the senses by which we perceive these, that our perception of common sensibles by those senses is incorrigible. We genuinely perceive them, and we may truly perceive them, but our perception cannot be said to be incorrigible under these circumstances. The fact that our visual perception of shape can act as an independent check upon our tactile perception of shape, and vice versa, suggests that we can be wrong in at least one of these perceptions. But if both kinds of perception agree, and if they are both made under the normal conditions peculiar to those kinds of perception, can we now be wrong about what we see? I think Aristotle's answer would be that we cannot be wrong, for *there is no other way* of deciding what shape something is and, this being the case, the only criteria that we could possibly have have been satisfied.

Note that what is incorrigible here is not the visual perception of shape, nor the tactile perception of shape – since these can at best only be true – but the joint perception of shape by the two senses. The difference between this case and that of the perception of special sensibles is that, for the perception to be incorrigible, in the latter case only those conditions which are normal *vis-à-vis* one sense need obtain, whereas in the former those conditions which are normal *vis-à-vis* more than one sense must obtain. Since the normal conditions for vision at best only overlap with those of touch it is clear that the normal conditions for both taken together will be more restrictive than those for each taken individually.

As far as liability to error is concerned, Aristotle places incidental perception after the perception of special sensibles and before common perception, thus making it clear that his earlier division of sensibles into those which are proper, i.e. special and common sensibles, and those which are incidental (*de An.*, 418[1]7–8) does not reflect degrees of liability to error. In discussing incidental sensibles, we should distinguish between two kinds. The first covers those sensibles which are the special sensibles of particular senses but can be perceived by other senses of which they are not the special sensibles. Sweetness, for example, is a special sensible of taste (*Metaph*, 1010^{b}23–6) but it can also be perceived by sight (*de An.*, 425^{a}21–4). Now because sweetness is a special sensible of taste it cannot be a common sensible, but the fact that it can be perceived visually makes it an incidental sensible of vision. Our visual perception of sweetness, under the conditions peculiar to vision, cannot be incorrigible but it can of course be true, in the way that our visual perception of a common sensible can be true under these conditions. This makes our liability to error in the perception of incidental sensibles the same as that in our perception of common sensibles by one sense. But there is a difference because our perception of incidental sensibles (of this kind) *qua* incidental sensibles cannot be incorrigible under any circumstances, and in this respect they differ from special and common sensibles (and from the other kind of incidental sensibles, as we shall see). But in fact Aristotle maintains at *De Anima*, 425^{a}3 that we never perceive a sensible *qua* incidental without at the same time perceiving it *qua* special since the perception of an incidental sensible (of this kind, but not of the other kind for reasons that will become obvious below) is always part of a *joint* perception involving both the sense to which the sensible is special and that to which it is incidental. Our joint perception of this sensible would therefore be incorrigible because one of its elements e.g. the taste perception in the case of sweetness, would be incorrigible, at least under the normal conditions peculiar to taste.

The second kind of incidental sensible, which is usually (and I think rightly) treated as being what Aristotle normally has in mind when speaking of incidental sensibles, is that of those sensibles which are incidental to all the senses, such as the son of Cleon (*De An.* 425^{a}24–6) or the son of Diares (418^{a}20–1). Since incidental perception is a genuine *aisthesis* not involving other faculties such as memory,[8] what is at issue in these examples is our perception of this white object (a special sensible) as the son of Cleon or Diares. What is not at issue is seeing someone whom we cannot place, or seeing someone whom we know as the son of Cleon but whom, due to a past revelation by Diares, we know *really* to be the son of Diares. Nor is it a case of our being able to tell the son of Cleon from someone cleverly disguised as the son of Cleon (unless we count disguise as being simply a violation of the normal conditions for vision, which is feasible). The kind of thing that is at issue here is much more simple than this, as is clear from Aristotle's own statement that

error is most likely in the case where the object of perception is far
away (*De An.*, 428ᵇ29–30).

What this statement suggests is that Aristotle is not concerned
with any major (or even minor) epistemological problems in his
mention of incidental sensibles. The kind of problem that we might
encounter in the perception of a white thing as the son of Cleon is one
of our not being able to see clearly who it is. If distance is the problem
then the solution is clear: we simply move up closer so that we can see
properly. And what we do here is simply to normalise (in the sense of
optimise) the conditions under which perception takes place. But
assuming we do this, and assuming that our eyesight is normal (i.e.
assuming that our eyes are fully developed and functioning as nature
intended), can we then say that our perception of this white object as
the son of Cleon is incorrigible? Again, I think Aristotle would
answer in the affirmative here, for if these conditions are fulfilled
then we have satisfied all the appropriate conditions: there are
simply no others.

The breakdown of the Aristotelian conception

Aristotle's broad conception of perceptual cognition covers both
'seeing' (in the case of special and common perception) and 'seeing
as' (in incidental and some cases of common perception), epistemological and optical–physiological questions, psychological and natural–philosophical questions, weaving them all together into an
account which takes as its core the case where something appropriate to one sense is perceived by that sense under optimal conditions.
Such perception, Aristotle considers, is not only veridical but constitutive of the very notion of veridicality. Note, however, that Aristotle's aim is not a 'search for certainty' in the Cartesian sense, and he
does not provide us with an epistemological justification of perception so much as an elaboration of why justification is not called for,
or even appropriate, in the core case of special sensibles. A number of
factors played a role in undermining Aristotle's comprehensive
account of perception, but I want to draw attention to the four that
seem to me to be the crucial ones.

The first factor is the Augustinian conception of philosophy.
Augustine undertook the complete 'Christianisation' of philosophy;
the translation of classical philosophy into Christian terms, with no
residue. Not only does Christianity supplement classical philosophy,

it appropriates the teachings of the ancients as its own and construes all issues in terms of Christian teaching. The philosophical vocabulary in which Augustine accomplished this is Neoplatonist, although whereas on the Neoplatonist account the link between us and God is made in terms of intellectual steps which the reflective mind takes, cutting itself off from the sensible world, on the Augustinian account the links take the form of the sacraments, devices by which God infuses us with grace so that we might know Him. The idea that the proper unaided use of the senses could lead us to know truths about the natural world is completely ruled out on this conception. According to Augustine's neoplatonically-inspired doctrine of divine illumination, presented in the *Soliloquia*, just as objects must be made visible by being illuminated before they can be seen, so too must truths be made intelligible by a kind of light before they can be known; and just as the sun is the source of physical light, so God is the source of spiritual light or truth. Spiritual illumination is needed to supplement our ordinary use of sensory/cognitive faculties if we are to grasp truths.[9] This Augustinian view of knowledge was largely unchallenged in the Middle Ages and was a crucial element in the seventeenth-century revival of Augustinianism, a revival in which both Malebranche and Arnauld had parts to play.[10]

There was of course also a revival of interest in Aristotle in the Christian West from the twelfth century onwards, and the Aristotelian account of perception was quickly taken over by philosophers. But it was glossed in Christian terms. The gloss at first appears somewhat minor. The doctrine that we have the sense organs we do because they naturally display to us the nature of the world we wish to understand becomes transformed into the doctrine that God has given us the sense organs we have so that we might know His creation (and know Him through His creation). Now if the Augustinian doctrine of illumination can be resisted, such an account might easily be made to yield the conclusion that the senses, when used properly and under optimal conditions (and with the qualifications about incidental and common sensibles), are automatically veridical. But on Aristotle's account the senses supply their own criteria for what is veridical, whereas on the scholastic account it is God who supplies such criteria, and He has chosen to make our sense organs operate in accordance with them. This is actually a very radical shift, for the core of Aristotle's position is that there is a form of perception which is constitutive of its own veridicality, and the degrees of liability to error of other forms of perception are to be judged against this core case. On the scholastic version, there can no longer be anything intrinsically reliable about the perception of special sensibles, or anything less intrinsically reliable about the perception of other kinds of sensible. Both the nature and the source of reliability in perception are changed.

The second factor affecting the acceptability of Aristotle's general view of perception was the rejection of Aristotelian natural philosophy in the first few decades of the seventeenth century, and its replacement by more or less mechanistic theories. When Mersenne began his extremely influential attacks on traditional natural philosophies in the 1620s, it was not scholastic Aristotelianism as such that was his target, but the various naturalistic, magical and neoplatonist natural philosophies of the Renaissance.[11] These postulated all kinds of powers, forces and activities in nature, many of them lying beyond human knowledge. Mersenne's objection to scholastic Aristotelian natural philosophy was not so much that it was mistaken but that it was ineffectual in rebutting these various other natural philosophies, which were objectionable on theological and empirical grounds. In its place he proposed a natural philosophy which effectively stripped nature of any active powers or forces: mechanism. But mechanism not only got rid of the traditional occult powers, it also removed from nature a number of properties which virtually everyone had assumed to be in nature: colours, sounds, odours, etc. The consequence of this for an Aristotelian account of perceptual cognition is obvious. If these properties and qualities which perception, under optimal conditions, tells us are in nature are actually not in nature at all, then not only would our perceptual cognition under normal or optimal conditions not automatically be veridical, it would be systematically misleading. This is a consequence that Descartes, Malebranche and Arnauld all accept.

Third, Aristotle's conception was to be challenged in the early seventeenth century by substantive results in astronomy and mechanics. His view would appear to have the consequence that observations which result from the proper use of the senses under normal or optimal conditions cannot be mistaken. There is some evidence that Aristotle embraced this consequence of his view. He does occasionally speak, in physical contexts, of the testimony of the senses as being 'decisive' (e.g. *De Caelo*, 306^{a}16ff. – the word he uses is '*kurios*'). This was to be challenged in a quite devastating way in

Galileo's work. Aristotle's account of perception is, for example, impossible to reconcile with any use of optical instruments which yields results contrary to the testimony of the senses under normal conditions. One such case occurred very early on in the use of the telescope: because the telescope reduces the irradiation effect, the stars look smaller relative to the planets through a telescope than they do with unaided vision. Better still – since the case does not involve perception at a great distance, which might be considered as abnormal circumstances – the Aristotelian notion of the reliability of perception cannot be reconciled with theories such as the earth's motion (whether diurnal or annual), since this theory, as presented by Galileo, for example, involves a violation of the standards of perception in that it denies that we can perceive certain kinds of motion correctly under normal circumstances, if at all (as in the case of those motions in which we and the earth share, on Galileo's account, and as in the case of inertial motions, on the Newtonian account).

Fourthly, Aristotle's conception came to be challenged by developments in optics and ocular anatomy. One of the most popular parts of Aristotle's account of vision in the Middle Ages was his account of the transmission of forms or species from the object perceived to the eye, and the mind's grasp of this form in its own right. In Aristotelian natural philosophy, all material things are composed of matter and form. The form of something may either be 'substantial', in which case it constitutes its essence, or it may be 'accidental'. Aristotle had construed accidental forms in terms of those basic qualities characteristic of the four elements – hot and cold, wetness and dryness, density and rarity, heaviness and lightness – although accidental forms became much more numerous and complicated in late medieval and renaissance philosophies. Colour, Aristotle maintained, was derived from a mixture of black and white, the former being associated with earth and the latter with fire (*de Sens.*, 439ᵃ18–440ᵇ23), so the colour of a body derived exclusively from the proportion in which these two elements stood in a body. Now the form of the object, both accidental and substantial, is transmitted through the medium and causes an impression upon the sense organ. This impression resembles the object perceived because the properties it has are caused by the same thing that causes the original object to have these properties, namely its form. In vision, for example, the quality of the object is actually assumed by the seeing part of the eye: when a white object is seen, the watery substance (in medieval accounts the crystalline humor) constituting the seeing part of the eye becomes white (*de Sens.*, 438^{b}19–20). In medieval faculty psychology, a great deal of attention was devoted to the various processes that succeed this. In Aquinas, for example, the sense organ taking on the form of the object known causes the faculty of the imagination to produce a material image – a *phantasma* – from which the 'active intellect' abstracts what Aquinas calls the 'intelligible species'. These intelligible species are not representations of the object known but are simply the form that the object known takes in the intellect. The crucial point here is that when we know an object we know its form, and this form can have both a physical existence in the object itself or an intellectual existence in the intellect. It is the same form in each case, and in grasping the substantial form of the object the intellect grasps the essence of the object.

Seventeenth-century philosophers and scientists objected to this kind of account on a number of grounds. The alleged species or forms which are supposed to be transmitted through the medium were undetectable, and were in any case quite incompatible with what was beginning to be discovered about the nature of light and its transmission. But it was Descartes' linking of the theory of the formation of the retinal image to a number of mechanist assumptions that provided the death-blow to the Aristotelian account, and it is to this that we now turn.

Descartes' account of perception

A crucial ingredient in Descartes' account of perceptual cognition is his commitment to mechanism. Just how important such natural–philosophical considerations are is clear from the difference between his account and that offered in Kepler's *Ad vitellionem paralipomena* (1604). The *Ad vitellionem* is a pathbreaking work which revolutionised the study of optics. Kepler presents his material in what he refers to as the 'natural way' (*naturalem methodum*), discussing the nature of light, then reflection, then refraction, and finally the optical anatomy of the eye. Descartes' approach to reflection and refraction is the same as that of Kepler, and he fully accepts Kepler's demonstration that, in perception, the image is formed on the retina and not in the crystalline humor, as was traditionally thought. Indeed, Descartes learnt these things from Kepler. However, there are two respects in which Descartes' approach differs from Kepler's. First, Kepler is not interested in what happens after the formation of the retinal image, arguing that this is something quite different from the question he is dealing with.[12] Descartes, on the other hand, is very interested in the physiological, psychological and epistemological aspects of what happens after the formation of the retinal image. This is not merely a difference in approach, reflecting different interests, as it might at first seem. The kinds of information contained in the retinal image on Kepler's account are quite comprehensive, and it does indeed look as if one has a good deal of the perceptual story once one has given an account of the formation of the retinal image. On Descartes' account, the retinal image contains a great deal less than we see, and the subsequent processes are of paramount importance if we are to get any idea of the overall perceptual process. This difference in the two accounts is largely due to a second difference between them: the difference between their natural philosophies.

That their natural philosophies should be so different is at first sight surprising. Both are committed to the idea that physical reality is mathematical (geometrical) in structure. Indeed, both come close to treating physical reality as if it were ultimately just mathematics: Kepler explicitly, and Descartes because of the well-known problems he faces in distinguishing material extension from a purely geometrical extension, i.e. from empty space. But while mechanism provides the motivation for Descartes, the sources of Kepler's natural philosophy lie in Neoplatonism. For Kepler, the real world is ultimately the mathematical harmony underlying physical appearances.[13] He takes over a view of light as being simply the radiation of power, a view developed in the ninth century by al-Kindi and then taken over in the thirteenth by Grosseteste and Roger Bacon. On this account, light is construed on a par with fire, magnetic attraction and repulsion, and indeed any form of radiation of power (including speech on some versions), but all causation tends to be conceived on the analogy of light, which gives optics a special significance in this tradition.

In the first chapter of the *Ad vitellionem*, Kepler maintains that light is a constituent of all physical phenomena. Material bodies are necessarily confined to particular regions of space, but by means of powers like light or magnetism they are able to act beyond their own boundaries. Now, on Kepler's account, light and magnetism are not made up of material corpuscles, but they do consist of a kind of matter which is subject to conservation and has geometrical dimensions.[14] Rays of light are emitted from their source equally in all directions, so that they are distributed over a spherical surface whose degree of illumination is inversely proportional to the square of the distance from the source. Light is treated as a movable spherical surface, as the locus of infinitely many light rays, which terminates on the surface of the body on which light falls. On Descartes' account, on the other hand, light is conceived in straightforwardly corpuscularian terms, although because the Cartesian universe is a plenum these corpuscles are not to be conceived as atoms but rather in terms of regions of matter distinct from other regions of matter because of their motion relative to those other regions of matter. The corpuscles have, as well as a linear velocity, a rotational velocity which is determined by the nature of the surface of the body from which they are emitted or reflected, and it is this rotational velocity that is responsible for our perception of colour. But it is our mind that perceives colour, not our eyes. Kepler's claim that 'just as the eye was made to see colours, and the ear to hear sounds, so the human mind was made to understand, not anything you please, but quantity'[15] has resonances of Aristotle's teleological approach to the sense organs, but, more importantly, it separates a *perceptual* or *sensory* process – vision – which results in Kepler's theory in the formation of the retinal image and in Aristotle's in the imposition of form on the humor of the eye, from a *cognitive* process – call it 'understanding' – which abstracts quantitative relations in Kepler's theory and universal in Aristotle's. Descartes' approach breaks down this distinction and this, I want to argue, is both the source of his problems and the source of his achievement.

Let us begin with the systematic exposition of perceptual cognition set out in Rule 12 of the *Regulae*. Descartes starts by distinguishing four faculties: the intellect or understanding, the imagination, memory and sensation. The latter three are conceived as aids to the intellect, which can either act alone or apply itself to ideas in the imagination.

The first stage of the perceptual process is the stimulation of the external senses. Descartes only allows stimulation by contact with bodies, and the only means such bodies have of affecting our sense organs is by transfer of motion. Sense-perception, he tells us, 'occurs in the same way in which wax takes on an impression from a seal'.

He continues: 'It should not be thought that I have a mere analogy in mind here: we must think of the external shape of the sentient body as being really changed by the object in exactly the same way that the shape of the surface of the wax is altered by the seal' (CSM I, 40). This is effectively to model all perceptions on contact senses such as touch. While this is a crucial part of the mechanist programme, it harbours a potential problem for, in the case of distance perception such as vision, it renders it at best problematic how we can perceive an object which we are not in contact with, and at worst it leads us to the view that what we perceive is the body which is in contact with our sense organ – e.g. the light corpuscles – rather than the body itself, which we believe we are looking at. Descartes certainly does not hold the latter view, but the problem is how he is to avoid it. The difficulty can be brought out by contrasting his account with Kepler's. In Kepler's Neoplatonic and Hermeticist natural philosophy, phenomena such as light and magnetism provide ways in which a body can exercise influence other than in the spatial region where it is located. But it is axiomatic to the mechanism that Descartes adheres to that bodies can only act where they are: action at a distance is completely ruled out. Consequently it is hard to avoid the conclusion that what acts on our sense organ is the thing immediately in contact with it.

Descartes' commitment to a plenum seems to be of some help here, for in a plenum everything is in some sense in contact with everything else. In describing the next stage in the perceptual process – the passage of the figure or shape which the sense organ receives as a result of being stimulated by the object to the common sense – Descartes says that no real entity has been conveyed, and he describes the process in these terms:

In exactly the same way I understand that while I am writing, at the very moment when individual letters are traced on the paper, not only does the point of the pen move, but the slightest motion of this part cannot be traced out in the air by the tip of the quill, even though I do not conceive of anything real passing from one end to the other. (CSM I, 41)

But surely this applies not just to internal parts of the body, but also to everything else, no matter how distant, in a universe which is a plenum, for motion in one part will always necessarily result in matter in at least some other parts, if voids are not to be opened up and matter is not to penetrate other regions of matter. So perhaps Descartes can have the advantages of the Keplerian view without any of its disadvantages. But there is still a problem: some things are distant from us, and in visual perception we not only see these things, *we see them as being at a particular distance from us*. How could the light corpuscles impinging on the surface of the eye convey this information? The Epicureans had suggested that the atoms of light reflected from distant bodies become worn down the further they have to travel, which is why things at a distance look smaller, but the view suffers from the obvious deficiency that, were this to happen, we would only see the centres and not the edges of distant bodies. Descartes, with the benefit of a comprehensive optics behind him, does not advocate such a view, although he does think (much more plausibly) that the distinctness of the retinal image is an indication of distance. Another way of accounting for distance vision that he offers in his *Treatise on Man* (AT XI, 159–60) is in terms of the accommodation of the lens of the eye – the muscles regulating the shape of the lens, and hence its focal length, will contract and expand depending upon the distance of the object seen, and we are somehow aware of this. But this does not help with the current problem, for it simply presupposes that we see things at a distance, without telling us how it is possible to see something we are not in contact with. The crucial ingredient in Descartes' account of distance vision – because

it is the ingredient that tells us how something in contact with the eye can convey information about the distance of its source – is his theory of the eye's 'natural geometry'. He compares our distance vision to a blind man holding out two sticks so that they converge on an object, and calculating the distance of the object from the base angles of the triangle so formed, where the base is simply the distance between the sticks in the man's hands. Note that the blind man does not know the length of the sticks, but this he can calculate by a 'natural geometry' from the length of the base and the base angles. Analogously with the eyes: here the base is the distance between the eyes, the base angles are given by the angles at which the corpuscles strike the eye, and apparently innate 'natural geometry' enables us to calculate the distance of the object on this information:

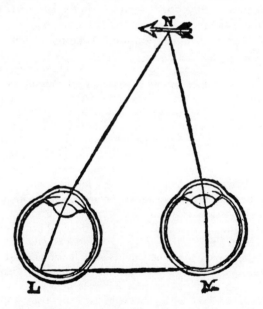

This account secures both the restriction of all influence to contact action, and the possibility of genuine distance vision. It also secures that 'no real entity', as Descartes puts it, travels from the object to the sense organ, thereby doing away with the 'species' of the Scholastics and the 'simulacra' of the Atomists.

Descartes' account of the transmission of the shape imposed on the sense organ to the 'common sense' – i.e. the faculty which co-ordinates impressions from the five senses – and the subsequent imprinting of these impressions, which he terms 'figures or ideas', on the imagination, is relatively straightforward and need not detain us.[16] The imagination itself 'is a genuine part of the body and is large enough to allow different parts of it to take on many different shapes' (CSM I, 41–2). It in turn moves the nerves, to which it is connected in the brain. This is sufficient to move our limbs, and indeed the process as described up to now is a complete account of what occurs in animals, 'even though we refuse to allow that they have an awareness of things, but merely grant them a purely corporeal imagination. It enables us to understand how there occur within us all those operations which we perform without any help from reason' (CSM I, 42).

Up to this stage, what has been described is what we might call the 'perceptual' part of perceptual cognition. In the *Dioptrics* Descartes spells out the differences between his approach to this part of the topic and that offered on the traditional Aristotelian approach:

We must take care not to assume – as [scholastic] philosophers commonly do – that in order to have sensory perceptions the soul must contemplate certain images transmitted by objects to the brain; or at any rate we must conceive the nature of these images in an entirely different manner from that of the philosophers. For since their conception of the images is confined to the requirement that they should resemble the objects they represent, the philosophers cannot possibly show us how the images can be formed by the objects, or how they can be received by the external sense organs and transmitted by the nerves to the brain. Their sole reason for positing such images was that they saw how easily a picture can stimulate our mind to conceive the objects depicted in it, and so it seemed to them that, in the same way, the mind must be stimulated, by little pictures formed in our head, to conceive the objects that affect our senses. We should, however, recall that our mind can be stimulated by many things other than images – by signs and words, for example, which in no way resemble the things they signify. And if, in order to depart as little as possible from accepted views, we prefer to maintain that the objects that we perceive by our senses really send images of themselves to the inside of our brain, we must at least observe that in no case does an image have to resemble the object it represents in all respects, for otherwise there would be no distinction between the object and its image. It is enough that the object resembles the image in a few respects. (CSM I, 165)

In other words, the traditional account subsumed the optics and physiology of the process to the purely epistemological constraint that the image resemble the object perceived. But this was not consistent with the result of mathematical research in geometrical optics, and empirical research in ocular anatomy and the structure of the nerves. Nevertheless, we should not let Descartes mislead us into thinking that his own account derives exclusively from his optical and anatomical studies. Mechanism is the central ingredient of his account: it legislates about what kinds of properties inhere in the world, it shapes his account of the transmission of light, and it provides the framework for his account of how information is conveyed from the sense organ to the brain. All of this it does in quite an *a priori* way.

The other part of the act of perceptual cognition is the actual cognition. This occurs, on the *Regulae* account, when the mind inspects 'ideas' in the imagination. Now I said above that, unlike Kepler, Descartes does not separate a perceptual or sensory stage – 'seeing' – from a cognitive stage – 'understanding' – in the process of perceptual cognition. I take his stress on the idea that the transmission of the image from the eye to the imagination is instantaneous to indicate that he is not thinking of perceptual cognition as a temporal process with distinct stages, but rather as an act which has conceptually but not temporally distinct parts. There is, however, one respect in which the fact that we can distinguish between parts of the act is useful, even if it is not necessary. The question which we are about to consider, the question central to the dispute between Malebranche and Arnauld, is whether what we know are only the ideas in the imagination, or what these ideas represent. This question must be kept distinct from the question we have just discussed, namely whether what we perceive, in the case of vision, is only the light corpuscle in direct contact with the eye, or whether we see the body from whose surface this corpuscle has been emitted or reflected.[17] The latter problem is one raised by, and ultimately solved by, Descartes' mechanism. The mind must play a role of course, since a calculation of distance is involved, but it does not matter here whether the mind is conceived dualistically, or materialistically (e.g. in purely mechanical terms), or naturalistically (e.g. as the inseparable 'form' of the body). The problem of ideas involves much more than mechanism, and is an altogether deeper philosophical question. Unfortunately, there has been an occasional tendency to run the two questions together since Descartes. Berkeley, for example, in Section 41 of *An Essay towards a New Theory of Vision*, cavalierly states that: 'From what hath been premissed, it is a manifest consequence, that a man born blind, being made to see, would, at first, have no idea of distance by sight; the sun and the stars, the remotest objects, as well as the nearer, would all seem *to be in his eye, or rather in his mind'* (my italics).[18] It is crucial that we grasp that the problems in the Cartesian account which provide the fuel for the dispute between Malebranche and Arnauld derive from whether we see things 'in the mind'; we definitely do not see them 'in the eye', as Descartes had shown to the satisfaction of all Cartesians, whether revisionary, like Malebranche, or more orthodox, like Arnauld.

Descartes and the doctrine of ideas

In Rule 12 of the *Regulae*, we are told that our ability to know things in the strict sense is purely spiritual, and that a single power or ability is involved in such knowledge. Descartes continues:

the cognitive power is sometimes passive, sometimes active; sometimes resembling the seal, sometimes the wax. But this should be understood merely as an analogy, for nothing quite like this power is to be found in corporeal things. It is one and the same power: when applying itself along with the imagination to the common sense, it is said to see, touch, etc.: then addressing itself to the imagination alone, in so far as the latter is invested with various figures, it is said to remember; when applying itself to the imagination in order to form new figures, it is said to imagine or conceive; and lastly, when it acts on its own, it is said to understand . . . According to its different functions, then, the same power is called either pure intellect, or imagination, or memory, or sense perception. (CSMI, 42)

What are we to make of the claim that the pure intellect and sense perception are the same power? To claim this is at least to deny that the intellect is merely an ingredient in sense perception: as it would be, for example, if it were simply the cognitive 'part' of what I have been calling perceptual cognition.

There are a number of parallels here with Descartes' treatment of inference, which differs radically from those medieval accounts of cognition which insist on a sharp separation between the corporeal faculties and the intellect. On Aquinas' account, for example, the raw material on which the intellect works must derive from our corporeal faculties: the body, via the senses, provides the *phantasiai* which are the basis of all knowledge. But Aquinas draws a sharp distinction between the limits of cognitive grasp afforded us by the intellect or understanding (*intellectus*), and the reasoning (*ratio*) which is the cognitive activity of our corporeal faculties. The *intellectus/ratio* dichotomy is a complex one in Aquinas, but the general thrust of the distinction is to mark out a form of direct intuitive grasp of truth from a limited, piecemeal, and often less reliable form of cognitive activity, which is the only route we have to understanding, but which is far from being an infallible route to such understanding. Moreover, and this is a crucial point, when *ratio* does lead to understanding it annihilates itself: it has served its purpose and disappears in favour of true knowledge, which is conceived on an intuitive basis.[19] The central contrast is, then, between direct intuition on the one hand, and the ratiocinative processes of imagining, remembering, perceiving and inferring on the other. I have argued elsewhere in a detailed examination of Descartes' conception of inference[20] that, for Descartes, inference is not something that our corporeal organs engage in so that the information provided thereby can be passed on to the incorporeal intellect, which unfortunately cannot get its information in any other way. Rather, this is what our intellect, when it is acting through what Descartes calls an 'intuition' (*intuitus*), *tells* us is knowledge. In other words, in the context of inference, the corporeal faculties are not regarded as mere aids to knowledge: rather, their proper exercise, guided by the mind, is constitutive of knowledge.

The cases of inference, memory, imagination and sense perception are each significantly different, but the situation with perception is at least analogous. Yolton, for example, has maintained that 'knowing (perceiving) is not reading off from our sensations properties of the world. Perceptual knowledge is the having of these sensations.'[21] This interpretation of Descartes is effectively that offered by Arnauld, and this in itself must give it some weight, in the light of Descartes' remark to Mersenne that Arnauld 'has entered further than anyone else into the sense of what I have written' (AT III, 331).[22] But while there can be no doubt that this is plausible as an interpretation of Descartes, it is certainly not the only possible interpretation, and there are other strands in Descartes' thought which, if they do not actually conflict with it, at least force us to be circumspect.

Of central importance here is the way in which one construes the role of ideas in the act of perceptual cognition. On the interpretation favoured by Arnauld and Yolton, one does not perceive ideas, and their role in perception is not that of a mere ingredient. Rather, to have an idea of *p* and to perceive *p* are the same thing. A crucial passage in this respect occurs in the first chapter of *Le Monde*. Descartes writes:

> Now if words, which signify nothing except by human convention, suffice to make us think of things to which they bear no resemblance, then why could nature not also have established some sign, which would make us have the sensation of light, even if the sign contained nothing in itself which is similar to this sensation? It is not thus that nature has established laughter and tears, to make us read joy and sadness on the faces of men. (CSM I, 81)

In short, there is in nature a sign which is responsible for our sensation of light, but which is not itself light; nor indeed does it resemble light. Now it is a consequence of Descartes' mechanism that nature itself is colourless, so there is nothing we would recognise as light in nature. Since black and white are colours, nature itself is not darker or lighter, or even of uniform illumination: it is quite different from our perceptual awareness of it. But Descartes wants there to be an objective correlation between phenomena in nature and our perceptual awareness of these phenomena, even though this correlation cannot amount to resemblance. In the case of light, the correlation is between the rotational velocity of the fine corpuscles making up the ray striking the eye and the colour we are aware of, where the speed of rotation is determined by the surface of the body from which the light has been reflected or emitted. The sign here is the rotational motion of the fine corpuscles making up the ray, and what we experience when we grasp the sign is light. In more general terms, physical motion is the sign, and what is signified is what is experienced in the sensation.

The point of describing the act of perceptual cognition in this way is to avoid the language of causation. Because of the problems attendant on any attempt to establish a causal connection between two such different substances as body and mind, Descartes must avoid saying that processes in the world *cause* us to have the sensations we do. Sometimes he avoids this in a way suggestive of occasionalism. One of the most interesting passages in this respect occurs in his *Comments on A Certain Broadsheet*.[23] He is concerned there to rebut Regius' theses that the mind does not need innate ideas, that 'its faculty of thinking is all it needs for its own acts', and that all common notions derive from observation or verbal instruction. In response, he argues:

But this is so far from being true that, on the contrary, if we bear well in mind the scope of our senses and what it is exactly that reaches our faculty of thinking by way of them, we must admit that in no case are the ideas of things presented to us by the senses just as we form them in our thinking. So much so that there is nothing in our ideas which is not innate to the mind or the faculty of thinking, with the sole exception of those circumstances which relate to experience, such as the fact that we judge that this or that idea which we now have immediately before our mind refers to a certain thing situated outside us. We make such a judgement not because they transmit the ideas to our mind through the sense organs, but because they transmit something which, at exactly that moment, gives the mind occasion to form these ideas by means of the faculty innate to it. (CSMI, 304)

It is indicative that sensation and innate ideas are so closely connected here, for the doctrine of innate ideas is central to Descartes' account of signification. The rotational motion of the fine corpuscles making up the light ray is a natural sign of light only for a creature fitted to respond to it in a particular way, and such a response occurs in the mind in virtue of a 'faculty innate to it'. The source of this faculty, and of innate ideas generally, is of course God. There are unmistakable echoes here of the medieval doctrine that God has given us the sense organs and corporeal faculties we have so that we might know His creation. On Descartes' account, the activity of these sense organs and corporeal faculties cannot be separated from the general act of perceptual cognition, so it is not our sense organs or corporeal faculties but our mind that God must shape or 'fit out' in the requisite way. This He does by providing us with the requisite innate ideas. It is not that there are natural signs in nature *and* that there are innate ideas, as if the conjunction were merely fortuitous. The former would simply not be natural signs for us unless we had the innate ideas we have.

The connection between the signs and the innate ideas is clearly more intimate than any causal connection would be, for it is the innate ideas that make the signs what they are, whereas effects can never make causes what they are. The semantic relation involves an element of reciprocity not to be found in the causal relation. This element of reciprocity is a crucial ingredient in the unified nature of perceptual cognition, something which is central to Descartes' understanding of this act. It is important to appreciate this for Descartes sometimes describes perceptual cognition in terms which suggest a process with discrete stages. In the first chapter of *Le*

Monde for example, just after the passage quoted above, he argues:

But perhaps you will say that our ears really cause us to perceive only the sound of our words, and our eyes only the countenance of the person who is laughing or weeping, and that it is our mind that, recollecting what the words and countenance signify, represents their meaning to us at the same time. I could reply that by the same token it is our mind that represents to us the idea of light each time our eye is affected by the action which signifies it. (CSM I, 81)

This is a reply to a hypothetical objection made from the standpoint of an account of perception antithetical to Descartes' semantic account. And in his reply he is obliged to offer a different kind of description of perception from the one he has just given. It is a description which responds to a faculty psychology approach in its own terms, and for this approach the crucial thing is to identify the stage of the perceptual process at which the distinctive cognitive element enters the picture. Such an approach requires an element of interpretation, and Descartes talks of the mind *representing* the idea of light to us when we are affected by the action which *signifies* it. The first description is of a single integrated act; the second, addressed to those who wish to construe what happens in terms of faculty psychology, introduces the notion of *ideas* being represented to us. This second description is the one that has caused the difficulties, for it suggests that some third representational entity is involved in perception, and Descartes' discussion of the objective reality of ideas, which he takes *inter alia* as a means of providing us with an account of the 'being' of objects in the understanding, only serves to reinforce this view. Now it is possible, as Yolton has shown,[24] to reconcile this account of the objective reality of ideas with the semantic interpretation, by taking the 'being' of objects in the understanding as their 'being understood' or 'being perceived'. Yolton has, I believe, shown that the semantic interpretation has more claim than any other to be taken as Descartes' considered view of the matter, but the distinctive approach of faculty psychology intrudes so regularly into his formulations that it cannot be said confidently that he ever finally and unequivocally accepts or even fully understands it.

Malebranche and the doctrine of ideas

The Preface to *The Search after Truth* begins:

The mind of man is by its nature situated, as it were, between its creator and corporeal creatures, for, according to Saint Augustine, there is nothing but

God above it and nothing but bodies below it. But as the mind's position above all material things does not prevent it from being joined to them, and even depending in a way on a part of matter, so the infinite distance between the sovereign being and the mind of man does not prevent it from being immediately joined to it in a very intimate way. The latter union raises the mind above all things. Through it, the mind receives its life, its light, and its entire felicity, and at many points in his work Saint Augustine speaks of this union as the one most natural and essential to the mind. The mind's union with the body, on the contrary, infinitely debases man and is today the main cause of all his errors and miseries. (ST, xix)

The bulk of the *Search* is devoted to an account of how these errors due to the mind's union with the body arise, and the first five Books are devoted to the senses, the imagination and the pure intellect (these three coming under the rubric of the understanding), and the inclinations and the passions (these two coming under the rubric of the will). I propose to look at the first and the third of these. It is worth bearing in mind from the outset, however, that Malebranche's advocacy of the Augustinian doctrine of illumination marks a significant departure from Descartes' own view. While Descartes does not discuss the relation between God and the mind in anything like the detail he discusses the relation between God and corporeal extension, and mind and corporeal extension, it is clear from his doctrine of method that reason is self-sufficient, requiring no help from God other than in His initial guarantee that what we perceive clearly and distinctly is true. To the Cartesian doctrine that the mind can grasp things in a reliable way only if it grasps them clearly and distinctly, Malebranche adds the doctrine that such a grasp is dependent upon divine illumination. This latter is a doctrine to which Arnauld also subscribes, so it is not at issue in the controversy with Malebranche, although it surely lends support, in a way that no doctrine to be found in Descartes does, to the view that we know all things in God, a view that Malebranche advocates and Arnauld vehemently rejects.

The first Book of the *Search* deals with sensation, and we are immediately presented with the distinctive and indeed core Cartesian doctrine that the senses are not designed to reveal the nature of bodies to us. This doctrine, as I have already indicated, is due less to an analysis of the perceptual act than a number of largely *a priori* mechanistic assumptions about the structure of the corporeal world. But whatever its source, it raises the fundamental question of what the function of the senses is; or, to put it in seventeenth-century terms, why God has provided us with the senses we have. Malebranche's answer is that they simply help us identify and satisfy our own body's needs in a quick and straightforward way. Indeed, Malebranche's view is that Adam did not rely on his senses for information about the nature of bodies (ST, 22). Since the Fall, however, we have become very dependent on our bodies, and as a result we have mistakenly relied upon our senses to tell us about the nature of bodies. Put in this way, it is clear that it is not our senses as such that deceive us, but rather the natural judgements that invariably accompany sensations, and which we make involuntarily. The degree of error involved varies. In the case of what we would now call primary qualities, while we are right to believe that bodies have shape, size, speed, etc., sensation is untrustworthy as a basis for ascribing particular shapes, sizes and speeds to particular bodies. In the case of 'sensible qualities' such as colour, heat, sound, odour, etc., on the other hand, we are completely misled by sensation, for these are only modifications of the mind and have no independent existence.

Our mistaking something which is merely a mode of the mind for an independently existing external quality occurs, Malebranche argues (ST, 52 ff.), because we confuse four things. The first is the action of the object on our sense organ; the second is the transmission of this action along the nerve fibres to the brain; the third is the modification of the mind that occurs when this happens; the fourth is the natural judgement we involuntarily make about this sensation. In acting on our sense organ, what happens is that the minute particles of the body that is sensed press against the surface of our skin, but because these particles are imperceptibly small, we suppose that what we sense is a property of the body. Consequently, 'almost everyone believes that the heat he feels, for example, is in the fire causing it, that light is in the air, and that colours are on coloured objects' (ST, 54). But when the object that occasions[25] the sensation is actually visible, such as when we are pricked by a needle, or when we are tickled by a feather, 'we do not judge on this account that there is anything resembling these sensations in the objects causing them' (ST, 54). Malebranche concludes that whether or not we take the sensory quality to be a property of the body is a function of the extent to which the cause of (or, more strictly speaking, 'what occasions') the sensation is visible to us. The particles that occasion/cause us to have a sensation of light are among the smallest and therefore the least perceptible, and this is why, at least when we rely exclusively on sensation, we are led to think that bodies are coloured. Malebranche next supplements this account with an equally *a priori* explanation of the relation between the intensity of a sensation and its source (ST, 57). In the case of strong sensations, we are told, we take the quality to be in ourselves, whereas with weak sensations we take it to be in the body. For example, when we immerse our hand in water so hot that we have a burning sensation, we take the pain to be in us and not in the water. But when we immerse our hand in lukewarm water, we take the quality to be in the water and not in us. There may also be intermediate cases, such as that where we immerse our hand in moderately hot water, and here the quality seems partly in us and partly in the water.

These accounts, reminiscent of Epicureanism in the naive belief that, providing we posit small enough particles, any qualitative phenomenon can be accounted for, would account at best only for how we come to mistake modifications of the mind for real qualities inhering in bodies. But we also need to explain why such a mistake should arise in the first place, and the explanation for this, Malebranche argues, lies in the fact that we have a clearer grasp of the modifications of extension (primary qualities) than we do modifications of the mind (secondary qualities) because our idea of extension is clearer than our idea of mind. This provides a major source of disagreement between Malebranche and Arnauld, Arnauld taking the more orthodox Cartesian line that we know nothing better than our own souls (see Chapter 23 and 24 of the text). Rather than pursue this issue, or the plausibility of the distinction that Malebranche makes between primary and secondary qualities,[26] I want to focus on his idea of the function of perception.

If, as Malebranche argues, sensation (or at least the natural judgements accompanying it) misleads us so seriously, and if God has given us our sensory organs, does it not follow that God deceives us? In arguing that He does not so deceive us, Malebranche maintains that it is to our benefit that we do not experience our sensations as mere modifications of the mind. The purpose of sensation being to make us aware of the body's needs, we often need to be alert to these immediately. If we experienced sensations as modifications of our mind, then we would have to make a conscious inference from the state of our bodies, thereby failing to attend to the body's needs immediately. Our false belief that pains are in our body, for example, is crucial if we are to remove our body from something harmful to it.

Similarly, colours enable us to distinguish bodies immediately. Our false beliefs about sensible qualities are crucial to our everyday activities and ultimately to our survival. The culpable error comes only when we consciously endorse these involuntary natural judgements, and say that they really tell us about true properties of bodies. On this question of the function of sensation, Malebranche and Arnauld are not in any great disagreement. And indeed what Malebranche offers is an obvious and potentially fruitful direction to go in. Descartes himself, while rejecting the Aristotelian and medieval accounts of the function of the sense organs, namely the view that they are designed to display to us the nature of the world, had not elaborated in any detail upon what the function of our sense organs actually is. Malebranche addresses himself explicitly to this problem, and his solution meets both the mechanist constraint that nature cannot be as we perceive it, and the constraint offered by intuitive, theological and other considerations, that it is not wholly accidental that we have the sense organs we have. I shall return to this question below.

Book 2 of *The Search after Truth*, on the imagination, largely follows Descartes' physiological psychology,[27] and is not of any special relevance to the Malebranche/Arnauld controversy. Book 3, however, is absolutely crucial, dealing with the cognitive part of perceptual cognition. The soul or mind has a somewhat intermediate standing in Malebranche: it is united to the body and it is united to God. In so far as it is united to the body it experiences sensations and various representations issuing from the phantasy and memory. In so far as it is united to God it is capable of clear and distinct ideas. Now, following Descartes, Malebranche thinks that the mind can either apply itself to ideas in the imagination, or it can act as pure intellect. It is in his account of the pure intellect that Malebranche moves most decisively away from the Cartesian doctrine.

Descartes had argued that certain clear and distinct ideas are innate, and that they are modifications of our mind, just as sensations are. Malebranche wants to make a sharp distinction between ideas that result from the mind-body union and those that result from the union of mind and God. What Descartes thinks of as innate ideas, Malebranche construes as eternal archetypes which can only exist in an eternal, unchanging being: God. God is an 'intelligible world' of archetypal essences[28] and it is in Him that we see the essences of things. These exist not as modifications of the mind, as ideas derived from sensations do, but actually in God.

Malebranche restricts the term 'idea' to our concepts of primary qualities, which resemble the bodies that they represent. He is explicit that primary qualities are those which we can conceive mechanically, quantitatively and geometrically: in other words, those that mechanism identifies as existing in corporeal extension. Our concepts of sensible qualities (secondary qualities), on the other hand, merely signal or signify to the mind some bodily state, which they do not resemble in any way, and Malebranche reserves the term 'sensations' for these. Now both ideas and sensations are needed in perception. The intellect only perceives intelligible extension, whereas if we are to distinguish bodies we need to endow them with sensible qualities such as colours. On Malebranche's view, because we need to so endow bodies with sensible qualities in order to be aware of them visually, aurally, etc., we do not perceive them directly. He interprets Descartes' account of perceptual cognition in representational terms: what we perceive are representations of the bodies, or 'ideas'. In the second Part of Book 3 of the *Search*, Malebranche examines the nature and source of our ideas in detail. He asks in turn of the three kinds of substance – body, mind and God – whether they could be the source of our ideas.

In considering whether bodies themselves can be the source of our ideas of bodies he considers only action at a distance and a scholastic transmission of 'species' account (ST, 220–1), neglecting Epicureanism, which would also fall into this category. He has no difficulty rejecting the scholastic account, along fairly standard Cartesian lines. It is crucial to bear in mind here that while Descartes thinks our ideas of bodies are due, at least in part, to bodies themselves, he does not think our clear and distinct idea of extension derives from them, and the latter is all that Malebranche is concerned with.

He considers next the view that mind creates in itself the idea of extension (ST, 225–6). It could not do this *ex nihilo*, for this power is confined to God, so it would have to do it by imitating something, but the only thing it could imitate in order to have an idea of extension would have to be itself an idea of extension, which leaves us with the original difficulty. Nor does God put ideas of extended things in the mind (ST, 226–8), either all together at the time He creates the mind, or individually whenever a body acts on the sense organs. If He created in our mind a fund of ideas for the infinite number of figures that we can conceive, then this fund would itself have to be infinite, and it is hard to imagine how a finite mind could contain an infinity of things. And in any case, it is unclear on such a view how we would be able to call forth the right ideas at the right times. If, on the other hand, God produces the idea of the object each time an object acts on our sense organs, then we cannot explain how we can have a confused but actual perception of an infinite number of ideas. Finally, Malebranche considers the view that the mind, while not containing these ideas, can know them by reflecting on its own nature (ST, 228–9). This possibility is rejected, as Malebranche has already argued that the mind knows itself very obscurely whereas it knows extension clearly.

How, then, does the mind come to know the nature of extension? Malebranche concludes (ST, 230–5) that we must perceive the idea of extension in a being (i) which is different from us, i.e. from our mind, (ii) to which our mind can nevertheless be united, and (iii) which is such that, unlike our mind, it can contain an infinite number of things. In other words, we see all things in God: 'the mind can see God's works in Him, provided that God wills to reveal to us what in Him represents them' (ST, 230). He then goes on to provide five independent arguments for this thesis. In brief, they are as follows. (1) It is a mark of God's perfection that He always produces things by the simplest means, and it is surely simpler to display His archetypal ideas to our minds than to provide us with an infinite fund of ideas, even if this were possible (ST, 230–1). (2) Everything depends wholly on God, and He is the immediate cause not just of creation but of our knowledge of creation (ST, 231). (3) When we want to think about a particular thing, 'we first glance over all beings and then apply ourselves to a consideration of the object we want to think about'; but 'we would desire to see a particular object only if we had already seen it, though in a general and confused fashion', and the only way we could already have seen it in the general case is if we saw it in God, who contains all things in His intelligible extension (ST, 232). (4) Some of our ideas are general, whereas we only know particular things, so these ideas must have come from elsewhere, and earlier arguments show that this can only be from God (ST, 232). (5) Nothing can act immediately on the mind unless it is superior to it, for only God can alter modifications of the mind (ST, 232).

Arnauld devotes a good deal of *On True and False Ideas* to

challenging these arguments, and I shall not elaborate on them here. The second argument, however, does merit some further clarification as it raises the question of occasionalism, which has often been misunderstood in this context. Malebranche presents the second argument as follows:

> The second reason for thinking that we see beings because God wills that what in Him representing them should be revealed to us . . . is that this view places created minds in a position of complete dependence on God – the most complete there can be. For on this view, not only could we see nothing but what He wills that we see, but we could see nothing but what He makes us see. (ST, 231)

In its exclusion of 'secondary causes' from knowledge, this argument is effectively a radical extension of occasionalism. Now no Cartesian is free from occasionalism, and Descartes himself shows tendencies towards occasionalism in a number of passages. It is important, therefore, that we be clear about exactly what occasionalism is and what it commits one to.

Although it has often been assumed that occasionalism was a seventeenth-century reaction to the mind–body problem, the occasionalist doctrine that God is the direct and sole cause of every natural event had been defended as early as the tenth century by Al-Ash'ai, and would have been familiar to seventeenth-century philosophers from Aquinas' attack on the doctrine in his 'Disputed Questions' on the power of God (*De potentia*, Book 1, qu. 3, art. 7). Moreover, occasionalism is a doctrine not just about the relation between things of a different substance, such as mind and body, but equally about the relation between things of the same substance, because in its most general form it is a doctrine about how bodies can communicate their modes to one another. Descartes was generally thought to have been an occasionalist in some domains in the seventeenth century, and both Malebranche and Arnauld construe his writings on the question of physical bodies communicating their modes to one another in this way, for example. There is some justification for this. Descartes considered that all change is due to bodies communicating their motion to one another, and he treats motion as a mode of bodies. But a mode is an inseparable property of a body, so how can it be transferred from body to body? When Henry More puts this question to Descartes, he replies that just as motion is a mode of a body in the same way that shape is, the power that causes that motion is the power by which God conserves the same amount of motion that He put in the extended world at the first instant (AT V, 403–4), and this He does by recreating the world at each instant, since on Descartes' conception of extended substance it contains no powers within itself, not even the power to conserve itself in existence. So God causes extended things to exist at each instant, and He causes them to exist in a definite state of rest or motion. But if that is the case, what real role could the second causes play? Descartes' treatment of this question is ambiguous. In a letter to Princess Elizabeth on 6 October 1645, he writes that 'the scholastic distinction between universal and particular causes is out of place here . . . [for] God is the universal cause of everything' (AT IV, 314). On the other hand, in the first article of Part II of the *Principles* (CSM I, 223) he appears to argue that we must ascribe an independent effectivity to second causes since, if we were to argue that God is the sole cause of all our sensations, then we would have to consider Him a deceiver.

An occasionalist construal of the interaction between physical substances was common amongst Cartesians, despite Descartes' own hesitation on this question.[29] Mind–body occasionalism, although not Descartes' considered position nor that of many Cartesians, was held by both Arnauld[30] and Malebranche. But only Malebranche went so far as to advocate the view that God is the immediate cause not merely of the world but of our knowledge of the world, and this forms the crux of the controversy between him and Arnauld.

Arnauld's criticism of Malebranche's doctrine of ideas

On True and False Ideas is a polemical treatise devoted to showing the falsity of Malebranche's claim that what we perceive are representations, and that these representations exist in an intelligible extension contained in God. The central thrust of the book is that it is above all a misunderstanding of the nature of ideas that leads Malebranche to the doctrines that we do not perceive material objects but only intelligible ones, that these intelligible objects can exist only in an infinite intelligible extension, and that this infinite intelligible extension can only be contained in God, so that we end up finally with the doctrine that we see all things in God, which Arnauld considers manifestly absurd.

A crucial role in his overall rejection of Malebranche's doctrine of ideas is played by the definitions he provides in Chapter 5, for these reveal not only the basis of his argument against Malebranche but also the basis of his own position. In the second definition, we are told that thinking, knowing and perceiving are the same thing, something which I have indicated is implicit in Descartes' account, but which Arnauld is the first to present and defend in an explicit way. Indeed, Arnauld is the first to develop an account of the perceptual act explicitly on this basis. In the third definition, we are presented with the crux of the difference between his view and that of Malebranche, when he claims that the 'idea' of an object and the 'perception' of an object are one and the same thing. He elaborates upon this in a way designed to reveal the difference between his construal of ideas and that of Malebranche. This idea–perception stands both in a relation to the mind, and to the object perceived in so far as it is objectively in the mind. The former relation is most aptly captured by the term 'perception' while the latter is most aptly captured by the term 'idea'. So while perception is unequivocally a single act, the two complementary ingredients of this act can be designated differently. The errors arise only when, like Malebranche, one construes the having of the idea and the perception as two distinct things or processes. When one does this one is led to introduce a completely superfluous entity over and above the object and the perception, namely the 'idea' as a hypostatised representation, something which is also encouraged by a conflation of 'the idea of an object' and 'that object conceived'.

Now Arnauld accepts that all thought or perception is representational. As he puts it in Definition 7, 'it is clear to whoever reflects on what occurs in his mind that all our perceptions are essentially *representative* modalities.' Moreover he does not deny that we see ideas immediately and objects mediately, but because of the way in which he construes ideas, this should not be taken to mean that ideas are separate entities which stand proxy for objects. In Chapter 6, he makes the point explicitly: 'not only in the case of material things but generally in regard to all things, it is our ideas that we see immediately and which are *the immediate object of our thought*. This does not prevent us from also seeing, by means of these ideas, the object that contains formally what is *objectively* in the idea.' In other words, it is by means of ideas that we see external objects, but this does not mean that we do not genuinely see the objects: on the contrary, ideas provide the means by which we genuinely see them. Arnauld is explicit in the eighth Definition that we must not model our perception of objects by means of ideas on the way in which paintings represent objects. The former is a cognitive relation involving the mind, whereas the latter is something purely corporeal, and 'what has thrown the question of *ideas* into confusion is the attempt to explain the way in which objects are represented by our ideas by analogy with corporeal things.'

Arnauld presents a number of objections to Malebranche's doctrine, in the form of 'demonstrations' each directed against particular claims. In the first of these, he looks at Malebranche's claim that we do not perceive material objects external to us by themselves. This expression 'by themselves' is equivocal, he tells us. Taken in its first sense, it results in the claim that the objects themselves are not the cause of what we perceive. Arnauld accepts this as true, and adopts the occasionalist doctrine that our mind sees the sun on the occasion of our eyes presenting the sun to the mind. Taken in the second sense, it amounts to the claim that we know objects only by means of representations, construed as something over and above the object and the perception itself. This contentious claim should not be conflated with the first and, Arnauld argues, simply presupposes what Malebranche has undertaken to show.

One of Malebranche's claims that Arnauld devotes a good deal of attention to is the claim that the mind can only know objects that are present to it. This kind of view results, Arnauld argues, from misunderstandings about the nature of corporeal vision, compounded by an attempt to model mental vision on corporeal vision. The principal misunderstanding is the view, encouraged no doubt (but certainly not entailed) by the mechanist rejection of action at a distance, that for a body to be perceived it must be spatially present to us. This is clearly false, however, and as Arnauld points out, if it were the case we should never see anything, for we cannot see objects which are too close to, or in contact with, the eye. Moreover, to say that objects known must be present to the mind does not mean that they must be *spatially* present but that they must be objectively in the mind. A second prevalent misunderstanding about corporeal vision that Arnauld points to is the belief that, in reflection (e.g. in a mirror), what we see is the image of the object and not the object itself. But what we actually see, if we take care to examine the case carefully, is the object by means of a reflected image.

Malebranche had claimed that the idea of the object must be present to the mind if we are to perceive it. Arnauld detects an equivocation here, and argues that if we take 'idea' as 'perception' then it is uncontentiously true, since we perceive many things in our mind without there being anything external corresponding to them, whereas if we take the term as 'representation', i.e. as something which does the representing, then the claim is false and question-begging. Moreover, Malebranche's further claim that we see only representations is in conflict with his explicit statement that God works in the simplest ways, as it introduces a completely unnecessary type of entity, as well as construing the process by which God enables His creation to be revealed to us as being quite devious, for no apparent reason.

Much of *On True and False Ideas* is devoted to Malebranche's claim that, for something to be perceived, it must be intimately joined to our soul. This leads him to the claim that what we perceive must be, not real objects, but only *intelligible* objects, and this is given so much attention because it leads directly to the doctrine that we see all things in God. Arnauld's discussion of these claims is almost exclusively negative, and his own doctrine of the nature of ideas is not further developed in it.

Arnauld and the question of the function of perception

On True and False Ideas, although principally concerned to rebut a particular view of the nature of ideas and to put in its place a semantic understanding of the role of ideas in the perceptual act, also touches upon a larger question. I said above that Arnauld and Malebranche did not disagree on the general question of the function of sensation. Both take the orthodox Cartesian view that the function of our sense organs cannot be to display to us the nature of the corporeal world, for both accept a mechanist conception on which the world of appearances is quite different from the world as revealed in physical theory. Likewise, both assume that it is not purely accidental that we have the sense organs we do, since God has provided us with these sense organs. Arnauld unequivocally takes the view that we have the sense organs we do so that we might conserve our body from harm, seek nourishment for it, etc. Malebranche's view is complicated somewhat by his doctrine that God acts only through a general will. We cannot say that God has specifically given us our senses in order to preserve our bodies, since God's sole aim is to manifest His attributes;[31] however, as a result of this manifesting His divine attributes, we are given the capacity for sensations which may, on occasion, inform our body of its need. Arnauld, on the other hand, is very concerned to develop an unequivocally functional understanding of perception, principally in the belief that a correct account of the function of perception will show the error of postulating intermediate representations in the perceptual act.

Although Arnauld poses the question in terms of why God has given us our sense organs, the philosophical issues remain the same if we pose the question in more modern evolutionary terms. The problem can then be put as follows. Our perceptual faculties have evolved. They could have evolved in ways quite different from the way they have in fact evolved, and consequently we can ask why they have evolved in the way they have. Now the obvious answer to the evolutionary question is to say that the way in which they have evolved is the one which best fits us to survive (or at least is one of the ways which best enables us to survive), and this is why they have evolved in the way they have. We can then ask what it is about the way in which they have evolved that best enables us to survive, and this question can be seen in either epistemological or in functional terms. If we believe that the perceptual organs display to us the world as it actually is, then of course we will say that what it is about them that enables us to survive is their ability to display the world as it is to us. This option is not open to a mechanist like Arnauld, although he can accept, and indeed insists (like any good Cartesian), that there is a systematic connection between how the world is and how it appears to us.

The attention of commentators has focused on this epistemological question. But the functional question has an interest in its own right. I have been concerned to show how a unified conception of perception came to break down around the seventeenth century and how epistemological, psychological, optical and natural–philosophical questions came to be separated. The unifying feature of the Aristotelian conception was the teleological view that we have the sense organs we do because they display the world to us as it is. This view was rejected on a number of relatively independent grounds, as we have seen, but the question of what the function of perception is, a question whose answer would have the potential to reunite the disparate areas in which perception was discussed, was not resolved. Attention focused instead on problems of representation, the distinction between primary and secondary qualities, and so on. *On True and False Ideas* has a contribution to make in these areas, but it is largely negative. It makes a positive contribution, however rudimentary, in its exploration of the question of the function of perception. This question was only revived in the twentieth century in the theories of the Gestalt school, and more recently in the work of J. J. Gibson, where the perceptual act is examined in the context of 'exploring organisms' actively seeking information from the environment in which they live, an environment which may please, threaten or support them, etc.[32] This is an approach which integrates physiological, psychological, ecological and other questions, and its reliance on the idea that the determinants of our visual impressions are to some degree innate accords well with the thrust of the Cartesian doctrine. Its relation to what answer we provide to the epistemological question is a complex one, and in seventeenth-century terms it would have been thought no less philosophical than the epistemological question. The connection between the positive thesis about the function of perception and the theses offered about the epistemological relation between perceptual cognition and the corporeal world should be kept in mind if one wants to understand the full extent of the problem of perceptual cognition as it presented itself in the seventeenth century. This was above all a problem of drawing together disparate fields and developing a coherent and unified picture of just what perception is, and Arnauld's contribution to this was surpassed by no one.

Notes to the introduction

1 See Richard A. Watson, *The Downfall of Cartesianism, 1673–1712* (The Hague, 1966).

2 This section draws on my 'Aristotle on the function of sense perception', *Studies in History and Philosophy of Science* XI (1980), 75–89. A fuller account can be found in this paper.

3 Aristotle's argument here is obscure. See the commentary in D. W. Hamlyn, *Aristotle's De Anima, Books II, III* (Oxford, 1968), pp. 115–17.

4 I. Block, 'Truth and error in Aristotle's theory of perception', *Philosophical Quarterly* XI (1961), 1–9.

5 I take it as given that these really are perceptions and do not involve higher 'faculties'. Although it has occasionally been thought that common

and especially incidental perception do involve such higher faculties – e.g. by J. I. Beare, *Greek Theories of Elementary Cognition* (Oxford, 1906), pp. 285–7, and by F. Solmson, 'Greek philosophy and the discovery of the nerves', *Museum Helveticum* XVIII (1961), 150–97 – this view is now generally considered to be mistaken. Cf. T. J. Slakey, 'Aristotle on sense perception', *Philosophical Review* LXX (1961), 470–84, and C. H. Kahn, 'Sensation and consciousness in Aristotle's psychology', *Archiv für Geschichte de Philosophie* XLVIII (1966), 43–81.

6   Cf. *De Sensu*, 447^{a}2–4. This is Aristotle's mature view. Earlier he had advocated an intromission theory (e.g. *Topics* 105^{b}6) but it is unclear whether this earlier view would have meant construing the process in temporal terms.

7   On touch, see Richard Sorabji, 'Aristotle on demarcating the five senses', *Philosophical Review* LXXX (1971), 55–79.

8   See S. Cashdollar, 'Aristotle's account of incidental perception', *Phronesis* XVIII (1973), 156–75.

9   For details, see Etienne Gilson, *The Christian Philosophy of Saint Augustine* (London, 1961), pp. 77 ff.

10   See Henri Gouhier, *Cartésianisme et Augustinianisme au XVIIe Siècle* (Paris, 1978).

11   For details see Robert Lenoble, *Mersenne ou la naissance du mécanisme* (Paris, 1971).

12   See David C. Lindberg, *Theories of Vision from al-Kindi to Kepler* (Chicago, 1976), pp. 202–5.

13   See Alexandre Koyré, *The Astronomical Revolution* (London, 1973), Part II; D. P. Walker, *Studies in Musical Science in the Late Renaissance* (London, 1978), Ch. 4.

14   J. Kepler, *Gesammelte Werke* (ed. Max Caspar, Munich, 1937 ff.), vol. 2, pp. 19–41.

15   Quoted in E. A. Burtt, *The Metaphysical Foundations of Modern Physical Science* (London, 1932), p. 57.

16   This is not to say that the account is entirely problem-free. For some obscure reason Descartes thinks that the physical forms in the external senses have to be incorporealised and then recorporealised on reaching the imagination. See John W. Yolton, *Perceptual Acquaintance* (Oxford, 1984), p. 20.

17   Descartes discussed the geometrical aspects of the transmission of light as if light consisted of a stream of atoms travelling in a void. This is a simplifying assumption at odds with his physical optics, and for the more comprehensive picture the streams of atoms must be replaced by something like rotating rods of fine corpuscular matter. The speed of rotation of the 'rod' determines the colour that will ultimately be seen by the mind, although it will be registered in the imagination by a two-dimensional pattern of lines (see CSM I, 40–1 for the account in the *Regulae*; the most

detailed account occurs in the discussion of the rainbow in the Eighth Discourse of the *Meteorology*, AT VI, 325 ff.).

18 I am grateful to David Armstrong for drawing my attention to this passage.

19 See J. Peghaire, *Intellectus et Ratio selon S. Thomas d'Aquin* (Paris and Ottawa, 1936).

20 See my *Cartesian Logic* (Oxford, 1989), Ch. 2.

21 Yolton, *op. cit.*, p. 26.

22 See also Descartes' prefatory remarks to his replies to Arnauld's objections to the *Meditations* (CSM II, 138).

23 Cf. *Treatise on Man* (CSM I, 102); *Dioptrics*, Discourse Six (CSM I, 167); *Principles of Philosophy* IV, art. 197 (CSM I, 284).

24 Yolton, *op. cit.*, pp. 31–9.

25 I shall look at the question of occasionalism below.

26 Malebranche's construal of this distinction ultimately tends to make primary qualities like secondary ones. See, for example, his first reply to *On True and False Ideas*, summarised below in the Appendix. Berkley's response to Locke parallels Malebranche's reply to Arnauld (and Locke's response to Malebranche in turn owes a good deal to Arnauld). On the Berkeley/Locke dispute over primary and secondary qualities, see Jonathan Bennett, *Locke, Berkeley and Hume* (Oxford, 1971), Ch. 4. On Locke's indebtedness to Arnauld see C. J. McCracken, *Malebranche and British Philosophy* (Oxford, 1983), Ch. 4.

27 Malebranche (OC XVIII, 48–52) tells us that his chance reading of Descartes' *Treatise on Man* in 1664 made his heart palpitate with excitement, and he obviously takes the physiological psychology offered by Descartes as a revelation.

28 This doctrine gave Malebranche some considerable trouble. Arnauld takes it to pieces in *On True and False Ideas*, and it led to charges of Spinozism against Malebranche.

29 Everything taken into account, I think we must conclude that Descartes *does* allow second causes an independent effectivity. See M. Gueroult, 'The metaphysics and physics of force in Descartes', and A. Gabbey, 'Force and inertia in the seventeenth century: Descartes and Newton', both in S. Gaukroger (ed.), *Descartes* (Sussex, 1980).

30 See Steven N. Nadler, *Arnauld and the Cartesian Philosophy of Ideas* (Manchester, 1989).

31 See Malebranche's reply to Arnauld, summarised in the Appendix.

32 See J. J. Gibson, *The Ecological Approach to Visual Perception* (New York, 1979). For an assessment of Gibson's earlier writings. see D. W. Hamlyn, *The Psychology of Perception* (London, 1969). There is a good discussion of Gibson's writings in relation to Descartes in M. Grene, *Descartes* (Sussex, 1985), Ch. 8.

Antoine Arnauld

On True and False Ideas

against the Teaching of the Author of
the Search after Truth

Contents

On True and False Ideas

A demonstration that what the author of the *Search after Truth* says about these rests upon false premises, and that there is nothing as baseless as his claim that we see all things in God.

Sir, I have told you of my plan to look at the *Treatise on Nature and Grace* and to make public my judgement of it.[1] I did not doubt that you would show my letter to its author, or that you would consider, as you did, that it was really directed to him, for in my view it is more honest and Christian to act frankly than to attack a friend secretly and to conceal from him something which I do not believe would displease him, as that would suggest that I suspected him of being insincere in his claim that he strives only for truth.

I am glad that I did not think this of my friend, and it gives me great pleasure to learn from your reply that I was not mistaken in thinking that St Augustine did not mean this when he said that it is wrong to prefer others to be in error than to discover that oneself is: *nimis perverse seipsum amat, qui alios vult errare, ut error suus lateat.* For you assure me that, having shown him my first letter, which you knew I had intended him to see, he indicated that he agreed with me on the question of writing against the opinions of one's friends, and that he was not at all annoyed that I had written against the *Treatise.* Thus I have no worries in this respect. But I'm afraid you won't be surprised when you see that this is not the work you've been waiting for, but merely a preamble to it. The reason is this. Our friend advises us in the second edition of his *Treatise* that if we are to be able to understand it we must first grasp the principles established in his *The Search after Truth*, and in particular his findings on the nature of ideas, i.e. his view that we see all things in God. Thus I set about studying this question. But having applied myself to it diligently, I found so little truth in what our friend teaches, to say the least, that it seemed to me that I could do no better than to begin by showing him that he has more reason than he thinks to doubt a number of assumptions which he takes as certain, so that he may be persuaded by sense experience to try to understand the mysteries of grace through the teachings of the saints rather than by himself.

I am sure, Sir, that you will agree with me when you realise just how much he contradicts himself on the question of ideas, and the extent to which he has failed to follow the rules of reasoning which he rightly prescribes for others. This you can judge for yourself from what follows. I would only add that if I have thrown some light on a question which up until now has seemed very obscure and complicated, this is due solely, on the one hand, to my having been guided by those clear and distinct ideas which everyone can find in himself if only he pays attention to what is in his mind, and on the other, to my having observed the following rules, which I believe should be presented first so that, once they are accepted, the same truths can be reached by the same route by all.

Chapter 1

Rules that must be kept in mind when one is seeking the truth in this question of ideas and in many similar questions

These rules are, in my opinion, so reasonable that I do not believe that there is any man of good sense who does not agree with them, and who would not at least agree that one can do no better than observe them whenever possible, or agree that they can provide the true means of avoiding many of the errors that one often unwittingly makes in the natural sciences.

The first is to begin with those things that are clearest and simplest, and which cannot be doubted, provided one pays attention to them.

The second is not to obscure something known clearly by trying to explain it further in terms of notions which are confused. To do this is to attempt to illuminate light by means of shadows.

The third is not to seek reasons *ad infinitum*, but to stop when we get to what we know to be the nature of a thing, or what we know with certainty to be a quality of it. One must not ask why extension is divisible, for example, or why mind is capable of thought, for it is the nature of extension to be divisible, and that of mind to think.

The fourth is not to ask for definitions of terms that are clear in themselves, and which can only be obscured by trying to define them, since we would be forced to explain them in terms of notions which are not as clear. Such are the words *think* and *exist*, for example, in the proposition 'I think therefore I exist'. Hence the objection made against Descartes in these terms in the *Sixth Objections* is a very weak one:

In order that you might know that you think, and conclude from this that you exist, you must first know what thinking is and what existence is. And since you do not yet know either of these, how can you be certain that you exist, since in saying *I think* you do not know what you say, and you know even less when you say *therefore I exist*? [CSM II, 278]

Descartes replies to this that no one knows so little that they do not know what *thinking* is or what *existence* is, so there is no need to define these words in order to be assured that one is not mistaken when one says 'I think therefore I exist.'

The fifth is not to confuse questions which must be answered by providing a formal cause with those which require an efficient cause, and not to ask for the formal cause of a formal cause – something that is the source of many errors – but only for its efficient cause. An example will help us make this clearer. If I am asked why this piece of lead is round, I can reply by giving the definition of roundness, i.e. by providing the formal cause, and say that it is because, if one conceives of straight lines drawn from as many points as one wishes on the surface to a particular point inside this piece of lead they will be equal. But if one continues to ask how it comes about that the surface of the lead is as I have described it, how it comes about that it is not shaped as it would be if the lead were a cube, then a Peripatetic will seek another formal cause, saying that it is because the lead has received a quality called roundness which has been drawn from the depths of its matter in order to make it round, and that it does not have any other quality which would make it a cube. But good sense required us to reply by providing an efficient cause, by saying that the exterior surface of this piece of lead is due to its having being melted down and thrown into a hollow mould whose concave surface made the lead's surface convex, so that all its points, etc.

The sixth is to take great care not to conceive of spirits as bodies, nor bodies as spirits, by attributing to either what is peculiar to the other. This occurs when one attributes a fear of a void to bodies, or when one attributes to minds the requirement that bodies be spatially proximate if they are to be perceived by them.

The seventh is not to multiply beings unnecessarily, as so often happens in everyday philosophy. This occurs, for example, when one wants to account for stone, gold, lead, fire and water solely in terms of the diverse arrangements and configurations of the parts of matter while still retaining substantial forms of stone, gold, lead, fire and water, where these are in reality quite different from anything that can be imagined in terms of the arrangement and configuration of parts of matter.[2]

I now want to show what, I believe, can be discovered easily if we follow these few rules about how the soul and its operations are to be conceived, in regard to one of its faculties, the understanding.

Chapter 2

The principal things that can be known about one's soul through a little careful deliberation.

St Augustine recognised long before Descartes that if we are to discover the truth we can begin with nothing more certain than the proposition that 'I think, therefore I exist.' He considers, in respect to the *I think*, all the different ways in which we think, whether it be knowing something with certainty (which he calls *intelligere*) or doubting or remembering. For it is certain, he says, that there is nothing at all that we can do that does not at the same time bring with it compelling proof of our own existence [*City of God*, XI, 26]. He concludes from this that, for the soul to know itself, it has only to distinguish itself from those things which are distinct from its thought, and what remains will be what it is. That is to say, the soul can only be a substance that thinks or is capable of thinking. It follows from this that we can know what we are only by attending seriously to what occurs in our minds. In this we must take particular care not to include anything of which we are not certain, and to reflect when we find it difficult to explain things in words which, since they have usually been invented by men who have only been attentive to what happened in their bodies and those around them, are scarcely suitable for relating the operations of the mind to the individual senses which provide us with the occasion to think of them.

Now when the mind, having freed itself of childhood prejudices, has come to know that its nature is to think, it easily recognises that it would be as unreasonable to ask why it thinks as it would be to ask why extension is divisible and capable of taking on different shapes and moving in different ways. For, as I said in the fifth Rule, when one has come to know the nature of a thing, there is no longer anything, by way of formal causes, left to seek. Consequently, I can only ask myself why mind exists, and why extension exists. And I must reply here by giving the efficient cause, which is that God has created both of these.

Thus just as it is clear that *I think*, it is also clear that I think of something, i.e. that I know and perceive something. For that is what thought is essentially. Consequently, since it is not possible for there to be thought or knowledge without an object known, I can no longer ask for the reasons why I think of something, since I cannot think without thinking of something. But I can of course ask why I think of one thing rather than another.

The changes which occur in simple substances do not cause them to be something different from what they are, but only to be in some other way than they were. And this must be what distinguishes things or substances from modes, or ways of being, which can also be called modifications. But true modifications cannot be conceived without conceiving of the substance of which they are the modifications; so if it is my nature to think, and I can think of different things without changing my nature, then these different thoughts can only be different modifications of the thinking which constitutes my nature. Although it is not necessary for my argument, perhaps we could speculate that there is in me some thought which does not change and which can be taken as the essence of my soul. I can find two thoughts which one might consider to be like this: the thought of a universal Being and that of my own soul. Both of these are to be found in all other thoughts: that of the universal Being, because it contains the idea of being in its entirety, whereas our soul only knows something under the notion of possible or existent being; and the thought that our soul has of itself because, whatever it is that I know, I know that I know by an implicit reflection that accompanies all my thoughts. Thus I know myself in knowing other things. And it seems to me that the principal way of distinguishing those beings which are intelligent from those which are not is that the former *sunt conscia sui et suae operationes* [are conscious of themselves and their actions] whereas the latter are not. That is to say, the former know that they exist and that they act, whereas the latter do not, the Latin capturing this better than the French.

But no matter how much care we take in our deliberations, we are not aware of anything else in our soul's thoughts which can change – and which we therefore judge to be only modifications of the soul, and to occur only in things which do not change. For in neither do we see anything but the perception and knowledge of an object. We will therefore only confuse ourselves and make our heads swim if we seek to understand how the perception of an object can be in us, or what one is to understand by this. If we pay careful attention we will find that this is the same as asking how matter can be divisible and have shape. For since it is the nature of the mind to perceive objects, some necessarily, so to speak, and others contingently, it is ridiculous to ask how it comes about that our mind perceives objects. As for those who are not prepared to understand the perception of objects by deliberating upon it, I do not know how to make them understand better.

Hence as regards the formal cause of our perception of objects, there is no question to be asked. This is because nothing could be clearer, provided only that one fastens on to what one understands clearly onself and does not run this together with things which one does not understand clearly but mistakenly wishes to include. This is the cause of all man's errors concerning his soul, as St Augustine correctly points out in Book X of *On The Trinity*.

The only legitimate question which could be asked about the cause of our perceptions is one concerned solely with the efficient cause of our contingent perceptions, namely, what is the cause of our thinking of one object at one time and of another at another time? As far as necessary perceptions are concerned there can be no doubt that these are due to God, and we shall postpone discussion of this until the end of the treatise.

Chapter 3

That the author of *The Search after Truth* gives a different account of ideas in the first two Books to that given in the third, where he deals with them explicitly.

What I have just said concerning the soul and its perceptions corresponds so closely to our natural conceptions that the author of *The*

Search after Truth himself speaks in the same way as long as he confines himself to the first ideas that come into his mind on this question, and as long as he does not muddle these up with other philosophical notions, which he too readily assumes to be fundamentally correct and in need only of amendment.

We can see that in his simple and natural judgements on this question, there is very little that does not accord fully with what we have said. There are nevertheless some expressions which are perhaps ambiguous, and what he has done is to take these badly understood ideas in the wrong sense, although in themselves they can also be taken in a truthful way. At the beginning of the third Book, he says in general terms: 'But if, by the essence of a thing, one understands what is first conceived in the thing, that on which all the modifications that are noticed in it depend, one cannot doubt that the essence of the mind consists in thinking [ST, 198 note *a*]. In the first Chapter of the first Book, in a comparison of matter and spirit, he explains at greater length what occurs in the soul:

Matter or extension has two properties or faculties. The first faculty is that of taking on different shapes, the second is the capacity for being moved. The mind of man likewise contains two faculties. The first, which is the *understanding*, is that of receiving various *ideas*, i.e. of perceiving various things. The second, which is the *will*, is that of receiving various inclinations, or of willing different things. We shall first explain the relations between the first of the two faculties belonging to matter and the first of those that belong to mind. [ST, 2]

Notice the words 'receiving various ideas, i.e. perceiving various things'. In what follows one would only have to substitute this definition for the *definiendum* to exclude the false notion of *ideas* that he presents elsewhere when he wants us to conceive of them as particular *representations*[3] of objects which are actually distinct from the perceptions and the objects. [He continues:]

Extension can receive two kinds of shape. Some are only external, like the roundness of a piece of wax. Others are internal, and these are the ones which are characteristic of all the small parts of which the wax is composed, for it is indubitable that all the small parts that make up a piece of wax have shapes very different from those that make up a piece of iron. That which is external I call simply *shape*, and I call *configuration* the shape which is internal and which is necessary for wax to be what it is. Likewise, it can be said that the ideas of the soul are of two kinds, taking the term *idea* generally to cover everything which the mind perceives immediately. The first represent to us something outside of us, such as a square, a house, etc. The second only represent to us what happens in us, such as our sensations, sadness, pleasure, etc. For it will be seen in what follows that these latter ideas are nothing but a way of being of the mind, and it is because of this that I will call them modifications of the mind. [ST, 2]

It is a matter of choice how one defines words. Nevertheless, it is annoying that the generic name should be given to one species and denied to the other, for this may lead one to think that the latter does not share in the notion of the genus at all. To avoid this drawback, I may also be allowed to devise my own dictionary and say that the perception of a square is a modification of my soul just as much as is the perception of colour, for the perception of a square is something in my soul. Since it is not its essence, it must be a modification of it. Moreover, on Malebranche's account, there is an analogy between my soul having a perception of a square and extension having a shape. Now shape is a modification of extension; thus to receive the notion of a square, i.e. to perceive a square, is a modification of my soul. Nevertheless, it must be noted here that he takes the word 'idea' as a *perception* and not as the *representation* which he maintains elsewhere we need in order to perceive things. And this agrees with Book 3, Part II, Chapter 1, where, in regard to sensations, i.e. perceptions of colour, light and so on, he says that the soul had no need of *representations*, and yet he calls these perceptions *ideas*. [He continues:] 'These inclinations of the soul can also be called modifications of the same soul because it has been established that the inclination of the will is a way of being of the soul and therefore it can be called a *modification of the soul*.' This is sufficient as far as I am concerned. Whatever other reasons he believes he has for not referring to it as a *modification*, I am happy to consider it as such and to call it by that name if indeed, as he acknowledges, it is one.

He goes on to say that our soul is completely passive with regard to perceptions but not with regard to inclinations. I shall draw some important conclusions from this but I will do that elsewhere, since they concern the cause of ideas and not their *nature*. It is the *nature of ideas* with which I am presently concerned. This is why I confine myself to noting that the author of *The Search after Truth*, having spoken of these ideas extensively in the first chapter of his book, indicates in a number of ways that *ideas of objects* and *perceptions of objects* are the same thing. And it is worth noting, in case one thinks that this has escaped his attention, that he continues to take the word *idea* in the same way in Part [2] of Book 2, especially in the [fifth] Chapter. For what he refers to in the title of this chapter as 'the mutual relations of ideas in the mind and traces in the brain', he calls in the same chapter 'the natural and mutual correspondence of thoughts in the soul and traces in the brain'. Thus he takes *ideas* to be the same thing as *thoughts*. And one only has to read this chapter to be convinced that *ideas* and *thoughts* are synonymous terms throughout. Nevertheless, when he discusses the *nature of ideas* at a fundamental level in the second Part of Book 3, and in the *Elucidations of the Search after Truth*, it is clear that what he is calling *ideas* is no longer *the thoughts of the soul* or *perceptions of objects*, but particular *representations of objects* distinct from these perceptions, which he says 'really exist and are required for the perception of material objects'.

I have no wish simply to point out the apparent contradiction here, for it may not be so much a contradiction as a lack of exactness, in that he has used the same word in two different senses without having alerted us sufficiently to this. But I do maintain two things. First, that ideas taken in the latter sense are in fact chimeras. They have been invented solely in order that we might better understand how our soul, which is immaterial, can know the material things that God has created. But the manifest failure of these speculations results in an attempt to persuade us, in a roundabout way, that God has given our souls no means at all by which to perceive the real and true bodies that He has created, but only a means of perceiving intelligible bodies which are outside our souls and resemble real bodies. Secondly, the author is a man of the world who speaks with the greatest force against those who abandon the clear ideas which they find in themselves and follow confused notions which remain with them as childhood prejudices. Yet he himself has fallen into the extraordinary views that I am undertaking to refute only because he has not been able to rid himself entirely of these prejudices and has retained a false principle which he holds in common with almost all scholastic philosophers, but which has led him to much stranger views than others because he has pushed it further than they. As in the case of those who have turned from the true path, they stray furthest who move the fastest.

I shall begin with the second point, as the falsity of the paradoxes that he advances on this question can be recognised more easily when their cause has been discovered. I apologise for using strong language. It is, I believe, just the love of truth and the desire to understand it better that compel me to do so, for without this I would cease to respect the person whom I am refuting. What I find here is only a striking example of human infirmity, which causes minds that are otherwise very clear and penetrating to fall into very great errors when they philosophise on these abstract matters, when they allow themselves inadvertently to take as true some common principle that they have not taken sufficient care to examine, and which turns out not to be true. For falsity is as fertile as truth. A false principle which one carelessly takes as true can lead to our becoming entangled in many absurd opinions just as a true one can lead us to discover many new truths.

Chapter 4

What the author of *The Search after Truth* says concerning *the nature of ideas* in his third Book is based merely on fancies deriving from childhood prejudices.

As all men have first been children, and were then concerned with almost nothing but their body and what affected their senses, they were not aware for a long time of any vision but corporeal vision, which they attributed to their eyes. And they could not help noticing two things about this vision. First, if we are to see the object it must be before or *present to* our eyes, and because of this they regarded the presence of the object as a necessary condition of seeing. Second, one also occasionally sees visible objects in mirrors or in water or in other things which represent them to us, and in this case it is thought, erroneously, that what one sees is not these same bodies but their images. This was for a long time the only idea they had of what they called *seeing*, and through habit they became accustomed to associate the idea behind this word with either the case where the object is present in direct view, or that where the object is seen only by its image reflected in a mirror. The difficulties in separating ideas which are habitually found together in the mind are well known, and this is one of the most common causes of error.

But, with time, men have perceived that they know various things that they cannot see with their eyes, either because they are too small, or because they are not visible, like the air, or because they are too distant, like the towns of foreign lands which we have never visited. It is this that has made them believe that there are things which are seen with the mind and not with the eyes. They would have done better to have concluded that we see nothing with the eyes, only with the mind, albeit in a different way. But they need more time to reach this conclusion. In any case, having imagined that the mind's vision is similar to the vision they have attributed to the eyes, they apply this word 'vision' to the mind, as usual with the same conditions that they imagine obtain in the case of the eyes.

The first such condition is the presence of the object. For they do not doubt – indeed they take it as certain – that, for the mind just as for the eyes, the object must be present if it is to be seen. But when philosophers – i.e. those who believe they know nature better than the vulgar and have not allowed themselves to be influenced by any principle before they have examined it properly – when they attempted to use it to explain the mind's vision, they encountered great difficulties. Some recognised that the soul is immaterial, whereas others, who believe it to be corporeal, considered it as a subtle matter shut up in the body, which it cannot leave in order to seek objects outside, nor can objects outside come in to join it. How then can one see, since an object cannot be seen if it is not present? To overcome this difficulty they introduce another sense of seeing which they are accustomed to calling 'seeing' in the case of corporeal vision. This is the case where one sees things not by themselves but by means of their images, as when one sees a body in mirrors. For as I have already indicated, they, and almost everyone else, believe that in this case it is not bodies that one sees but only their images. They stick to this and the belief has such force for them that they do not accept that there is any doubt as to its truth. Consequently, taking it as a certain and incontestable truth, they are no longer worried about finding out what these images or *representations* could be, which the mind needs in order to perceive bodies.

Something else, which in fact derives from what we have just said and is not really that different from it, reinforces this opinion still more, and this is that we have a natural inclination to want to know things by example and comparison since, provided we are careful, we can appreciate that it is vexing to believe something remarkable without being able to give an example of it. Thus when men begin to realise that we see things with the mind, instead of reflecting on and noting what they perceive clearly happening in their minds when they know things, they imagine that an analogy will improve their understanding. Since we have become afflicted by sin, our love for the body is all the greater, this causes us to think that we know corporeal things much better and more easily than spiritual things. Thus they believe that they will find some analogy in the body which will allow them to understand how we see with the mind everything that we conceive, and above all material things. But they do not realise that this is not a means of clarification but rather a means of obscuring what would be very clear to them if they were only to reflect upon it, for the mind and the body are two substances which are wholly distinct and, as it were, opposites, so their properties should have nothing in common. Only confusion can result from trying to explain the one by the other, and one of the most pervasive sources of error is our constant application of the properties of the mind to bodies and the properties of bodies to mind.

But however that may be, they are insufficiently enlightened to avoid this pitfall. They try with all their might to construct an analogy with bodies in order, they believe, that they and others might better understand how our mind can see material things. And this is what they did, and what one finds all the harder to understand. And they had no difficulty in establishing the analogy. It almost presents itself ready-made, as a result of another prejudice, namely that there must at least be a great resemblance between those things having the same name. As I have already indicated, they give the same name to corporeal and to spiritual vision, and as a result they argue that what happens in mental vision must be roughly similar to what happens in bodily vision. In the case of the latter, we can only see what is present, i.e. what is before our eyes; or, if we occasionally see things which are not before our eyes, these are only images which represent these things. Thus it must be the same with the mind's vision. And they do not hesitate to make an indubitable principle out of the maxim that we see with our mind only those objects present to our soul. But they do not mean this in the sense of *objective presence*, by which a thing is only objectively in our mind in virtue of our mind knowing it. If this were what they meant it would just be a different way of saying that the thing is objectively in our mind (and consequently *present to it*) and is known by our mind. They do not take the word *presence* in this way, but rather intend it as a prerequisite for the perception of an object, as something which is necessary if the object is to be in a state whereby it can be perceived, something they found to be necessary in vision, or so they thought. And from this they quickly pass to another principle, namely, that since all the bodies that our soul knows cannot be individually present to it, they must be present in the form of images which represent them. And philosophers have a stronger attachment to this than others, for they hold the same view in the case of corporeal vision. They imagine that our eyes only perceive objects via images which they call intentional species, and they believe they have a convincing proof of these, for when we close off a room except for a single hole, and place in front of this hole a glass in the shape of a lens, stretching behind it at some distance a white canvas, then light from outside forms images on this canvas which represent perfectly, to those who are in the room, the objects which are outside and opposite the hole.

Thus they adopt another principle which they take to be incontestable, namely, that the soul only sees bodies via images or species which represent them. They draw different conclusions from this, depending on the procedure adopted by the particular philosopher, and some of them are very poor. Gassendi reasons in the following way, or at least these are the opinions he proposes as objections to be answered by Descartes:

Our soul can know bodies only by means of ideas that represent them. Now these ideas are not able to represent material things unless they are themselves material and extended. Hence they are such. But if they are to serve the soul in knowing body they must be present to the soul, i.e. they must be received in the soul. Now that which is extended can only be received in something which is itself extended. Hence the soul must be extended and therefore corporeal.

However damnable this conclusion, I do not see that it is easy to disallow it if one accepts these principles, and hence it must be concluded that the principles are not true.

Other philosophers, however, fearing such a conclusion, have claimed that they can avoid it by maintaining that these ideas of bodies are at first material and extended, but that before being received into the soul they are spiritualised, just as gross matter is refined by being passed through an alembic. I do not know if they use this analogy, but it comes down to the same thing when they maintain that ideas of bodies, which they call impressed species, being material and sensible to begin with, are made intelligible and immaterial by the active intellect, and this renders them capable of being received in the passive intellect.

I am astonished that the majority of philosophers have reasoned in this way and have as a result blindly accepted as incontestable two principles: *that the soul can only perceive objects which are present to it,* and *that bodies can be present to it only through particular representations called ideas or species which, being similar to them, take their place and are in immediate contact with the soul in place of them.* Nothing indeed is more atonishing than that the author of the *Search after Truth,* who professes to follow a completely different path, should accept these and other principles without any further scrutiny. For he knows better than anyone that the comparison of corporeal and spiritual vision, on which this is all apparently based, is false in every respect. This is not only because it is the soul and not the eyes that see, but also because even if it were the eyes that saw, or the soul in so far as it is in the eyes, one would find nothing in this vision to support the claim of the scholastic philosophers that one ought to find two things in the mind. The first is the presence of the object, which they say should be in immediate contact with the soul. This is in fact quite contrary to corporeal vision, for although in ordinary parlance one says that the object should be present to our eyes if we are to see it (something which has been a source of error), it is the other way round entirely if we speak exactly and philosophically. The object must be absent from the eye, since it must be some distance from it, for what is in the eye or too close to it cannot be seen. The same holds for the second thing, which is that we see particular representations which, being similar to objects, enable us to know them. He is well aware that neither our eyes, nor our soul by means of our eyes, see anything like this. He knows that when one sees oneself in a mirror it is oneself that one sees and not the image which I have already spoken of and which the Schools call *intentional species,* which are mere chimeras. Finally, he is well aware that, although the objects that we see form perfect enough images on the back of our eye, it is certain nonetheless that what our eyes see are not these small images painted on the retina, and that vision does not take place by means of these, but in another way, as Descartes shows in the *Dioptrics.*

It is certainly surprising that, knowing full well the falsity of everything that follows from these opinions, he is so persuaded by them that he takes them, without any hesitation, as the unassailable foundation for all he has to say on the matter. For this is what happens in Book 3, Part II, entitled *On the Nature of Ideas*. It is clear from the title of the first chapter – *What is meant by ideas; that they really exist and are needed for the perception of objects* – what he seeks to show, and this is how he undertakes to establish his principles:

I believe, he says, that everyone agrees (it is as if someone were speaking who wanted everything judged by everyday prejudices) that we do not perceive objects which are outside of us by themselves. We see the sun, the stars, and an infinite number of objects outside of us, and it is not likely that the soul leaves the body and as it were strolls about the heavens in order to contemplate all these objects. Thus it does not see them by themselves, and the immediate object of our mind when it sees the sun, for example, is not the sun but something which is in immediate contact with our soul, and this is what I call an *idea*. Thus by the word *idea* I understand here nothing other than what is the immediate object, or what is closest to the mind, when it perceives something. It must be noted that if the mind is to perceive some object, it is absolutely necessary that the idea of the object itself be actually present to it. This is indubitable. [ST, 217]

This, Sir, is how he broaches the subject. He does not examine what he assumes to be indubitable, because belief in a commonplace should be accepted without investigation. He does not doubt that. He takes it as one of his first principles that one only needs to consider it briefly to put it beyond doubt. He does not put himself to the trouble of convincing us by proving it. It is sufficient to tell us that 'everyone agrees with it'.

Nevertheless, it is clear from what we know from the first chapter, namely that 'the idea of an object' is the same as 'the perception of that object', that he is presenting us with something completely different here. For it is no longer *the perception of bodies* that he calls an *idea*, but rather a particular *representation* of bodies which he claims is needed to make good the absence of any body that can be joined intimately to the soul, so that the *representation* is thereby *the immediate object and what is closest to our mind when it perceives it*. He does not say that it is in the mind or that it is a modification of it, which he would say if he had meant by it only the perception of the object, but only that it is 'the closest to the mind', because he regards this *representation* as being actually distinct from our mind as well as from the object.

This can be understood better in the following way. To say that the soul and everything in it, such as its thoughts and modes of thinking, are understood without ideas is a manifest contradiction if, by 'idea of an object' one understands 'only the perception of that object'. For that would be to say that the soul perceives without perceiving and that it knows without knowing. Thus it is clear that he wishes to indicate by his statement that for the soul to know itself it has no need of a *representation* to compensate for something absent, since it is always present to itself.

I speak principally here of material things, which surely cannot be in contact with our soul in the way necessary for it to perceive them, because, since they are extended and the soul is not extended, there is no relation between them. Besides which, our souls do not leave the body in order to gauge the grandeur of the heavens, and consequently they can see external bodies only by means of the ideas which represent them, and with this everyone must agree. [ST, 219]

It would be impossible to speak more confidently if one were presenting the axioms of geometry. And he continues in the same tone:

Thus we maintain that it is absolutely necessary either (a) that the ideas that we have of body and or all other objects that we cannot perceive by themselves come from these bodies of these objects; or (b) that our soul has the power of producing these ideas; or (c) that God produced them in us when He created the soul, or produces them every time we think about an object; or (d) that the soul has in itself all the perfections that it sees in bodies; or finally (e) that it is joined to a wholly perfect being who contains all the perfections of created beings. [ST, 219]

If these alleged *representations* of body are not to be purely chimerical, I freely grant that they must be in our soul in one of these five ways. But as I am convinced that they are only chimeras, I am greatly astonished that our friend, who has destroyed so many other chimeras, should succumb to these.

The conclusion has the same air of confidence, but does contain some modest words which will be instructive for those who are convinced that nothing has been proposed which is not of the greatest clarity:

We can only conceive objects in one of two ways. Let us determine which is the more probable, without either prejudice or fear of the difficulty of the question. We can perhaps resolve the question clearly enough, even though we do not claim to provide demonstrations which everyone will find beyond question, but only proofs which are very convincing at least to those who consider them seriously, for it would appear presumptuous to maintain otherwise. [ST, 219]

And I, Sir, am not afraid of appearing presumptuous in saying two things to you. This first is that since ideas taken as *representations* distinct from perceptions are completely unnecessary for our soul to see bodies, it is consequently completely unnecessary that they be in it in one of the five ways. Secondly, the least likely of the ways, and the one which explains least how our soul can see bodies, is the one which our friend prefers to the others.

Chapter 5

That it is possible to prove geometrically the falsity of *ideas* taken as representations. Definitions, axioms and questions serve as principles in these demonstrations.

I believe, Sir, that I can demonstrate to our friend the falsity of these *representations*, provided he is willing, in good faith, to go back to what he himself has said, on many occasions, should be observed if one wishes to discover the truth in metaphysics just as in the natural sciences; that is, one must take as true only what is clear and evident: and one must not make use of alleged *entities* of which we have no clear and distinct idea in order to explain the effects of nature, whether corporeal or spiritual. I shall try to prove this by the geometrical method.

Definitions

(1) I call *soul* or *mind* the substance which thinks.
(2) To *think*, to *know* and to *perceive* are the same thing.
(3) I also take the *idea* of an object and the *perception* of that object to be the same thing. I leave to one side whether there are other things that can be called *ideas*. For it is certain that there are *ideas* in this sense, and that they are attributes or modifications of our mind.
(4) I maintain that an object is present to our mind when our mind perceives and knows it. I leave open for the time being whether there is another sense in which an object is present to the mind,

namely that where the object must be present in a knowable state prior to our knowledge of it. But there can be no doubt that the sense in which I say an object is present to the mind when the mind knows it is one which cannot be questioned; and this is what leads us to say that a person we love is often present to our mind, because we think of them often.

(5) I maintain that a thing is *objectively* in my mind when I conceive it. When I conceive of the sun, a square or a sound, then the sun, the square or the sound are objectively in my mind, whether or not they are external to my mind.

(6) I have said that I take *perception* and *idea* to be the same thing. It must nevertheless be noted that, while this thing is single, it stands in a twofold relation, to the soul that it modifies, and to the thing perceived in so far as this latter is objectively in the soul, and the word 'perception' more directly refers to the former relation, the word 'idea' to the latter. Thus the *perception* of a square has as its most direct meaning my soul perceiving the square, whereas the *idea* of a square has as its most direct meaning the square in so far as it is *objectively* in my mind. This distinction is of great use in resolving many difficulties which are based on insufficiently understanding that it is not a question of two different entities, but rather a single modification of our soul which necessarily contains both these relations, for I cannot have a perception which is not the perception of my mind as a perceiving mind, and the perception of what it is that is perceived, and moreover nothing can be objectively in my mind (what I call the *idea*) which my mind does not perceive.

(7) In so far as I reject them as superflous entities, I understand by *representation* only what is imagined to be really distinct from ideas taken as perceptions. I am not denying that there are *representations* or *representative modalities*, since I believe it is clear to whoever reflects on what occurs in his mind that all our perceptions are essentially *representative* modalities.

(8) To say that our ideas and our perceptions (taking these to be the same thing) represent to us the things that we conceive and that they are their images, is to say something completely different from saying that pictures represent their originals and are the images of them, or that spoken or written words are the images of our thoughts. For in the case of ideas we mean that the things we conceive are *objectively* in our mind and in our thought. And this *way of being objectively in the mind* is so peculiar to the mind and to

thought, since it is what specifically gives them their nature, that one seeks in vain anything similar outside the mind and thought. As I have already remarked, what has thrown the question of *ideas* into confusion is the attempt to explain the way in which objects are represented by our ideas by analogy with corporeal things, but there can be no real comparison between bodies and minds on this question.

(9) When I say that *idea* and *perception* are the same thing, I understand by perception everything my mind conceives, whether this be in its first awareness of things, or the judgements that it makes about them, or what it discovers about them through reasoning. Thus, although there are an infinite number of figures whose nature I know only after lengthy reasoning, when I have engaged in this reasoning I do not hesitate to count the idea I have of these figures as being as true as the idea I have of a circle or a triangle, which I can conceive straight away. And, although it is perhaps only by reasoning that I am completely certain that there really exist outside my mind an earth, a sun and stars, the idea which represents to me the earth, the sun and the stars as actually existing outside my mind merits being called an idea no less than if I had it without any need for reasoning.

(10) There is yet another equivocation that needs disentangling. We must not confuse *the idea of an object* with *that object conceived*, at least as long as one does not add 'insofar as it is objectively in the mind'. For *being conceived, in regard to the sun that is in the sky*, is only an extrinsic denomination, i.e. only a relation to the perception which I have of it. This is not what should be understood when one says that *the idea of the sun is the sun itself, in so far as it is in my mind*. To say that something *is objectively in the mind* does not just mean that it is the object which my thought is about, but that it is in my mind *intelligibly*, as is customary for objects which are in my mind. And the idea of the sun *is the sun, in so far as it is in my mind*, not formally as it is in the sky, but *objectively*, i.e. in the way in which objects are in our thought, which is a way of being much more imperfect than that by which the sun actually exists, but which nevertheless is not such that it derives from nothing or needs no cause.

(11) When I say that the soul does this or that, and that it has the faculty of doing this or that, I understand by the word 'do' the perception that it has of objects, which is one of its modifications. I

am not concerned with the efficient cause of this modification, with whether God provides it or whether the soul provides its own, for this does not bear upon the nature of ideas, only upon their origin, and these are quite different questions.

(12)   I call a *faculty* the power that I know with certainty that a thing has, whether it be spiritual or corporeal, acting or acted upon, or existing in such-and-such a way, i.e. having such-and-such a modification.

(13)   And when this *faculty* is indubitably a property of the nature of this thing, I then say that it has it from the author of its nature, who can only be God.

Axioms

(1)   If one claims to know things scientifically, one should take as true only those things that one can conceive clearly.

(2)   Nothing should cause us to doubt whatever we know with complete certainty, whatever difficulties are put forward against it.

(3)   It is a manifest confusion of the mind to wish to explain what is clear and certain by obscure and uncertain things.

(4)   One should reject as fictitious those *entities* of which one does not have a clear idea and which one knows to have been invented solely in order to explain things which are considered inexplicable without them.

(5)   This is even more beyond dispute when they can be explained properly without these entities invented by the new philosophers.

(6)   Nothing is more certain for us than the knowledge we have of what occurs in our soul, when we restrict ourselves to this. I am very certain, for example, that I conceive of body when I believe I do, although I cannot be certain that the body I conceive really exists or is as I conceive it.

(7)   It is certain, whether by reason, supposing that God is not a deceiver, or at least by faith, that I have a body and that the earth, the sun, the moon and many other bodies that I know exist outside my mind actually do exist outside my mind.

(8)   The act necessarily presupposes the power, i.e. it is certain that what does something (taking the word 'do' broadly as in Def. 11) has the power to do it, and hence that it has this faculty as defined in Def. 12.

Questions

I ask that everyone reflect seriously on what occurs in his mind when he knows various things, by considering everything that he notices in the one simple thought, without reasoning or otherwise seeking comparisons with corporeal things, and in only stopping himself when he comes to something so certain that it cannot be doubted.

And if you cannot do this by yourself, I ask that you follow me and examine in good faith whether what I maintain is clear to me will not also be clear and certain for you.

(1) I am sure that I exist because I think, and thus that I am a substance that thinks.

(2) I am more certain that I exist than I am that I have a body, or that there are other bodies. For I can doubt that there are bodies, whereas I cannot doubt in the same way that I exist.

(3) I can conceive of perfect being, being itself, universal being. Thus I cannot doubt that I have an idea of it, taking 'the idea of an object' as 'the perception of an object', following Def. 3.

(4) I am sure that I conceive of bodies when I can doubt whether any exist, for it is enough that I know them as possible. And when I take a body to exist which does not exist, I am mistaken, but it is no less the case that this body will be objectively in my mind even though it does not exist outside my body, and thus I will know it in the way described in Def. 4.

(5) When my senses cannot assure me of the existence of external things reason will convince me, by adding the fact that God is not a deceiver. And if I cannot be entirely assured by reason, I can at least be assured by faith (I say this so as to give the matter the greatest certainty, even for the author of *The Search after Truth*). Hence to me, since I have faith as well as reason, it is very certain that when I see the earth, the sun, the stars, and people who converse with me, these are not imaginary bodies or people that I see, but the works of God, and they really are men whom God has created just as He has created me. And it does not matter to me that among thousands of these objects there may be some which exist only in my mind. It is sufficient for my point that, wherever my certainty comes from, whether from reason or from faith, the bodies that I believe I see are as a rule actual bodies that exist outside me.

(6) I am no less certain that I know an infinite number of objects in general, and not only in particular, such as the even numbers in

general, which are infinite, or the square numbers in general, and so
on for the others. The same holds for bodies, for I know with
certainty a cube in general, a cylinder and a pyramid, even though
there are infinitely many different sizes of each of these types of body.

(7)   It is also beyond doubt that I know things in two ways, either
by seeing them directly or by explicit reflection, as when I reflect
upon the idea or the knowledge that I have of a thing and examine it
with more attention in order to determine what is contained in that
idea, taken in the sense of Def. 3.

If I had a little Erastus, I would interrogate him as is done so
ingeniously in the *Christian Conversations*,[4] and I am sure that he
would answer me on all those things of which he is completely
confident. If, on the other hand, I were to ask him whether, in
addition to everything else, one must accept these other ideas, these
representations, etc., I am no less sure that he would say to me that he
knows nothing of them, that he has nothing to say about them, and
that he only gives answers concerning things of which he has a clear
conception, which he does not have in the case of *representations*.
And as for the author of *The Search after Truth*, I would consider
that I had done him an injustice if I had the slightest doubt that he
would not recognise, in good faith, that there is nothing here which is
not very certain.

But I have still to explain other terms and expressions which I said
nothing about in the *Definitions*, because it seemed to me that they
called for more discussion if they were to be understood properly and
if difficulties due to mere equivocation, which have still not been
disentangled, were to be forestalled. I turn to this matter now.

Chapter 6

An explanation of some expressions: 'We do not see things
immediately'; 'It is the ideas of them which are the immediate object
of our thought'; and, 'It is in the idea of each thing that we see its
properties.'

At first sight it would appear that the following expressions – 'We do
not see things immediately', 'it is the ideas of them which are the
immediate object of our thought' and 'it is in the idea of each thing

that we see its properties' – cannot be accepted as true without adhering to the philosophy of imaginary ideas. For it is difficult to understand how these ways of speaking can be correct if there is, over and above the objects that we know, nothing in our minds which represents these objects.

I do not reject these ways of speaking. I believe them to be acceptable if properly understood, and I can even accept the last implication. But I deny that it follows from this that one must allow ideas other than those which I have defined in the preceding chapter, Defs. 3, 6 and 7; these have nothing to do with *representations* distinct from perceptions, which is all I argue against, as I indicated specifically in Def. 7.

To understand this fully, two or three points must be made. The first is that our *thought* or *perception* is essentially reflective upon itself: or, as it is said rather better in Latin, *est sui conscia*. For I do not think without knowing that I think; I do not know a square without knowing that I know it; I do not see the sun or, to avoid any doubt, I do not imagine I see the sun, without being certain that I imagine I see it. I may not remember sometime later that I have seen it, but at the time I conceive it I know that I conceive it. See what St Augustine says on this in Ch. 10 of the tenth Book of *On The Trinity*.

The second point is that, as well as this implicit reflection which accompanies all our perceptions, there is also something explicit, which occurs when we examine our perception by means of another perception. This is easily shown and it occurs above all in the sciences, which are constituted through the reflections men have made on their own perceptions, as when a geometer finds in examining his perception of a triangle that, having conceived it as a figure bounded by three straight lines, it must have three angles, and that these three angles are equal to two right angles.

There is nothing in these two points that can reasonably be contested. Combining them with what we said in Defs. 3, 6 and 7, it follows that, since every perception necessarily represents something and for this reason is called an *idea*, it cannot be essentially reflective upon itself and its immediate object is not this *idea*, i.e. the *objective reality* of the thing that my mind is said to perceive. For example, if I think of the sun, the objective reality of the sun, which is present to my mind, is the immediate object of this perception; and the possible or existing sun, which is outside my mind, is so to speak its mediate object. It is clear from this that, without invoking *representations* distinct

from perceptions, it is true in this sense that, not only in the case of
material things but generally in regard to all things, it is our ideas that
we see *immediately* and which are *the immediate object of our
thought*. This does not prevent us from also seeing, by means of these
ideas, the object that contains formally what is only *objectively* in the
idea; for example, my conceiving the formal being of a square which
is *objectively* in the idea or perception that I have of a square.

In case it is thought that I have made all this up so as to extricate
myself from difficulties, I should point out that Malebranche will
find the same thing in Descartes's *Meditations*, when he undertakes
to prove geometrically the existence of God and the immortality of
the soul, in replying to the second set of objections. We can confine
ourselves to the second and third definitions of this geometrical
demonstration, which I give in Latin and in French, as the Latin
seems to me clearer:

Ideae *nomine intelligo cujuslibet cogitationis formam illam, per cujus*
immediatam *perceptionem ipsius ejusdem cogitationis conscius sum; adeò
ut nihil possim verbis exprimere intelligendo id quod dico, quin ex hoc ipso
certus sim in me esse ideam ejus quod verbis illis significatur.*

Per *realitatem objectivam* Ideae *intelligo entitatem rei representatae per
ideam quatenus est in idea, eodemque modo dici potest perfecto objectiva,
artificium objectivum, etc. Nam, quaecumque percipimus tamquam in idea-
rum objectis, ea sunt in ipsis ideis objectivè.*

By the term *Idea*, I understand that form of any of our thoughts the
immediate perception of which gives us knowledge of these same thoughts;
so that, so long as I understand what I say, I can express nothing in words
without this very fact making it certain that I have in me the idea of the thing
signified by the words . . .

By the *objective reality of an idea*, I understand the entity or being of the
thing represented by the idea, insofar as this entity is in the idea. We can talk
in the same way of objective perfection, objective artifice etc. For everything
we conceive as being in the objects of ideas is objectively or by representation
in the ideas themselves. [CSM II, 113–14]

From these two definitions, as well as from many other things that he
says in the third and fifth of the *Meditations*, it appears that what he
calls an *idea*, and what he subsequently bases his demonstrations of
God and the soul upon, is not really distinct from our thought or

perception, but is rather our thought itself insofar as it contains *objectively* what is formally in the object. And it would appear that it is this idea which, he says, is the *immediate* object of our thought, *per cujus immediatam perceptionem*, etc., because the thought is known itself, and because I do not think of nothing, *cujus non conscius sim.* Hence he did not need, any more than I do, to have recourse to a *representation* which is distinct from my thought in order to accept these propositions which, when properly understood, are very true: 'that it is the ideas of things that we see immediately and these are the immediate object of our thought'.

It is again only in this sense that he understands the word 'idea' in the proposition that 'everything that I perceive clearly as being in the idea of a thing can correctly be asserted of that thing', which he claims, with good reason, to be the foundation of all the natural sciences. If, examining the idea that I have of a triangle (by reflecting on the perception that I have of it), I find that the equality of its three angles to two right angles is contained in this idea or perception, I can correctly assert that every triangle has three angles equal to two right angles.

And finally, it is by always taking the word 'idea' in this sense, and not as a representation distinct from the perception itself, that he proves the existence of God by means of an argument which the author of *The Search after Truth* [at III.2.6] calls 'the most beautiful proof; the loftiest, the most solid and the first, i.e. that which presupposes the least'. Here is the proof:

Everything that is manifestly contained in the idea of a thing can be correctly asserted of that thing.

Necessary existence is manifestly contained in the idea that we have of an infinitely perfect Being.

It can thus be asserted that an infinitely perfect Being is and exists.

It is evident that in this demonstration the word 'idea' must be taken as the perception of a perfect Being and not as the perfect Being itself, for it is in immediate contact with our soul and takes the place of the representation supposedly needed in order for us to conceive of material things. For if we were to take the word 'idea' in the latter sense, the demonstration which our friend says is so beautiful, so lofty and so solid would merely be that sophism known as *petitio principii*, for I could only draw the conclusion 'thus the perfect Being exists' by supposing in the minor premise that it is *itself intimately joined to my soul*, and hence that it exists.

I shall look at this in more detail below. For the moment, my only conclusion is that I need recognise no ideas other than those which I have defined as not being different from perceptions if I am to recognise the truth of the expression 'we do not see things immediately' and 'it is our ideas that are the immediate objects of our thoughts'. It is also clear from this what must be understood when it is said that 'it is in the idea of each thing that one perceives its properties', and nothing could be more useless in this context than *representations* distinct from perceptions, supposedly needed for our minds to conceive of number and extension.

In clarifying this I believe I can do no better than offer an example in which I assume nothing which anyone would not recognise as occurring in his own mind, provided his attention does not wander and he is not distracted by wondering how something occurs in him which he cannot doubt occurs.

The philosopher Thales, having to pay twenty workers one drachma each, counted twenty drachmas and paid each worker. He would not have been able to do this unless there were at least two perceptions in his mind: one of twenty men and one of twenty drachmas. And I remind you for the last time that *idea* and *perception* are the same thing in my dictonary, and thus that, when I make use of the expression 'idea' and 'idea of an object', I understand by this the *perception of an object*.

Having some spare time he began to reflect, and thinking about what the two *perceptions* or *ideas* have in common, namely that there is 20 in both, he abstracts from what is particular in them the abstract idea of the number 20, which can subsequently be applied to twenty horses, twenty houses, twenty stadiums. This is a third idea or perception.

He then takes it into his head to reflect on this abstract idea of the number 20, i.e. he considers it with greater attention, with a reflective vision that is one of the most admirable faculties of the mind. And the first thing that he discovers is that it can be divided into two equal halves, for he easily sees that if he puts 10 on one side and 10 on the other this makes 20. And he sees at the same time that if he adds 1 to 20, the number 21 cannot be divided into two equal parts, because the closest one can get to an equal division is to put 10 on one side and 11 on the other. This leads him to judge that we may usefully employ different words to designate numbers that can be divided into equal halves and those that cannot, calling these *even* and *odd* respectively. Then, still considering what is contained in this idea or perception of the number 20, he asks what its factors are, i.e. what numbers taken together make exactly 20. He begins with *unity*, and sees immediately that unity must be one of the factors, since 1 taken twenty times makes 20. From this it is easy to derive the general rule that 1 is the factor of all numbers, since it is its own factor, 1 being 1, and all of the other numbers are only definite multitudes of 1s.

Next he takes 2, and finds that 2 is a factor of 20, for in counting in 2s – 2, 4, 6, etc. – he arrives at exactly 20. He takes 3 and discovers that this is not a factor of 20, for counting in 3s – 3, 6, 9, 12, etc. – he finds that after having done this six times he arrives at 18, after which there is only 2 left before 20. Then he takes 4 and finds that it is a factor of 20, because 4 taken five times is exactly 20. He finds the same for 5, for 5 taken four times is exactly 20. He next finds that neither 6, 7, 8 or 9 can be factors of 20, for the same reason as he found 3 not to be. But 10 is a factor because 10 taken twice is 20. Neither 11, 12, 13, 14, 15, 16, 17, 18 nor 19 can make exactly 20, when taken any number of times, so they cannot be a factor of it. But 20 can be a factor because 20 taken once is 20. From this various reflections follow:

First, because there can be numbers having no other factor than unity and themselves, it is a good idea to give them a name which distinguishes them from the others, and they can be called *prime numbers*.

Second, all the even numbers, since they are divisible into two equal parts, have 2 as a factor.

Third, 2 is the only even number which is *prime* because it alone of all the even numbers has only unity and itself as a factor.

There is no need to continue the list. Here are my thoughts on what I have said. First, I have not presupposed any *representations*, only that this philosopher has, first of all, two direct perceptions of twenty men and twenty drachmas, without troubling how he comes by these, for I am happy to allow, if you wish, that it is God who has given them to him on the occasion of corporeal motions which occur in his sense organs and his brain. However this may be, and whatever opinion one holds on the matter, it cannot be denied that he has these two perceptions, since it is granted that he perceives, that he is acquainted with these twenty men and twenty drachmas, and that it is not at the same time possible that he does not see, that he is not acquainted with these twenty men and twenty drachmas, provided he has these two perceptions, however he has them, for this is something which has to do not with the *nature* of his ideas but their origin.

Secondly, once these two *perceptions* which I call *ideas* are granted, it is undeniable that the mind has the faculty of doing everything which this philosopher does, for it is an everyday occurrence, and thus we are assured that we can do it *certissima scientia et clamante conscientia* [by a very certain science and with a cry from our conscience], as St Augustine puts it. Strictly speaking, it is this that should be called 'seeing the properties of things in their ideas': seeing in the idea of extension that it must be divisible and movable, seeing in the idea of mind that it must be a substance completely distinct from extended substance, seeing in the idea of God, i.e. in the idea of a perfect Being, that He must necessarily exist, seeing in the idea of a triangle that its three angles must necessarily be equal to two right angles. For this, one need not know that our mind has the power of reflecting on its own thoughts or, once the object has been perceived, that it can consider it more attentively.

This is undeniable, and all the sciences depend on it, especially the more abstract ones such as methaphysics, geometry, arithmetic and algebra. For in these all one does is to conceive the simplest objects clearly and distinctly, and use these in forming definitions. By relating these simple objects in the most straightforward way, axioms are formed. And from these simple reflections on our basic knowledge (and not on some imaginary *representations*), one draws this wonderful series of conclusions, which, by their obviousness, force all reasonable minds to yield to them, because of this single principle: that everything that is contained in the true idea of a thing (i.e. in the clear perception that we have of it) can be truthfully asserted. And it must be God who has given us an unshakeable inclination to assent to this, and to take it as the foundation of all human certainty. For those who say that they disagree with it cannot really do so, for it would seem that the sciences in which one applies oneself solely to examining these ideas, i.e. the natural perceptions which we have of things, and to penetrating the content of these ideas, sciences such as arithmetic, algebra and geometry, are considered by everyone to be indubitable.

But my principal aim in this chapter being to undo the equivocation in the word 'immediately', I declare here that if, by conceiving of the sun, a square or a cubed number *immediately* one understands this to be the opposite of conceiving them by means of ideas, such as I have defined these in the last chapter, i.e. as the same things as perceptions, then I agree we do not see them *immediately*, for nothing could be clearer than that we only see, perceive or know them by means of the perceptions that we have of them, in whatever way it is that we have these. But it is clear also that this is no less true of the manner in which we conceive of God and our soul than it is of our manner of perceiving material things. But if by not knowing them *immediately* one understands only the ability to know them through representations distinct from perceptions, I maintain that, in this sense, it is not only mediately but also immediately that we know not only God and our soul but material things also. That is to say, we can know them without any intermediary between our perceptions and the object, and I say 'our perceptions' here because I acknowledge that we often need reflective perception as well as direct perception in order to know them properly.

If the above is granted then I can, I believe, show the falsity of the hypothesis of *representations*, for to show this I need only do two things. The first is to demonstrate clearly and evidently that none of the principles and demonstrations on which this edifice of ideas has been built have solid foundations. The second is to show that, in order to know those things that God has wished us to know, we have no need of representations distinct from perceptions. This will, I hope, be clear from the following demonstration.

Chapter 7

Arguments against ideas construed as *representations* distinct from perceptions.

Propositions to be proved

In its knowledge of material things our soul does not need *representations* distinct from perceptions which, it is claimed, are necessary to compensate for the absence of everything which cannot itself be united to our soul.

First demonstration

Any principle which rests only on an equivocal expression, which is true only when its sense does not bear upon the problem that one wants the principle to resolve, and which, in its other sense, presupposes without proof what is in question, should be banished from philosophy. Now the very first thing that the author of *The Search after Truth* takes as the principle underlying what he wishes to prove concerning the nature of ideas is of this kind.

Thus he could not sin more explicitly against his own rules than by beginning his treatise 'On The Nature of Ideas' [ST, Book 3, Part II] with it. He claims that it is indubitable only because he has not thoroughly examined it, and to be a belief commonly held by philosophers only because he has not taken the care to recognise it as something left over from childhood prejudices, something no more secure than a hundred others which he rejects.

We cannot deny the major premiss, and Malebranche can deny it even less, considering the care that, throughout *The Search after Truth*, he says he has taken in the sciences not to admit as true anything whose truth is not clearly known to us, nor to take such a thing on trust on the authority of anyone.

Thus it remains only to demonstrate the minor premiss, which is easy. His words are: 'Everyone agrees that we do not perceive objects which are outside us by themselves.' The equivocation lies in the words 'by themselves', for this can be taken in two senses. In the first sense, it means that they make nothing known to our mind *by themselves*, i.e. they are not the cause of what we perceive, and they do not produce in our mind the perceptions that we have of them, in the same way that it is said that matter does not move of or by itself, because it does not provide its own motion. This is true but irrelevant to the question, which concerns the nature of ideas and not their origin. It is also clear that Malebranche does not understand the words in this sense for, maintaining as he does that God is the source of all our sensations, he would have to put the soul as well as material things amongst those things that we do not perceive by themselves, since according to him it is God, and not our soul, who causes in our mind the perception by which we perceive it.

Thus there remains only the second sense in which he can take the words 'by themselves', by contrasting *being known by itself* (as he believes is the case with the soul when it knows itself) with being known by representations of objects *distinct from perceptions*, which we have already said so much about. Now to take them in this sense is manifestly to suppose what is in question before having shown it, and something so easily established should be rejected as false, or at least as doubtful, unless he has examined it in the light of his own rules and reflected on the matter, as he does in other cases.

For if, instead of referring us to this alleged 'everyone' who he says agrees with this and that, he had reflected and considered attentively what occurs in his mind he would have seen clearly that he knows bodies, that he knows a cube, a cone, a pyramid and that, turning towards the sun, he knows the sun. I do not say that his corporeal eyes see these, for the corporeal eyes see nothing, but rather it is his mind that sees them on the occasion of his eyes presenting him with them. And if, proceeding further, as he must do according to his own rules, he stops at the thought 'I know a cube, I see the sun', in order to ponder on it and consider clearly what is contained in it, I am sure that, confining himself to this, it would be impossible to see in it anything other than the perception of a cube, or the cube objectively present to the mind, or the perception of the sun, or the sun objectively present to the mind. He will never find the least trace of that *representation* of the cube or the sun, distinct from the *perception* of them, which is needed to make good their absence. In order to find it, he must put it there himself, relying on a remnant of a prejudice that he has not taken care to cast aside. That is to say, he has only found it there in the way that the defenders of substantial forms find them in all bodies in the universe, because it is imagined that they are both relevant to and indispensible in explaining what one observes in these bodies. And since this manner of philosophising, in terms of what is or is not contained in the clear notions that we have of things, is for him a convincing reason for rejecting, as an idle invention, the postulation of substantial forms in all bodies in the way in which the Scholastic philosophers understand this, he must also reject, as a still more insubstantial fantasy, the speculative postulation of these *representations* of bodies which have been invented in the same way as substantial forms, and whose notion is even more obscure and confused than that of these forms.

Chapter 8

Second demonstration

It is contrary to good philosophical practice to deal with an important matter by starting off taking as a general principle something which is not only not clear, but contrary to something which is so clear and evident to us that it is impossible for us to doubt it.

This is what the author of *The Search after Truth* does in his treatise 'On the Nature of Ideas'. It is impossible to reason less precisely than he does in this matter, or in a manner more opposed to that which he follows in almost all others.

Only the minor premiss requires proof. What he supposes first, as a clear and indisputable principle, is that our mind can only know objects that are present to our soul. And this leads him to say:

> We see the sun, the stars and an infinite number of objects outside of us, and it is not likely that the soul leaves the body and, as it were strolls about the heavens so as to contemplate all these objects. It does not see them by themselves, and the immediate object of our mind when it sees the sun, for example, is not the sun but something which is in immediate contact with our soul, and this I call an idea. [ST, 217]

A man who speaks in this way manifestly supposes, as a clear and indubitable principle, that our soul cannot perceive objects that are removed from it. And from this he concludes that, the sun being at a distance from us, if our soul is to see it then either it must go to find the sun, or the sun come to find it. The first, quite reasonably, seems improbable; 'for it is not likely', he says, 'that the soul leaves the body, and that it strolls about the heavens.' Thus the sun must come to find the soul. But it is even more embarrassing to want the sun to leave its own place and go to find all the souls that want to see it. What then does one do? Is it impossible for us ever to see the sun? We have found a solution, say the scholastic philosophers and the author of *The Search after Truth*, and people should be thankful that we have, for without it everything would be lost. In spite of men's assertions that they see the sun, we have demonstrated to them that they are dreamers, and that it is impossible that they see it. The argument is conclusive. It is indubitable that our soul can only see objects which are present to it. Now Cassini says that the sun is more than thirty million leagues from our souls.[5] It would be necessary, in order to make itself seen by our soul, either that the sun approach it or that it approach the sun. Now you believe neither that your soul leaves your body in order to go and find the sun, nor that the sun leaves the sky in order to come into immediate contact with your soul. Thus you are dreaming when you say you see the sun. But do not grieve, for we will extricate you from this embarrassment and give you the means of seeing it. Instead of the sun, which does not appear to regularly leave its own place (this would be too embarrassing), we have very ingeniously found a certain *representation* which takes its place, and which makes good its absence by coming into immediate contact with our soul. And it is to this *representation* of the sun (irrespective of what it is and where it comes from, for this is something that we do not yet agree on) that we have given the name *idea* or *species*.

But, joking aside, our friend has certainly assumed, in what he says here, as well as in everything else he says in his treatise 'On the Nature of Ideas', that our soul cannot see, know, perceive (for these are the same thing) objects at any distance from it so long as they remain at any distance.

Now not only do I doubt this alleged principle, but I maintain that it is totally false, for it is as evident as can be that our soul can know an infinite number of things at a distance from it, and that it can do this because God has enabled it to do so. The proof of this is easy. By Axiom 8, the act necessarily presupposes the power, i.e. it is certain that what a thing does (taking the word 'do' broadly, as in Def. 11) it has the power to do, and consequently it must be allowed that it has this faculty, by Def. 12, and that it derives this from the author of its nature, on whom it is dependent, by Def. 13.

Taking the fifth question and Def. 9 together, it is clear to me that my soul has seen the sun, the stars and the other works of God and men on an infinite number of occasions and these men are not spirits but true men, created by God like me: Thus I am certain that my soul has the faculty of seeing all things and that, as it is dependent on the thought which constitutes its nature, it derives this from its author, God. That is to say, God, having made it a substance that thinks and sees, also gives it the faculty of seeing all the things that I have just mentioned.

Now all these things, the sun, the stars, the men with whom I converse, and in general all the bodies in nature, other than what is in immediate contact with my soul, are at a distance from my soul. Thus my soul has the faculty of seeing bodies at a distance from it, and God, in creating it, has given it this faculty, because it is something dependent on its nature, by the last definition.

I do not see that there is any reply to this. This is all the more convincing when one considers that God has, on the one hand, created man to be a spectator and admirer of His works and that, on the other, having joined the soul to the body, He must have given man the faculty, i.e. the power, of seeing, perceiving and knowing not only the body to which he is joined, but also those others which surround him, which can injure him or help him to conserve himself. It was thus necessary that he was given the power to know bodies at a distance from him, i.e. at a distance from the body to which he was joined.

But how does it come about, tell me, that everyone lets himself think that the soul cannot know objects at a distance from it, that something must serve to make them present and that this requires ideas or species? I gave the reason for this in Chapter 4. It results from the comparison of corporeal vision, poorly understood, with the mind's vision. And the equivocation in the word 'presence' helps a good deal here, as I have noted, for it is very common that the same word, when applied to the mind and the body, is understood very crudely by most people and accordingly in a way appropriate to the body, even when it is being applied to the mind. Thus the word 'presence' signifies *spatial presence* in relation to the body and *objective presence* in relation to the mind. With regard to the latter, objects are said to be in our mind when they are there objectively, i.e. when they are known by it, as specified in Def. 4. This *objective presence* being too spiritual for most people, and *spatial presence* being much better understood, two quite wrong meanings are ascribed to the equivocal proposition that *bodies must be present to the soul if they are to be known*. In the first, it is imagined that this presence is prior to the knowledge of bodies, and that it is necessary if bodies are to be in a knowable state, whereas the presence of objects in our mind, which is only an *objective presence* and no different from our mind's perception of an object, is thus far from preceding the knowledge that it has of them, since it is by means of this knowledge that it knows that they are present to it.

The second error they make is to crudely take this *presence* to be the *spatial presence*, which is appropriate to bodies. This is indeed how it appears to Malebranche, who locates the difficulty that the soul would have in seeing the sun itself in the fact that the sun is so far

from us and that it is unlikely that it would leave its body to seek the
sun in the heavens. He consequently regards *spatial separation* as an
obstacle which stops a body being in a state whereby it can be known
by our mind, and thus he believes that *spatial presence* is necessary
for our mind to see objects.

Nevertheless, as false opinions are never properly understood, and
as they always contradict themselves in some way, they say other
things which show that *spatial presence* doesn't make any difference.
According to them, even if God had allowed our soul to leave our
body to go and find the sun in order to see it, it would have a wholly
wasted journey, since it does not see it any more when it is not only
much closer but even inside that star than when it remains where it is.
For can our soul be more present to the sun than it is to its own body?
According to Malebranche, we do not see our own body by itself any
more than we see any other. Thus it is pointless to maintain that our
soul's being distant from the sun and not being able to leave our body
and journey around the heavens is something that prevents it from
seeing the sun. For whether present or distant, it makes no difference
to the soul, which is condemned by an irrevocable sentence of this
philosophy of false ideas never to be able to see any body by itself,
present or absent, near or far. And I would even want to remove the
words 'by itself', and say absolutely that it is condemned to seeing no
body at all, as we shall see in what follows.

One might perhaps say that this is the result of the body not being
able to be present to our soul in the way which is necessary if our soul
is to perceive it. But I do not know that our friend would approve of
this response. He hates vague unexplained terms too much to maintain that we should avail ourselves of them. Thus we must show what
it is for a body *to be present to our soul in a way necessary for our
soul to perceive it*. Now what distinct notion can he offer of this sort
of presence if his account is to convince us that it is neither *objective
presence* nor *spatial presence*? He must abandon the alleged necessity of the sun being spatially present to our soul if our soul is to see it.
And he cannot do this without conceding to me what I have undertaken to show, and without at the same time being obliged to
recognise that he has not taken enough care in what he has said when
he has advanced the spatial distance of the sun as a reason which
prevents our soul from seeing it until this obstacle can be overcome;
or because our soul's leaving our body to go and find the sun is
unlikely, or because some representation of the sun comes to be

united with our soul in order to make up for its absence. For, if he is now obliged to acknowledge that spatial presence or distance does not matter to whether a body can or can not be the object of our mind, what he says about the distance of the sun and our soul's not being able to leave our body to find it are as unreasonable as if I complained of not understanding someone from lower Brittany, who spoke to me in his own language, which I do not understand, because he spoke too softly – which would be ridiculous, for if the language is one that I do not understand, it does not matter whether it is spoken loudly or softly. It is easy to see the parallel between this and the present case.

If, so as to avoid this objection, he persists in explaining this presence in terms of *spatial presence*, then the argument I have advanced against it remains with full force. And there is another argument which I believe is equally compelling. It is certain, by Def. 6, that my mind does not only perceive single material things such as some particular square or triangle or cube, but that it conceives a square in general, a triangle in general, a cube in general; and without this there could not properly speaking be a geometry. For when a geometer demonstrates the properties of a square or a triangle he is not dealing with some particular square or some particular triangle, but with every square and every triangle. Now these kinds of objects, a square in general, a triangle in general, a cube in general, although corporeal exist in no way spatially, and what does not exist spatially cannot be either spatially present to or absent from my soul. And the same holds for the abstract numbers which are the object of arithmetic. Thus one cannot reasonably say that it is because they are absent from my soul that I need *representations* to make good this absence so that they might be known.

Here is another argument, a little more subtle but nonetheless a strong one. Since, for any object of the will to be loved, it is a necessary condition that it be good or appear to be good, it is impossible for our will to love any object except in so far as it is good. It follows from this, it seems to me, that if it is a condition that the object of the understanding be spatially present to the mind in order for us to know it, it must be the case that just as our will can love nothing in so far as it is bad, so our understanding is similarly unable to conceive of anything spatially absent from the soul. Now we cannot doubt that the mind conceives of an infinite number of things which are spatially separated from our soul: for example, when the mother of young Toby weeps bitterly when he is late coming home, it is certain that her mind conceives him as absent from her. Thus spatial presence is not at all a necessary condition of an object's being seen by our soul, and consequently spatial separation also make no difference to what can be seen.

One is only inclined to suppose the contrary because, since [original] sin, we devote ourselves almost exclusively to caring for the conservation of our body,[6] especially in childhood, which lasts for a long time in most people, and we have a lot of trouble in raising ourselves above matter and conceiving of spiritual things spirtually. We almost constantly confuse these with notions which belong only to body, and we imagine that by including them in the same genus we have thereby got them in a state where they are appropriate to minds, by conceiving of them, it seems to us, in a manner a little less coarse than when we attribute them to bodies. This is what makes St Thomas say, following Boethius, that there are maxims that are very clear and very certain which are nevertheless such only to the wise, and which are absent from the minds of the people, and he gives as an example that incorporeal things are not in a place: *Quaedam sunt communes animi conceptiones, et per se notae, apud sapientes tantum, ut incorporalia in loco non esse.* For there is no one who, though convinced that our soul is incorporeal, does not believe that it must be in some place if it is to exist, and that it would cease to be if it were nowhere. One must therefore not be surprised, if, almost without being noticed, *objective presence*, which alone is necessary for a body as well as anything else if it is to be known by the mind, but which is distinct from the knowledge of it, has been changed into *spatial presence*, the word 'presence' being associated much more closely with this notion than with the other. And suppose one then draws from the assumption that this *spatial presence* is necessary if an object is to be in a state whereby it can be perceived by our soul, all the bizarre consequences that result from these *representations* which must compensate for the absence of bodies, subject to our deciding what one understands by them and what their origin is, on the basis of what belongs generally and necessarily to these chimerical beings. For it is ridiculous enough for them all to begin by not doubting that it must be true that something exists because they think they need it to explain how our soul, without leaving the body, can see the sun which is millions of leagues from it; worse still, they subsequently look at their leisure for something that would provide them with the means of explaining something which they would see clearly does not need their purported explanations, if they wanted to take the trouble to consider what occurs in their own minds, without adding things which are not found there, and which are only appropriate to their body, such as considerations of spatial presence and absence.

Chapter 9
Third demonstration

This will be shorter. It will consist in showing that a proposition which he ties to the preceding ones, and which appears to be no less important, is also equivocal: in one sense it is entirely useless for his purposes, and in the other it is quite false and question-begging. The proposition is: 'It must be noted that if the mind is to perceive something, it is absolutely necessary that the idea of the object be actually present to it, but it is not necessary that there be something external which is like the idea' [ST, 217].

I have shown in Chapters 3 and 4 that at the beginning of his work he takes the word 'idea' as the perception itself, but that when he expressly deals with the *nature of ideas*, he takes it as a particular *representation* really distinct from the perception of the object. One cannot assess the proposition, therefore, without first ridding the word 'idea' of this ambiguity. And for this one must form two propositions out of it, substituting the definitions for the defined.

In the first proposition, we take the word 'idea' to mean the perception itself: 'One must note that for the mind to perceive some object, it is absolutely necessary that the idea of that object (taken as its perception) actually be present to it; this cannot be doubted; but it is not necessary that there be something external which is like the idea.' Nothing could be truer than the proposition taken in this sense, in both of its parts. For how could our mind perceive something if it did not have an idea of it, i.e. a perception of it? It is certain also that the perception of many things is really in our mind, although these things are not in fact outside us.

In the second proposition, we take the word 'idea' as in Book 3, Part II, Chapter 1, which is the passage that we are currently concerned with; here it is understood as some kind of representation which is distinct from perception, which compensates for the absence of objects, and in doing so puts the mind in a state whereby it can know them. 'It must be noted that for the mind to perceive some object, it is absolutely necessary that this representation, to which I give the name *idea*, is really present to it; this it is impossible to doubt; but it is not necessary that there be something external which is like the idea.' Construing the proposition in these terms, not only *is it possible to doubt it*, but I absolutely deny its first part, seeing no need for this alleged *representation* in knowing any object, whether absent or present. As for the second part, if it is not necessary that there be something external similar to this *representation*, then it is no longer necessary that there be outside us anything *existing* which is similar to the perception that I have of the sun. It follows from this that there is no reason why I must have recourse to these *representations* distinct from perceptions, which enable me to see the sun even if there were no sun. For as it would then be the possible sun that I conceived, and not the existing sun, although I may erroneously judge it to be the existing sun, the same would have to be said of the *representation* of the sun, supposing there were no sun, namely, that it represents to me the possible sun and not the existing sun, and this would also be an occasion for error if I judged from it that the sun exists.

Chapter 10

Fourth demonstration

Nothing could be more questionable to those who philosophise properly than those philosophical *entities* of which we have only very confused notions, and which it is easy to see have only been invented in order to explain certain things which, it is believed, cannot be explained without them. But there can be no doubt that they should be completely abandoned if it can be shown that we do not need them and can do very well without them. Malebranche would surely not contest this maxim.

It is thus only a matter of proving that these alleged *representations*, which he calls *ideas*, are like this, and that they are not needed for the role that he assigns to them, namely that of providing our mind with a means of seeing material things. This is quite easily shown.

(1)   God would not have wanted to create our soul, and place it in a body which would be surrounded by infinitely many other bodies, unless He had also wished that it be able to know those bodies, and consequently unless He had also wished that those bodies be conceived by our soul.

Now all God's wishes are realised: thus we can be certain that God has given our minds the ability to see bodies, and to bodies the passive faculty, so to speak, of being able to be seen by our mind. All this is clear as day. But see what follows from it.

God does not do in complex ways what can be done more simply: this is our friend's great principle, and he uses it in relation to this same question of the *nature of ideas*.

God having willed that our mind knows bodies and that bodies be known by our mind, it would surely have been simpler to make our mind able to know bodies directly, i.e. without *representations* distinct from perceptions (for it is in this sense that I take the word 'directly' here), and to make bodies able to be known directly by our mind, rather than having the soul unable to see them other than by *representations*, and in such a complicated way that there is no one who is sincere who could say in good faith that he understands it.

How then could Malebranche, who gives so much weight to the maxim that God always acts in the simplest ways that he sometimes takes it too far, convince himself that our soul cannot see bodies directly, but only by means of these alleged *representations*, which he unjustifiably calls 'ideas'?

(2)   Take the case where my soul is not thinking about a body, but is occupied with thinking about itself, or is seeking to determine whether a number has some property. The problem is to determine how it can move from this thought to that of a body *A*. You want it to be able to see the body *A* only by means of a *representation* of *A*. But I ask whether it is enough that this *representation* – whatever it be, created or uncreated – be intimately joined to my soul without modifying it in some new way, i.e. without its having a new perception. It is clear that it is not. For the *representation* is of no use unless the soul perceives it. Now suppose that the soul had not perceived the body previously; it follows that it must have had a new perception of the body. But will this new perception merely be a perception of the *representation*, which I shall call *B*, or will it also be the perception of the body *A*?

If it is of both, then both will be objectively in my mind at the same time. Thus the immediate object of my thought will be the perception of both, and neither will be the immediate object by themselves, for the reasons given in Chapter 6. If, therefore, it can be said that I see *B* directly and *A* indirectly, I would have to see them by two different perceptions, and the perception of *B* would have to be the cause of the perception of *A*.

If one says that the first perception is not the perception of the *representation*, there would then need to be a second perception which was the perception of the body *A*, for it is *A* that I need to see since it can be useful or injurious to the conservation of my body, whereas the *representation* which I am supposed to see first can do me neither good nor harm. Since we must, then, arrive finally at the perception of the body *A* – without which my soul, which needs to see it, would never see it, and with which it cannot fail to see it – why has the infinitely perfect Being, which always acts by the simplest means, not made it come about directly? And what shows that He must seek the useless detour He is made to take in order to realise His wish to make my soul able to see bodies, and bodies able to be seen by my soul. For, as I have already said, the relationship between knower and known must have been reciprocal and God's will must have applied to each of them. What prevents one being able to say that the soul itself is able to see bodies directly, i.e. without *represen- tations*, when it can see itself like that, is that bodies are too coarse and too far removed from the spirituality of the soul to be able to be seen directly.

But, since the difficulty can only arise from the latter argument, it is a good idea to examine it more specifically. Actually, nothing seems stranger to me than to say that bodies are too coarse to be able to be seen directly by our soul. For the coarseness and imperfection of bodies is legitimately raised when the question of whether they have knowledge is at issue, as it is all too often in everyday philo- sophy,[7] where one wants animals to know and plants to choose their food, and all heavy things to seek the centre of the earth as their place of rest, which is impossible without knowledge; but when it is simply a question of being known, what bearing can the imperfection of material things have on this? Knowing is doubtless a great perfection in the thing that knows, and hence the lowest degree of intelligent nature is something incomparable with, far greater than, and more admirable than all the highest achievements of corporeal nature. But being known is, from the point of view of the thing known, nothing more than being given a particular name, and for this it is enough that the object not be nothing, for only nothing cannot be known. And being knowable is, so to speak, a property inseparable from being, in the same way as being *one*, or being *true*, or being *good* are inseparable from being: or, rather, it is the same thing as being *true*, that which is true being the object of the understanding as that which is good is the object of the will. So it is the most baseless fantasy one could have to think that a body *qua* body is too different from the soul for it to be known by it.

It would also seem that Malebranche does not confine himself to the materiality of bodies in order to ensure that they are knowable directly by my soul, for, if one is to believe him, my soul cannot know the souls of other men either. And since he claims at the same time that we know them neither in themselves nor through ideas, he is reduced to saying [ST, 239] that we know them only by conjecture. There is much I would say on this, but it would take us too far from my subject.

What, then, does this come down to?: without doubt we have to come back to the *intimate union* which, it is claimed, all objects of the mind should have with our soul if they are to be in a state whereby they can be known directly. Now neither bodies, whatever they be, nor other men's souls can be intimately united with my soul, therefore I cannot know them directly.

But isn't this just to ascribe to God bizarre and baseless laws? Isn't it simply to subjugate Him to the vain imaginings of philosophers so as to oblige Him *who always acts in the simplest way* to follow the strange route which is wished upon Him in order to carry out His wish that material things be known to the soul? Accordingly, I would only have to say analogously that a body can only be conceived to leave its state of rest when it is pushed, and that it can only be pushed by some force [*vertu*], and continue in its motion only when this force continues to push it, and that this is what is called impressed force [*vertu impresse*]; and thus, since it is now desired that it is God who gives motion to all individual bodies, this must also be by means of an impressed force, which is no less universally recognised by scholastic philosophers than these *representations* of objects. This being the case, must one not also reject the latter if one is to reject the former?

It will be said that the need for this impressed force in maintaining the motion of a body that is thrown is a fantasy which has been assumed without proper examination, and without being based on a reliable argument. I say its alleged necessity is the same as that of the baseless supposition that all the objects of the mind must be intimately joined to our soul if they are to be in a knowable state.

It will be said that, leaving aside this *impressed force*, it is impossible to conceive that God could give motion to a body and it not move, and, were God's aim only to make the body move, it would be contrary to His wisdom to employ this *impressed force* as He can do without it.

Likewise, I say it is inconceivable that God could give to my mind the perception of body *A* and I not perceive *A*, and, were God's aim only to make me perceive *A* because this is necessary for my self-preservation, it would be contrary to His wisdom to employ a *representation* intimately joined to my soul, whatever this may be, for He can make me know *A* without this, and He never makes useless detours when He can act in simpler ways. I would be mistaken indeed if it could be shown that these points against the need for *representations* were not as basic and solid as those against the need for an *impressed force*.

The way in which we see the properties of things in their ideas can be seen from what I have said in Chapter 6. I have no doubt that it will be concluded from this that *representations* distinct from perceptions serve no purpose, since I find I have no difficulty explaining what occurs in human knowledge without them. And even those who assume them have to acknowledge that they are of no use to me unless I am acquainted with them, and that I am not acquainted with the objects they represent by means of these representations, i.e. unless I have the perception of the square by means of what is thought to be the requisite *representation* intimately joined to my soul. But as soon as I perceive a square, who can doubt that, if I seek the properties of a square, it will not be in the perception that I seek them? And consequently, as I have said in Chapter 6, when it is said that *this or that is contained in the idea of some thing*, the word *idea* signifies the perception that we have of this object, and not some alleged *representation* which the scholastics have invented in the belief that it is needed, but which certainly serves no purpose as they conceive of it.

Chapter 11

Fifth demonstration

For the man who reasons properly the most convincing demonstration of the falsity of a principle is when it leads him into errors
which are completely absurd and contrary to what he would have
taken as indubitable, and which is in fact indubitable, and which is
the very thing which he had claimed the principle explains.

Now this is the case with the way in which Malebranche uses the
principle 'that in order for an object to be in a state where it is
perceivable directly by our mind, it must be intimately joined to our
soul.'

For he has employed this principle only as a result of having taken
it as incontestable that we see an infinite number of bodies, and that
our mind perceives them, the problem being how we are to explain
how it can perceive them. In the title of Book 3, Part II, Chapter 1,
this leads him to say that 'ideas are necessary for us to perceive any
material object'. Hence he supposes that we do perceive them. For it
would clearly be ridiculous to say that we need refracting telescopes
to see the satellites of Jupiter and Saturn if we did not see the satellites
of these two planets even with these telescopes. Moreover, at the
beginning of this chapter, as we have seen, he says: 'we see the sun,
the stars, and an infinite number of objects outside ourselves' [ST,
217]. And a little further on:

everything that the soul sees is of one of two kinds: either it is in the soul or it
is outside the soul. Our soul has no need of ideas in order to perceive the
former: but as for those outside the soul, these we can perceive only by
means of ideas, given that these things cannot be intimately joined to it [ST,
218].

All this puts it beyond any doubt that we see things which are
outside the soul, as well as those which are in the soul. The problem is
to determine whether we need ideas to see the one and not the other,
and what the nature of the ideas that we need in order to see external
things is.

In Book 3, he continues to assume that we perceive material
things, but that this can only be by means of ideas. And he even
explicitly says, in Chapter 6, that one sees not so much the ideas of
things as the things themselves that the ideas represent. 'For', he says,
'when one sees a square, one does not say that one sees the idea of this

square, which is joined to the mind, but only the square which is outside.'

Nevertheless, in the *Elucidations*, carrying the natural implications of this philosophy of ideas still further, he suddenly transports us into unknown lands, where men no longer have true knowledge of one another, nor even of their own bodies, nor of the sun and the stars which God has created, but where everyone sees, instead of the men to which one turns one's eyes, only *intelligible men*; instead of one's own body one sees only an *intelligible body*; instead of the sun and the other stars that God has created one sees only an *intelligible sun and stars*, and instead of the physical spaces which exist between us and the sun one sees only *intelligible spaces*. Perhaps it will be thought that I say this only as a joke, and that these are merely inferences that he would not acknowledge and which I attribute to him unreasonably. Listen, then, to what he himself says [in the *Tenth Elucidation*]: 'It should be noted that the sun that we see, for example, is not the one we look at. The sun and everything else in the material world is not visible by itself, as I have already proved. The soul can only see the sun to which it is directly joined' [ST, 625].

This is manifestly contrary to the claim, that we have just seen him make, that: 'When one sees a square, one does not say that one sees the idea of this square, which is joined to the mind, but only the square which is outside'. One can only say that, having penetrated further into these mysterious ideas to the extent that he does later in the work, he recognises that the way in which he explained them earlier is not sufficiently precise and that it conformed too closely to popular language and beliefs to say that 'when one sees a square, it is the square itself outside of us that one sees, and not the idea of the square, which is joined to the mind', but that, speaking philosophically and with 'rigorous exactness', one must go beyond this and say clearly that our soul can only see the square which is joined to our soul, i.e. the *representation* of this square, distinct from the perception that we have of it, and not the square itself which is outside us: just as the sun that we see is not that which we look at, but another sun which is directly joined to our soul.

He explains himself on this issue at great length, and more assertively [in the *Sixth Elucidation*]: 'Take care: the material body we animate is not the one we see when we look at it, i.e. when we turn our bodily eyes towards it: it is an intelligible body that we see, as there are intelligible spaces between our body and the sun that we look at [ST, 573].

Nothing could be explained better or more clearly. He distinguishes between *looking at* and *seeing*. He defines *looking at* as merely turning our eyes towards an object, and *seeing* it to be understood as perceiving an object with our mind. Then he distinguishes even more carefully between what we *look at* and what we *see*. He advises us to *take care*, because this is something which is indubitable provided one pays attention to it. Thus he declares that when we *look at* our body, i.e. when we turn our eyes towards it, what we *see* by means of our mind, on the occasion of this looking, is not *the body which we animate* but an *intelligible body* which, not being material, can be intimately joined to our soul. And likewise, when we *look at* the sun by turning our eyes towards it, what we *see* with our mind is not the material sun that God has created but an *intelligible sun*. And he anticipates an objection deriving from the great distance that we see (with our mind) between our body and the sun, a distance which it seems could not be anything other than physical, for he claims that there are *intelligible spaces* between these *intelligible bodies* and the *intelligible sun* that we *see*, just as there are *physical spaces* between our body and the sun that we *look at*.

Is this not clearly what I have said? He has assumed first of all that our mind perceives material things. He has only concerned himself with *how* this occurs, with whether it is by means of ideas or without ideas, taking the word 'idea' to mean *representation* distinct from perception. And having philosophised on the nature of these *representations*, having gone over them thoroughly, and having been only able to locate them in God, his only reward is to be no longer able to explain how we *see* material things, which was all that was needed, but to say that our mind is incapable of perceiving them, and that we live in a continual illusion in believing we *see* the material things that God has created when we *look at* them, i.e. when we turn our eyes towards them, whereas we see not them but only *intelligible bodies* which resemble them.

Do we need anything more than this to reject what Malebranche says about the *nature of ideas*, for all the air of spirituality that he gives it? For what has he set out to prove?: that the ideas whose nature he seeks *are needed for the perception of material objects*? And what has he concluded after so many subtleties?: that our body turns its eyes towards material bodies, which is called *looking*, but that our mind is incapable of *perceiving* them, and that it perceives only *intelligible* bodies. How can one believe that someone accustomed to arguing well has started from sound principles when he infers from them something that is the complete opposite of what he set out to prove, or rather what he had taken to be incontestable and in no need of proof? It is as if someone had promised to show how human freedom can be reconciled with God's providence, and after much deliberation found that his only means of establishing this reconciliation was to deny that man is free.

I could stop here, but because there may be some people who would prefer to believe that, in *The Search after Truth*, Malebranche's error is to have assumed in the first place that our mind perceives material things, instead of starting from what he says in the *Elucidations*, namely that it only perceives intelligible things,[8] or that he has only failed to speak exactly, I want to look closely at whether this view, which seems so extraordinary, can have any foundation.

I do not wish to take advantage of the fact that anyone could find the proposal of such a strange doctrine surprising, it being so easy to turn it into ridicule. I know that there are some very true things that people are no less prejudiced against, and that there are many people who are scarcely less shocked when one tells them that animals are only automata which sense nothing and know nothing, than they are when they hear it said that we see only intelligible bodies. Let us put all prejudices to one side and use reason alone to judge the truth or falsity of this opinion, which is on the one hand very shocking to many people, and on the other seems to have something mysterious about it which makes it very agreeable to people who like mysteries, above all when they are clothed in noble terms such as 'intelligible'. But it is this very word which must be explained if its equivocation is to be uncovered. Just as one can say that what is objectively in our mind is there *intelligibly*, one can also say in this sense that what I see *directly*, when I turn my eyes towards the sun, is the intelligible sun, so long as one understands thereby only the idea of the sun which is not distinct from my perception, as I have explained in Chapter 6, and as long as one does not add that I only see the *intelligible sun*. For although I see this intelligible sun directly by means of a virtual image which I get from my perception, I do not stop there; rather, this same perception in which I see this intelligible sun makes me see the material sun that God has created at the same time. Now is this not what Malebranche wishes to say in *The Search after Truth*, and as it is certain that he understands by the *intelligible* sun something radically distinct from the perception that I have of the sun when he claims in the sixth and tenth *Elucidations* that we only see the intelligible sun, I implore those who would wish to persist in maintaining his paradox to reply to this argument:

My soul can see, and in fact it sees what God wished it to see.

God, having united my soul to a body, wished that it see not an *intelligible* body but the body it animates, not other *intelligible* bodies but the natural bodies which are around that to which it is joined, not an *intelligible* sun but the material sun which He created and which He put in the sky.

Thus it is false that our soul only sees an intelligible body and not the body it animates. And similarly for other bodies.

The major premiss cannot be denied without impiety, since this would be not to conceive God as He is, i.e. omnipotent; it would imply that He has not done everything He wishes to do. Thus it remains only to prove the minor premiss.

God, in creating my soul and placing it in a body, wanted it to look after the conservation of my body; He wished that, joined with my body to form a man, I should live in a society of other men who also have a body and soul like me, and this society consists in the mutual provision of the offices of charity.

Now for this it was necessary for me to know the body that I animate, and not an *intelligible* body, for I must know the body I am to conserve, and it is not an intelligible body that I am supposed to conserve but the body I animate. Similarly, if, when I feel very cold, I need to draw near to a fire, I must draw the body that I animate near to the physical fire, and not an *intelligible* fire. If, being exposed to the sun's rays in the middle of summer, I am made uncomfortable and, as it were, burned by it and I need a place where I can shelter from the sun's rays, these will be the rays of the physical sun and not of some intelligible sun. It is physical food and physical drink that I must take in through a physical mouth in order to sustain the body I animate and to replenish its losses. It is, then, all these things that I need to be acquainted with, and not *intelligible* food and *intelligible* drink which my mind could see being taken into an *intelligible* body through an *intelligible* mouth, for there is no indication that these are appropriate to the nourishment of my body. It is the same with the social intercourse I need with other men. I must be acquainted with them in order to assist with their needs or to be assisted by them; to instruct them or be instructed by them; and finally to render them, or receive from them innumerable charitable offices. Now it is sufficiently clear that it is not to *intelligible* men that I have these duties but to the men whom I see and who see me, who talk to me and to whom I talk.

Thus nothing is more baseless, to put it no more strongly, than this bizarre fantasy that when we turn our eyes towards material bodies, which is called *looking*, it is not material bodies but intelligible bodies that we see.

Perhaps it is hoped that empty subtleties will make us believe that these come down to the same thing, and that we would not fail to look after the conservation of our body, even though we see not it but only an *intelligible* body, and that we would act in the same way to other men even though we see not them but only *intelligible* men.

But let the proponents of this paradox push their refinements as far as they wish, without my bothering to refute them: I need only the argument that I have already given to render them useless.

God does not do in complicated, confused or involved ways what he can do in more simple ways. Malebranche is careful not to question this proposition since he puts it amongst the primary notions which no-one can doubt: 'Who would dare to say', he says [in the *Sixth Elucidation*], 'that God does not act in the simplest ways' [ST, 568].

Now although it may be true that what is achieved so naturally and easily in the supposition that God has made our souls able to know natural bodies, might also be realised by assuming that it cannot know them but only *intelligible* bodies, nevertheless it must be acknowledged that this is only the case in the latter supposition in a way which is not only much less simple than in the first but which is clearly confused and involved.

Hence the latter supposition must be rejected as wholly unworthy of God's wisdom, even though it can be made less improbable by means of empty subtleties.

Finally, this latter position would amount to saying that God, who created material bodies, should not have privileged our soul in a way contrary to the nature of material bodies; and hence one should not be surprised if our soul can neither see nor know *material* bodies but only *intelligible* ones, because it is the nature of the material bodies to be neither visible nor intelligible.

This is also the principle that Malebranche uses to condemn our soul not to see any material bodies. We have already seen this in the following passage [*Tenth Elucidation*]: 'It should be noted that the sun that one sees is not the sun that one looks at. The sun, and everything else in the material world, is not visible in itself, as I have proved elsewhere: the soul can only see the sun to which it is directly joined' [ST, 625]. And in this way he begins his elucidation *of the nature of ideas*, where he claims to explain the expression *as one sees all things in God*, which in his philosophy is the same thing as seeing only those bodies which, being in God, are intimately joined to our soul, which he otherwise calls *intelligible bodies*. For he lays down first a principle from which this must follow, namely that *bodies are not visible by themselves*. But instead of stopping there, allowing us to see only intelligible bodies, which would have left some mysterious obscurity to hide, to some extent, what is defective either in this alleged principle or in the consequences he derives from it, he completely spoils it by emphasising to us what he understands by the expression *being visible by itself*. He does this in a way which makes the principle true only by making it, at the same time, entirely useless for the purposes for which it is wanted. He says:

It is evident that bodies are not visible by themselves, that they cannot act on our mind nor represent themselves to it. This needs no proof, since it can be seen with a simple perception and with no need for reasoning. But it is certain only to those who silence their senses in order to listen to their reason. Likewise everybody believes that bodies move one another, because the senses say so; but we do not believe that bodies are by themselves completely invisible and unable to act on the mind, because the senses do not say so and seem to say the contrary. [ST, 612]

Hence we can see that he takes *to be visible by itself* and *to be able to act on our mind* as the same thing; and conversely, *to be by itself wholly invisible* and *to be unable to act on our mind*. Leaving to one side, then, the equivocal words *to be visible or invisible by itself*, and putting in their place the meaning he gives to them, which is *to be able or unable to act on our mind and represent itself to it*, i.e. to make itself known to it, we can see immediately that nothing is more inappropriate to establishing his claim *that we do not see material bodies but only intelligible bodies*. For he can only use this principle in his argument in virtue of the following major premiss:

What is unable to act on our mind, and make itself known to it, cannot be seen by our mind.

Material bodies are unable to act on our mind, and to make themselves known to it.

Hence the material bodies cannot be seen by our mind.

Hence, when we believe we see them, we see intelligible bodies in their place.

The inferences are quite correct, and one cannot deny them if the major premiss is true. But who will be persuaded that nothing can be known by our mind unless it acts on it so as to make itself known? As if *to be known* presupposed an active faculty in the thing known, whereas in fact one supposes it to be passive at the most. It is the same thing as saying that matter cannot be moved and that there must be something else that moves in its place, because it is not mobile in itself, i.e. it cannot give itself motion. It is easy to see how absurd this would be. Nevertheless, I do not see that it is any more absurd than what is being argued when one says: bodies are not visible by themselves, i.e. they cannot act on our mind; hence they are not visible; hence they cannot be known by our mind. This is the sophism logicians call *a dicto secundum quid ad dictum simpliciter.*

It remains for me only to say a word on another equivocation in the term 'intelligible', so that one can judge whether material bodies are or are not intelligible. And from this it will be seen that there is a very good sense in which the great philosophers were able to say *that the material world is not intelligible.*

It should be noted that the word *intelligible* comes from *intelligere,* and that strictly speaking it means *quod potest intelligi* [what can be known]. Now the word *intelligere* has two meanings. The first is general, where it is taken as 'to know', however this knowledge is acquired. The second meaning is particular, where it is restricted to a single way of knowing which is that of *pure intellection,* which comprises the way our soul knows its objects, without forming corporeal images of them in the brain in order to represent them: in this sense, *intelligible* is contrasted with *sensible* or *imaginable.*

In the first sense, *intelligible* signifies what can be known, as when one says something is *knowable,* and it is beyond doubt that material things are *intelligible,* since it is perfectly clear, as I have shown above, that our soul is able to know material things, and consequently that material things can be known by it.

In the second sense, particular material things, such as some particular cube or some particular cylinder, are not strictly *intelligible* but sensible, because we perceive particular bodies only by means of our senses. But in the general sense they are *intelligible*, and strictly speaking they alone are *intelligible*; for, since only particular bodies can stimulate our senses – as it is not possible for any cube whatsoever, i.e. the cube in general, which as I have already noted has no location, to make any impression on my eyes by stimulating the filaments of the optic nerve by rays of light which are reflected to it – it is necessary either that we know no bodies in general (which we cannot say since each of us is convinced of the contrary by his own experience), or we know them by pure intellection, and consequently they are *intelligible* without needing any ideas other than our perceptions, i.e. we do not need *representations* considered as distinct from these. We need only note that the perception of a single body, which we have only by means of the senses, can awaken in us the idea of a body in general, just as the shape of a square drawn on paper awakens in us the universal idea of a square being a pure *intellection*, even though it is accompanied by an image in the brain, because our mind is not constrained by the particularity either of the image in the brain or of that drawn on the paper, but applies itself solely to the abstract idea of a square in general, which can be traced neither in the brain nor on paper.

If one asks why God willed that particular bodies not be *intelligible* but perceivable by us only through our senses, the reason seems to me to be as follows. Since the capacity of our mind is limited and since it should not be employed exclusively in knowing bodies, God did not deem it appropriate for us to know every particular body, of which there are infinitely many. He believed, however, that there must be some rationale for our knowing some bodies rather than others, and that this was principally concerned with the conservation of our bodies. It was in order that we might do this that He gave us the senses, which are corporeal organs which, being struck in various ways by small bodies which cause movements in them, are the occasion for our soul to direct its attention towards the place from where the corpuscles striking our senses seem to originate. But the mind, receiving its perceptions or ideas of particular bodies in this way, can easily either make a general idea from them or remember one that it already possesses, by abstracting from what is peculiar to each idea, in the way we have specified in Chapter 8.

And in this way the content of the idea, i.e. of the abstract perception, becomes *intelligible,* because it can be perceived by pure understanding. And thus, however one considers material things, whether as particular or as universal, there is no reason to say that they cannot be perceived by the mind. It follows from this that, whatever one does, there is nothing that will give any credence to the strange paradox that, when we look at the bodies that surround us, and even at our own body, i.e. when we turn our eyes towards them, it is not these material bodies that we see, but *intelligible bodies.*

Chapter 12

On the way in which the author of *The Search after Truth* wants us to see all things in God. He has spoken inexactly or prevaricates about the things which he claims are seen in God.

We saw earlier that Malebranche went to so much trouble to provide a proper basis for his philosophy of *representations* distinct from *perceptions*, which he calls 'ideas', only to force us to recognise that it is very advantageous to religion that only God can have this *representative* role with respect to our minds, and therefore that it is in God that we see all things.

With this in mind, he assumes that these *representations* can only be united to our soul, and give our soul the means of seeing external things, in five ways, so that, having shown the disadvantages of the first four, there remains only the last, which must necessarily be adopted. And it is in this fashion that he begins the sixth Chapter [of Book 2, part II], entitled *That we see everything in God*: 'In the preceding chapters we have examined four different ways in which the soul might see external objects, none of which seems plausible to us. There remains only the fifth, which alone seems to conform to reason, and to be the most appropriate for showing the dependence that minds have on God in all their thoughts' [ST, 230].

There is much I could say on the demonstrations he uses against the first four of these five ways, for some of them seem to me very weak; but there is little to be gained from this since if the views have no semblance of truth it does not matter whether he has rebutted them well or badly.

It can also be noted that, although he is often so demanding about proofs that he claims that we should not accept any which do not force us to accept their conclusions by the evidence they offer, he is content with much less on this occasion, even though there is nothing in all his book of which he speaks so heatedly and with such zeal as this new discovery. For there is assuredly nothing which resembles true demonstrations less than the arguments he puts forward to establish this quite extraordinary opinion.

But I do not think they should be pursued further, for it is well known that good arguments cannot establish something which has no appearance of truth. It is sufficient, I believe, to present what he says by explaining in what way we see all things in God, so that we may recognise that nothing worse, more unintelligible or more inappropriate, has ever been devised to enable us to see the material objects that we seek to know.

One of the first insubstantial proofs of this new doctrine proposed to us as a marvellous discovery has nothing solid in it, and he sometimes speaks of it in one way and sometimes in another.

Exaggerations are out of place in dogmatic treatises, where only what is exactly true should be advanced. Why then say in a chapter title 'that we see *everything* in God'? Why repeat this many times in the same chapter? Why conclude one's demonstrations with the words: 'These are some of the reasons which might lead one to believe that minds perceive *everything* through the intimate presence of He who understands everything in the simplicity of His being' [ST, 235)?; and a little further on, that 'only God can enlighten us by representing *everything* to us', so as to end up saying that it is necessary that God, who is joined to our soul in the capacity of a *representation*, represents everything to us, when He represents to us neither our own soul, nor the souls of other men, nor the angelic spirits? And these are all things which should be far better represented to the soul than material things because they participate more in the perfection of His being, as they were created like Him and in His image.

Everything, then, is reduced to material things and numbers. But, even among material things, in the *Elucidations* he excludes all those which exist, and generally all particular beings, which add up to all the works of God; for this is what we are led to when he says:

It seems to me very worthwhile to ponder the fact that the mind knows external objects in two ways only: by illumination and by sensation. It sees things by illumination when it has a clear idea of them, and when, by consulting this idea, it can discover all the properties which they are able to have. It sees things by sensation when it finds in itself no clear ideas of these things to be consulted; when it is thus unable to discover their properties clearly; when it only knows them through a confused sensation, without illumination and without evidence. It is by means of illumination and a clear idea that the mind sees the essences of things, as well as numbers and extension. It is by means of a confused idea or by means of sensation that it forms an opinion of the existence of creatures and that it knows its own existence. [ST, 621]

Given this, there can be no doubt that he takes *to see by illumination* and *to see by means of a clear idea* to be the same thing. Now he says we see by light and by a clear idea only the essences of things, as well as numbers and extension. Hence these are the only things we see in God. Here we have a major restriction in the range of the term *everything*.

And in case it is thought that he introduced essences of things, numbers and extensions only as examples of things we see by illumination and a clear idea, rather than claiming that we see these alone in this way, i.e. in God, he explains himself so clearly on the following page that there is no room for doubt that he restricts what we see in God – or, what comes to the same thing, what we know by illumination or by a clear idea – to these three things. 'From this,' he says, 'we can judge that it is in God or in an immutable nature that we see everything that we know by illumination or clear ideas' [ST, 621]; thus he restricts what one sees in God to this, 'not only because we only see by illumination numbers, extension and *the essences of things*, which do not depend on a free act of God, as I have already pointed out, but also because we know these things in a very perfect way' [ST, *ibid.*]. Now everything that God has created depends on a free act of God. Thus, confining oneself to what he says in this passage, which contains his last thoughts on the matter, one should conclude that we do not see any of God's works in Him.

But how is this to be reconciled with what he says, in the same chapter, when he begins to speak in detail on this question, and to prove *that we see everything in God*: 'It is absolutely necessary that God have in Himself the ideas of all the beings that He *has created*, since otherwise He could not have produced them . . . Thus it is certain that the mind can see in God *the works of God*, supposing that God wishes it to discover what He has represented to it' [ST, 230]. And a little further on: 'We believe also that one knows in God changeable and corruptible things, although St Augustine only speaks of immutable and incorruptible things, because no imperfection need be ascribed to God for this to be the case, since it is enough that God shows us what in Him is related to these things' [ST, 239]. Hence, at that stage it was 'the works of God, the beings whom God has created, changeable and corruptible things', as well as immutable and incorruptible things, that we saw in God. But now this is no longer the case: we only see what does not depend on free acts of God, and everything He has created surely depends on these.

I do not even believe that he remains firm and constant in his restriction of the things we see in God when he confines them to *numbers, extension and the essence of things*. For in Book 3, Part II, Chapter 7, he says that there are four ways in which our mind knows things: (1) by themselves, (2) by their ideas (i.e. through the representations which, according to him, are only found in God), (3) by consciousness or inner sensation, and (4) by conjecture. Now he only puts *bodies or properties of bodies* in the second class of things, which he claims can only be known in the second way, i.e. by their ideas, which is the same thing as being seen in God. And this is linked to many other passages in the book where he reduced to material things whatever we cannot see by themselves but only through their representations, distinct from perceptions. Thus it would seem that by this criterion he should not include abstract numbers, which are the object of arithmetic and algebra, amongst the things which can be seen only in God, since these kinds of numbers are neither *bodies* nor *properties of bodies*, and they have nothing material in them, being applicable equally to spiritual and corporeal things.

And in fact I do not see why, on Malebranche's account, abstract numbers can only be known in God. For according to him the only things which must be seen through representations are those which are seen in God, and it is only whatever cannot be ultimately joined to our soul that needs to be seen by a representation. Now abstract numbers are intimately joined to our soul, since they exist only in our soul, though *numbered things*, so to speak, are outside it. Thus abstract numbers do not need to be seen in God.

I detect a similar prevarication in regard to immutable and external truths. He says in several places that we do not see them in God, and in others that we do see them in God. He declares [Book 3, Part II, Chapter 6] that 'his opinion is not that we see these truths in God', and that he does not agree with Augustine's opinion in these matters. 'We do not say', he says:

that we see God in seeing eternal truths, as St Augustine says, but in seeing the ideas of those truths; for the ideas are real, whereas the equality between ideas, which is truth, is not something real. When we say, for example, that the cloth that we measure is three ells, the cloth and the ells are real, but the equality between the ells and the cloth is not a real being, but only a relation found between the three ells and the cloth. When we say that twice 2 is 4, the ideas of the numbers are real, but the equality between them is only a relation. [ST, 135]

Hence we do not see truths in God, because these are only relations, and a relation is not real.

But I do not know how this accords with what he says [in Book 3, Part II, Chapter 3]: 'No one doubts that ideas are real beings, since they have real properties, or that they differ from one another' [ST, 222]. For can one deny that relations too have real properties, and that they differ from one another? Aren't some equal and some unequal, some larger and some smaller? Isn't the relation 3:4 equal to the relation 15:20? Isn't the relation 3:5 greater than the relation 4:7, and the relation 5:11 smaller than the relation 6:13? Hence one cannot say that relations are 'not something real'. If, taking the word 'being' as 'substance', one says they are not 'real beings', then abstract numbers are no longer 'real beings'; for three ells, insofar as they are *ells*, are a 'real being', but the number 3, abstracted from all 'numbered' things, so to speak, is not a 'real being', since it is not outside our thought. Why then are there 'ideas of numbers' but not 'ideas of relations'?

However this may be, according to what he says here one sees neither relations nor truths in God, since truths are only relations. Nevertheless, he seems to say the opposite in the *Tenth Elucidation*:

I see that 2 times 2 makes 4, and that my friend is to be valued more than my dog; and I am certain that there is no man in the world who is not able to see this as well as I. Now I do not see these truths in the mind of other people, just as other people do not see them in mine: thus it is necessary that there be a universal reason that enlightens me and all other intelligences. [ST, 613]

Isn't this to say that each of us, not seeing things in the mind of others, sees them in God? But he has just said that '2 times 2 makes 4' is only a relation, and my friend's having a higher value than my dog is only a relation too. Relations are, therefore, according to the last passage, seen in God.

Chapter 13

He prevaricates also in his explanation of the ways in which we see things in God. The first is by means of ideas. Starting from this he denies that there are in the intelligible world any ideas which represent each thing in particular, something that cannot be denied without error.

He prevaricates even more when explaining the way he thinks we see things in God. Having proposed one way in *The Search after Truth*, he retracts it in the *Elucidations*, where he takes a very different viewpoint, believing it to be better, whereas it is incomparably poorer and less suited to showing us what he wants us to believe concerning the union of our soul with God, so that we might see all things in Him.

This can be seen by comparing the following passages. The first is from Book 3, Part II, Chapter 6. Having assumed two things which are completely true – the first, 'that God has in Himself the ideas of everything that He has created', and the second, 'that God is intimately joined to our soul by His presence' – he concludes from these 'that the mind sees in God all His works, provided that God wishes to reveal to the mind whatever it is in Him that represents these works' [ST, 230]. Note that this condition involves two things: first, that God wishes to reveal to man something Malebranche baselessly assumes man needs if he is to know the works of God; secondly, that what God has to reveal to him in this way is what it is in God that represents each of His works, i.e. the ideas according to which He has made them, as St Augustine, and St Thomas after him, teaches. There is no doubt that if God wishes to reveal His divine ideas to man during his life this would be a very perfect way of knowing creation. But I deny that there is no other means of enabling him to know, and there are plenty of arguments to show that He does not use these means in order to provide knowledge of creation, above all during our life, since for this it would be necessary for Him to show Himself to us face to face, as He shows Himself to the saints.

Forestalling this objection, here is what he says:

But it must be noted that one cannot conclude that minds see the essence of God from their seeing all things in God in this way: because what they see is very imperfect, and God is very perfect. They see divisible, shaped matter etc., and in God there is nothing which is divisible or has shape, for God is all

being, since He is infinite and understands everything: but He is not being in
particular. Besides, it might be said that one does not so much see the ideas of
things as the things themselves that the ideas represent, for when we see a
square, for example, we do not say we see the idea of a square which is joined
to the mind, but only the square that is external to it. [ST, 231]

If such a poorly-founded principle is to have some likelihood, this
is the very least we can say if we are not to attribute to God
something unworthy of Him, supposing He wishes to use these
representations. But it is to conceive of the mind poorly to imagine
that an idea which is in God, and which our mind does not see, can be
used by it to know what this idea represents. It is like saying that the
portrait of a man whom I know only by reputation, when placed so
close to or so far from my eyes that I cannot see it, would not fail to
enable me to know the face of this man.

Perhaps this is also what makes him abandon this approach and
take up another which allows him to avoid this disadvantage,
although it draws him into several infinitely greater ones, as we shall
see below.

But I shall confine myself here to considering whether, in trying to
change his first way of seeing things in God, he achieved this by
denying something which is true and which he had previously
granted. For he had shown that this way consisted in God revealing
to us *each of His ideas*, and that is what he no longer agrees with in
the *Elucidations*, where he declares: 'When I said that we see
different bodies through the knowledge we have of God's perfections, which represent them, I did not exactly claim that there are in
God certain particular ideas which represent each body individually'
(ST, 627). This is connected with what he had said earlier: 'It should
not be imagined that the intelligible world is related to the material,
sensible world in such a way that there is, for example, an intelligible
sun, an intelligible horse, or an intelligible tree, which are meant to
represent to us a sun, a horse, and a tree' [ST, 627]. And I say that if
we remove the words 'to us' (for God's ideas represent nothing to us,
at least in this life, but it is to God himself, as we conceive Him, that
they represent His works) and then I maintain that it is not something we imagine but is something certain, that 'the intelligible world
is related to the material, sensible world in such a way that there is,
for example, an intelligible sun, an intelligible horse, or an intelligible tree, which represent a sun, a horse, and a tree'. And it is

impossible that matters should have been otherwise.

For the intelligible world is nothing but the material and sensible world in so far as it is known by God and represented in His divine ideas. And consequently, it is impossible for there not to be a perfect relation between them, and for everything which exists materially in the material world not to exist intelligibly in the intelligible world. This is exactly what must be understood by the ideas ascribed to God, and which St Augustine says one cannot avoid ascribing to Him, since to deny them one would have to believe that God had created the universe without reason and unknowingly. It was Plato, Augustine says [*Eighty-Three Different Questions*, Question 46 (1)], who was the first to give the name *idea* to what we must conceive to have been in God when He planned the creation of the world, and what he understood by this word has always been recognised by all those who have had a true knowledge of God. Now as *ideas* in God are the form and exemplar according to which He created each of His works, because there is nothing, however small, that He has not created, without a distinct knowledge of what He is doing, there must necessarily be individual ideas which represent to Him not only the sun, a horse, a tree, but also the smallest gnat and the smallest particle of matter.

This is an incontestable truth and it is proved by St Augustine in several places. In Question 46 of the *Eighty-Three Questions*, after having said that *ideas* are the forms, species and reasons according to which God created everything, he expressly declares that each thing has been created according to its individual idea. The Latin expresses his thought better than can be done in French:

Quis audeat dicere Deum irrationabiliter omnia condidisse? Quod si recte dici et credi non potest, restat ut omnia ratione sint condita: nec eadem ratione homo qua equus, hoc enim absurdum est existimare. Singula igitur propriis sunt creata rationibus. Ilas autem rationes ubi arbitrandum est esse, nisi in mente Creatoris?[9]

[Who would dare say that God has created all things without a rational plan? But if one cannot rightly say or believe this, then all things are created on a rational plan, and the same plan does not serve for a man and a horse, which would be absurd. Therefore individual things are created in accord with reasons specific to them. As for these reasons, can they be thought to exist anywhere but in the mind of the Creator?]

St Thomas, as was his custom, followed St Augustine as his master. He devoted a 'Question' to ideas in the first Part of the

Summa Theologica. It is the fifteenth Question, which has only three Articles. He proves in the first that there are ideas in God, in the second that there are several ideas, and in the third that each thing has its own individual idea, and that one must not make an exception for matter or individual things, as Plato seems to have done.[10] But it is worth looking at how, in the second Article, he explains how there can be several ideas in God, even though the idea is the same thing as the essence of God and God has only one essence, because this is of great help to us in disentangling the things that Malebranche constantly jumbles together in *The Search after Truth.*

Aquinas says:

It is easy to conceive of several ideas in God without this contravening His simplicity. One need only consider that the idea of a work is in the mind of the craftsman as that which is understood (*sicut quod intelligur*) and not as the form by which he understands it (*et non sicut species, qua intelligitur, quae est forma faciens intellectum actu*), i.e. as the very perception which is the formal cause, so to speak, of the fact that the mind actually perceives an object; for the idea of a house is in the mind of the architect as a thing which he knows, and in whose likeness he must make the material house that he undertakes to build. Now it is not contrary to the simplicity of God's understanding for Him to know several things, but it would be contrary to His simplicity if He knew them by means of a plurality of perceptions. And hence there are many ideas in God, as things understood by God (*unde plures ideae sunt in mente divina ut intellectae ab ipso*). And it will be judged that this is how things should be when one considers that God knows His essence perfectly, and that consequently He knows it in all the ways in which it can be known. Now it can be known not only as it is in itself, but also as it can be participated in by creatures according to some degree of likeness. But each creature has its own form or nature to the extent that it participates in something resembling the divine essence. Insofar as God knows His essence as capable of being imitated by such a creature, He knows it as the particular type or reason or idea of that creature. And similarly for other creatures. Thus one must conceive of God as having several *notions* or *reasons* of several things. And this is what makes one conceive that God has several *ideas* in Him.

When it is objected 'that art and wisdom are in God as much a principle of knowledge and action as the idea is, and that He cannot therefore have a plurality of ideas, since there is only one divine art and wisdom', he replied in this way:

The word 'art' and 'wisdom' denote in God that by which God knows (*quo Deus intelligit*), but the word 'idea' indicates what God knows (*quod Deus intelligit*). Now God knows several things at a single glance, and not only what they are in themselves, but also that by which they are known, i.e. He knows the notions and reasons of various things. This is the same as for an architect: for when he has in his mind simply the perception of the material form of a house, one then says that he knows a house; but, when he applies himself to considering the house insofar as it is in his mind, i.e. insofar as he expressly reflects on the perception that he has of it in virtue of knowing this house (*ex eo quod intelligit se intelligere eam*), this first perception, which was previously *id quo intelligitur* [that by which it is known], becomes by this reflection *id quod intelligitur* [that which is known], and one says then that he has the *idea* of this house. Now God does not only know several things through His essence, He also knows that He knows several things through His essence. And it is this that is called knowing several notions of things, or that there are in the understanding several divine ideas, insofar as these are known by Him: *Vel plures ideas esse in intellectu divino ut intellectas.*

It can be seen from this that St Thomas does not take the word *idea* as broadly as I have done in construing it as any *perception* which, properly speaking, is *id quo intelligitur* (although also in one way *id quod intelligitur* because of the implicit reflection that is essential to it), but that he restricts it to that perception which, by an *explicit* reflection on our knowledge, becomes more specifically *id quod intelligitur*. And this brings us back to what I said in Chapter 6, when explaining what it was properly speaking to see the properties of things in their ideas. If this were all then it would be merely a speculative *idea*; whereas the idea which an architect has of a house which he plans to build – an idea which he often turns over in his mind by means of knowledge reflecting on the first perception he has of it – is a practical idea, which is the same thing as an exemplary cause. But one sees in this no trace or vestige of those *representations* which precede any *perception* and which, it is imagined, our mind must have for it to be able to know.

And what is still more notable is that St Thomas recognises that God sees all things in a single, unique vision, both as they are in His divine understanding and as they are in themselves: '*Deus uno intellectu intelligit multas et non solum secundum quod in seipsis sunt, sed etiam secundum quod intellecta sunt*' ['God knows several things in a single glance, and not only what they are in themselves, but also as they are known']. And it appears that he considers the first kind of perception as a proof of the second. From which it follows that things are *objectively* in God like they are in themselves, and consequently a thing can be objectively in God, i.e. be known by God, without it being in Him formally. For a toad, a caterpillar and a spider are objectively in God because He knows them, although one cannot say that there are toads, caterpillars and spiders formally in God. And yet we shall see that it is because he does not distinguish between these things properly that Malebranche still often argues *a dicto secundum quid ad dictum simpliciter*, in almost constantly reasoning in the following way: 'God knows such and such a thing: now God only knows what is in Himself: thus this thing is in God.' For 'to be in God' may be understood, in the conclusion, either *objectively* or *formally*. If one understands it *formally* then it is the sophism that I have just indicated, *a dicto secundum quid ad dictum simpliciter*. For it does not follow that a stone is formally in my mind because I know it, only that it is *objectively* there.[11] And if this is not how it is to be understood in the conclusion 'Thus such and such a thing is in God', i.e. *if it is in Him objectively*, then it is trifling to argue in this way. For this is merely to conclude what is already in the major premiss, since there is no difference between the statements 'that God knows such and such a thing' and 'that such and such a thing is objectively in God'.

Chapter 14

The second way of seeing things in God, which is to see them in an *infinitely intelligible extension* which God contains within Himself. What is said concerning this is either completely unworthy of God or manifestly self-contradictory.

We have just seen that Malebranche, while remaining resolute in *The Search after Truth* in the belief that we see all things by means of the particular idea of them in God, subsequently changes his mind, declaring in [*Elucidation Ten*] 'that he did not claim' (he should say rather that he no longer claims) 'that there are in God particular ideas which represent each particular body, but that we see everything in God through God's applying intelligible extension to our mind in a thousand different ways' [ST, 627–8].

It thus remains to examine whether this second way of seeing things in God, which involves seeing them '*in an intelligible extension which God contains within Himself*, is any better than the first.

Now in order to assess this second way better, we must attend to his explanation of how he himself maintains this occurs. And, above anything else, we must note that what led him to take up this new theory is an objection which was put to him in these terms:

Objection: Nothing in God is moveable, and nothing in Him has shape. If there is a sun in the intelligible world, this sun never changes. The visible sun appears larger when it is near to the horizon than when it is far from the horizon. Thus it is not the intelligible sun that we see. The same holds for all other creatures: thus we do not see God's works in Him. [ST, 626]

And this is how he replies:

To reply to this is enough to bear in mind that God contains in Himself an infinite intelligible extension; and He knows this extension since He created it, and He can know it only in Himself. Thus, since the mind can perceive a part of this intelligible extension that is contained in God, it is certain that it can perceive all shapes in God, for every finite intelligible extension must be an intelligible shape, since shape is nothing but the limits of extension. Moreover, this shape of intelligible, general extension becomes sensible and particular through colour or some other sensible quality that the soul attaches to it, for the soul almost always projects its sensation onto the idea that strikes it vividly. Thus it is not necessary that there be any sensible bodies in God, nor any shapes in intelligible extension, in order for us to see them in God or for God to see them in Himself, even though He only considers Himself. If we also imagine that a shape of intelligible extension, made sensible by colour, be taken successively from different parts of this infinite extension, or if we imagine that a shape of intelligible extension can turn on its centre or successively approach others, we would perceive motion in sensible or intelligible shape without there being any motion in intelligible extension. For God does not see the motion of bodies in His substance or in the idea that He has of it in Himself, but only through the knowledge that He has of His volitions in regard to these bodies. Even their existence He perceives only in this way, because His will alone gives being to all things. God's volitions change nothing in His substance; they do not move it. Perhaps in this sense intelligible extension cannot be moved even intelligibly. Although we only see this infinite intelligible extension, immobile or otherwise, it seems to us to move because of the sensation of colour or because of the confused image that remains after the sensation, which we successively attach to different parts of the intelligible extension which furnishes us with an idea when we see or imagine the motion of some body. It can be understood from this why we see the intelligible sun sometimes greater, sometimes smaller, although it is always the same for God. For all that is needed for this is that we sometimes see a greater part of intelligible extension, and sometimes a smaller, and that we have a vivid sensation of light which we attach to this part of extension. Now as the parts of intelligible extension are all of the same kind, they can all represent any body whatsoever. [ST, 626–7]

I do not know, Sir, what to say of such a discourse: I am startled by it. For I find that it contains so many muddles and contradictions that all my effort will be devoted to untangling equivocations and finding the paralogisms in it.

(1)   I have already undermined in advance its main support by showing in what sense one can say that what God knows is in God. For the whole of this discourse revolves around the peculiar hypothesis that 'God contains in Himself an infinite intelligible extension'. And the only demonstration of this that he offers is 'that God knows extension, since He created it, and He can know it only in Himself'. On this kind of reasoning, there is nothing that one could not put in God, since I have as much reason to say that 'God contains in Himself millions of intelligible gnats and fleas; for He knows them, having created them.' And He can 'only know them in Himself'.

(2)   But these arguments are pure sophisms, for from the major premiss 'God knows everything in Himself' one can only argue as follows:

God knows extension, gnats, fleas, toads and all other creatures.
Therefore, He knows all things in Himself.

But it is a clear paralogism to conclude absolutely from this:

Therefore, all things are in God – extension, gnats, fleas, toads – and He contains them in Himself.

(3)   To reach this last conclusion with respect to extension, as Malebranche does, the major premiss must be 'God only knows what is in Himself', but this can only be said erroneously. For God knows what is in Him and what is outside Him, since He knows Himself and He also knows the creatures that He has produced outside Himself. St Thomas makes this an article of the *Summa* [*Theologica*], in Part I, Question 14, Article 5 – *Ultrum Deus cognoscat alia a se* [Whether God knows things other than Himself] – and he answers that:

God necessarily knows things other than Himself. For He could not know Himself perfectly unless He knows what His power extends to. Now His power extends to many things *outside Him*, since He is the cause of them; and moreover the essence of the first cause, God, is His own act of understanding, *ipsum intelligere*. Thus the effects which are in God as their cause are necessarily in Him, in a way which is appropriate to their being in an intelligence, namely being known in it.

He then explains in what way God sees things that are outside Him and in what way His perception of Himself differs from the perception 'that He has of His creatures': 'It is that He sees Himself in Himself, because He sees Himself through His essence; but He sees things that are different from Him, i.e. creatures, not in themselves but in Himself, inasmuch as His essence contains the likenesses of all the things to which He has given existence.'

And to the objection based on the claim of St Augustine, that *'Deus extra seipsum nihil intuetur'* [God sees nothing outside Himself], he says that this should not be understood as saying that God sees nothing of what is external to Him, but just that He sees what is external to Him only in Himself. And in fact what St Augustine says in the passage cited in St Thomas's first objection, which is from the Forty-sixth Question of the *Eighty-three Questions*, is far from meaning 'that God sees nothing outside Himself' (from which it would appear that one could conclude, as our friend does, that a thing must be in God if He is to know it) since he says only that God does not seek outside of Himself the exemplars that He needs in order to make the things that He has created: *'Non enim extra se quicquam positum intuebatur, ut secundum id constitueret quod constituebat; nam hoc opinari sacrilegium est'* [It would be sacrilegious to suppose that He was looking at something outside Himself as a model for creating what He did create].

St Thomas takes this still further in the following article, where he refutes, as being erroneous, the opinion of those who say that God knows creatures only according to the general notion of *beings* and not according to what each is in itself and in so far as they are distinct from one another. And he maintains that, although He knows them in Himself and through His essence, He nevertheless knows each of them by an act of knowing which is peculiar to each, because the divine essence includes whatever perfection each creature has and even infinitely more: *'Cum essentia Dei habeat in se quidquid perfectionis habet essentia cujuscumque rei alterius, et adhuc amplius, Deus in seipso potest omnia propria cognitione cognoscere'* [As the essence of God contains in itself all the perfection contained in the essence of any other being, and far more, God can know in Himself all of them with individual knowledge].

And in reply to the first Objection [of Book I, Question 14, Article 6 of the *Summa Theologica*] he reveals the illusion to which our friend almost always succumbs on this matter. This is his view that, as a rule, 'to know things according to the intelligible being that they have in the understanding of those who know them' and to know them 'according to what they are in themselves and external to the understanding' are two quite different things. But St Thomas shows that this distinction is so far from being one of opposition that the latter is a consequence of the former. For although one knows an object according to the intelligible being that it has in the understanding, this does not prevent it being known at the same time insofar as it is external to the understanding. Thus I know a stone according to the intelligible being that it has in my understanding when I know that I know it; and yet at the same time I know this stone according to what it is in itself, and according to its own nature. And although I only say all this to explain how God does not fail to see creatures in themselves, and by means of a knowledge which is peculiar to each one, even though He sees them in His essence, one can judge from this whether it is to speak theologically to say, as our friend does [*Elucidation Six*] that: 'God sees that there are spaces between the bodies that He has created; but He sees neither these bodies nor the spaces in themselves. He can see them only by means of intelligible bodies and intelligible spaces' [ST, 573]. There is something mysterious in these words which has enabled them to be accepted respectfully by many people. But the mysteries disappear as soon as one provides the correct understanding of the word *intelligible*, and doesn't have it so obscure that one can either conceive nothing distinctly, or that one conceives it as something completely different to what one should be conceiving when one reads the expressions: 'intelligible bodies', 'intelligible spaces', 'intelligible extension'. For an intelligible sun is, as we have just seen in St Thomas, nothing but the material sun according as it is in the understanding of he who knows it, *secundum esse quod habet in cognoscente*. This is not at all different from what it is in itself, above all in regard to God. Since God's knowledge is completely perfect, He can know each thing only according to what it truly is in itself. He therefore knows them, as St Thomas says, *et secundum esse intelligible quod habent in cognoscente, et secundum esse quod habent extra cognoscentum* [according to the intelligible being they have in my understanding, and according to how they are outside my understanding]. It is therefore not true that God sees the spaces between the bodies that He has created only through intelligible bodies and spaces; and that He cannot see these bodies and spaces by themselves, at least so long as this *by themselves* is not an equivocation which directs the mind to a meaning which is not in question here. For if *by themselves* refers to the *rationem cognoscendi* [the notions by which we know], God does not see bodies by themselves because He sees them in His essence, and His essence is what makes them known to Him. But if *by themselves* refers to the *rem cognitam* [thing known], God sees bodies by themselves and in their own essence, and not just according to the intelligible being which He has in the divine understanding. Consequently, this latter sense of *by themselves* being the only appropriate one when it comes to showing 'that God sees that there are spaces which He has created, but He only sees them through intelligible spaces', it is clear as daylight that this proposition is untenable in sound theology, since in God intelligible spaces are nothing but the real and physical spaces He has put between the bodies that He has created. Consequently, it is impossible that God should see these intelligible spaces and at the same time not see the real, physical spaces which He has put between these bodies, much less that knowledge of the former precludes knowledge of the latter.

(4) I cannot in good faith imagine what he wants us to understand by the *infinite intelligible extension* in which, he now claims, we see everything; for he says such contradictory things about it that it seems to me as difficult to form a distinct idea of it from what he says as it is to understand a mountain without a valley. It is both created and not created. It is both God and not God. It is both divisible and not divisible. It is not only in God eminently, but also formally; and it is in Him only eminently and not formally.

It is created, since it is the extension made by God. And it is the extension made by God since it is from this that he proves that God knows it. 'God', he says, 'contains in Himself an infinite intelligible extension; for God knows extension since He has made it, and He can know it only in Himself.'

And it is not created since, if it were, in seeing things in this *infinite intelligible extension* we would only see them in something created, whereas his aim is to show us that we see them in God.

Accordingly, it is necessary that it be God: but it can be neither God nor an attribute of God, by the same arguments as those which Malebranche uses to show 'that the soul does not contain intelligible extension as one of its modes of being'. For one need only apply the arguments to God to see easily that they are more effective in excluding intelligible extension from God's essence than they are in excluding it from that of our soul. Or, putting it better, on the true notion of *intelligible extension*, which I examined in the last chapter, these arguments do not prove that intelligible extension is not in our soul, and on his confused notion, if they show that *intelligible extension* is not in our soul they also show that it is not in God's. I shall begin by showing the first of these.

'This intelligible extension', he says, 'is perceived by itself, without our thinking of anything else, and one cannot conceive modes of being without perceiving the subject or being of which they are the modes' [ST, 624].

Reply: I deny the antecedent premiss, for *intelligible extension*, taken as the perception of extension, cannot be conceived unless at the same time one conceives the mind which perceives it.

'We perceive this intelligible extension without thinking about our mind' [ST, 624].

Reply: Again I deny this, for the reason I have just given; for one cannot think of *intelligible* extension without thinking of some mind in which it is perceived, since it is this very thing that makes us call it *intelligible*.

'The limits of this intelligible extension give it shape, but the limits of the mind cannot give shape to the mind' [ST, 624].

Reply: They give it an *intelligible* shape, which can be in our mind as easily as *intelligible* extension can. That is to say, both are there objectively.

'Since this intelligible extension has parts, it can be divided, but we see nothing in the soul that is divisible' [ST, 624–5].

Reply: I reply that there is nothing in our soul which is *formally* divisible. But our soul could not know extension, unless extension with all the properties of *divisibility*, *mobility*, etc., were present to the mind *intelligibly*, i.e. *objectively*: and thus it does not follow from the essential divisibility of extension that the soul cannot contain it within itself, even though extension can only be conceived as divisible.

If the author takes the phrase 'intelligible extension' in a different sense, I maintain that the same arguments must show that infinite intelligible extension cannot be God, i.e. cannot be an attribute of God. To show this we need only go back to his statement that 'this intelligible extension is perceived by itself, without our thinking of anything else; and one cannot conceive modes of being without perceiving the subject or being of which they are the modes'.

For still less can we conceive the attribute of a being without perceiving the being of which it is the attribute. Thus, if God contains within Himself *intelligible extension* as one of His attributes, it cannot be conceived without conceiving of God: 'now one can conceive of it without our thinking of anything else'. Thus it is not contained in God as one of His attributes.

'We perceive this intelligible extension without thinking about our mind.'

We perceive it also without thinking about God, for it is certain that the Epicureans and Gassendists do not think of God when they conceive of the space where their atoms move around as an *infinite intelligible extension*.

'We cannot even conceive that this infinite intelligible extension could be a mode of our mind.'

Even less can we conceive that it could be God, or an attribute of God.

'The limits of this infinite intelligible extension give it a shape, but the limits of the mind cannot give it a shape.'

This is even truer with respect to God, for one cannot conceive of God having limits; and when one pictures this to oneself, it is even more certain than their *not being able to have a shape*.

'Since this intelligible extension has parts, it can be divided, but we see nothing in the soul that is divisible.'

And it is even more evident that *there is nothing in God which is divisible*. Therefore, if he thinks it justifiable to conclude from all these arguments that 'intelligible extension cannot be a mode of our mind', how much more justifiable would it be to conclude that it cannot be God or an attribute of God?

And we must not imagine that the property of *infinity* that he ascribes to this *intelligible extension* renders it any more worthy of being admitted into God. The infinity which is appropriate to God bears no relation to the infinity that one can conceive in extension. And the infinity of extension, far from being contained in the idea of a perfect Being, excludes it no less certainly than it necessarily includes the former, for the greater the extension becomes the closer it approaches infinity, the more parts actually distinct from one another it will have, which manifestly goes against God's simplicity, which is one of the principal attributes of the perfect Being. But the infinity which is appropriate to God is far from containing anything which goes against this idea, since on the contrary the first thing one notices in it is Being itself, the fullness of Being, limitless being, and hence infinite Being.

It also turns out that this *infinite intelligible extension* is both divisible and not divisible. It is divisible because what essentially makes extension divisible is not the actual separation of one part from another; rather, it is sufficient that one part be external to another and that it not be the other.[12] Now we have just been told 'that a shape of intelligible extension can be taken successively from different parts of this infinite extension'. Thus it is conceived of as being divisible. But since it is God, as it must be if we are to see in God the things we see in this extension, it cannot be divisible, according to Malebranche, for it is so certain that God is not divisible on his account that it is one of the things which, he says, no one has any hesitation about. 'For where is the man who hesitates,' he says, 'when asked whether God is wise, just, and powerful, whether or not He is triangular, divisible, or mobile?' [ST, 568].

(5)   But what is most puzzling is knowing whether this *infinite intelligible extension* which he claims to be in God, since he says that God contains it, is *formally* or only eminently in Him. We need this distinction to explain how effects are in their causes. There are those who believe that every plant is in the seed from which it issues, with its parts distinguishable but in a smaller form, and Malebranche holds this opinion in Chapter 6 of the first Book of *The Search after Truth* [ST, 26f.][13] If this were the case, one could say that every plant is *formally* in the seed which produces it. But it is not in this way that creatures are related to God; they must be in Him as in their cause, but they cannot be in Him *formally*, for whatever being and perfection they have is limited and therefore imperfect. Now there is nothing imperfect in God. Matter is above all, by its nature, necessarily divisible and shaped, 'and there is nothing in God which is divisible or has shape', as our author says [ST, 231]. Thus, since creatures must be in God as in their cause, and cannot be there formally, we must find a word to indicate in what way they were in

Him, and we will find nothing more appropriate than to say that
they were in Him *eminently*, i.e. in a more exalted way than they
are in themselves, and which is free from all the imperfections
which are inescapably attached to their condition as creatures,
compared with the infinite perfection of the sovereign Being.
Descartes, who was not someone to use a scholastic distinction
unless he believed it to be well-founded, uses this distinction in
several places in his works, and especially in the *Replies to the
Second Set of Objections to the Meditations*, where he had to speak
with greater precision as he undertakes there to prove, by the
geometrical method, the existence of God and the real distinction
between our soul and body [CSM II, 113ff.]. Malebranche does not
use the same words, but his explanation is in terms which come
down to the same thing when he says 'that God is the whole of
being because He is infinite, and includes everything, but He is not
any particular being'. From this he concludes that, although (as he
deludes himself into thinking) we see everything in God, 'nevertheless we do not see God because what we see is only one or several
beings, and we do not understand the perfect simplicity of God,
who contains all beings'. This is connected with his remark that 'all
creatures, even the most material and terrestrial, are in God,
although in a way which is *completely spiritual, and which we
cannot understand*' [ST, 229].

It is very difficult to know in which of these ways he claims God
contains this *infinite intelligible extension* in Himself, in what way he
wants us to see all things. One would hope that this is only *eminently*,
for that would involve nothing unworthy of God. The only problem
would be to find out why – given that all the bodies that God has
created, and which we need to see, have a greater claim to be
eminently in God than this *infinite intelligible extension* – he has not
rather said that since each of these bodies is eminently in God, it is
there that we see them, instead of saying that we see them in this
infinite intelligible extension, if he believed that this was only
eminently in God, along with all the individual bodies. This argument already shows that he thought it was there *formally* and not
only *eminently*, but that this was sufficiently qualified by the word
'intelligible', which I do not see one can make any good sense of in
this passage.

This can also be seen in the fact that nothing can better show that
something is *formally*, and not merely *eminently*, extended than to

add to it the greatest imperfection of extension, viz. having parts actually distinct from one another, so that it has smaller and larger parts. And this is what he says about his *infinite intelligible extension*, as we have already seen in the passage quoted.

This can also be seen in the way in which he contrasts extension with sensible bodies and motion, for he does not want either sensible bodies or motion, even intelligible motion, to be in God in the same way that he imagines *extension* to be in God. This is explicit in the case of sensible bodies, for on the same page that he says that God contains extension, he says that 'there are no sensible bodies in God', and that this is not needed for us to see them in God. And as for motion, here is what he says in the same passage:

> We can perceive the motion of a sensible shape without there being any motion in intelligible extension. For God does not see the motion of bodies in His substance or in the idea He has of them in Himself, but only through the knowledge that He has of His volitions. Even their existence He sees only in this way, because His will alone gives being to all things. God's volitions change nothing in His substance, they do not move it. Perhaps in this sense intelligible extension cannot be moved in any sense, even intelligibly. [ST, 627]

I understand nothing in any of this and I cannot find a word of truth in it. If there is no motion in *intelligible extension*, then we might see motion by a perception we have of it from another source, but it is impossible for us to see it in this extension.

The proof that he provides for this, taken from the divine science of motion, makes a false assumption. God sees all things in His essence, both Himself and His creatures, and consequently He sees motion there as well as extension.

It is no less certain that He sees motion through the idea that He has of it in Himself, for as we have already shown, He created nothing of which He did not have an idea. Now He has created matter in motion, without which it would only have been a shapeless mass from which He would not have been able to make any of His works. Therefore He necessarily has the idea of matter in motion, not only because He has created it in this state, but also because He conserves it always in the same state since it is directly through Himself that He conserves the same quantity of motion in the world, by making it continually pass from one body to another. It is impossible for Him not to have the idea of motion in Himself since He makes nothing which He does not have an idea of, as I have shown above in St Augustine and St Thomas.

Malebranche thinks it false that God only knows motions through knowledge of His volitions, which produce them, for he assumes, in his *Treatise on Nature and Grace*, Discourse 1, Paragraph 13, 'that God, finding in the infinite treasures of His wisdom that an infinity of worlds are possible as necessary consequences of the laws of motion that He can establish, decided to create that world which can be produced and conserved in the simplest ways'. Hence He knew the laws of motion in the infinite treasures of His wisdom before knowing them in His volitions, since this occurred before He decided to create the world. Now He could not have known the laws of motion without knowing motion. Hence it is not true that it is only in deciding to produce motions that He knows them.

I also cannot understand why he says that God's volitions change nothing in His substance and that they do not move it. Is it because he fears that, if God were to know motion through His essence or substance and not exclusively through His Will, then His substance would thereby be changed? But in that case why does he not also fear that, if God knew extension through His essence and not exclusively through His will, His essence would be extended, which is no less contrary to the nature of an infinitely perfect Being than is its being in motion? Hence I do not see why a stationary, immobile extension seems to Him more worthy of being admitted into God than an extension which is moving or movable. Certainly he has not consulted 'the vast and immense idea of the infinitely perfect Being' sufficiently in thinking about it in this way.

But, what I believe is much more important, he seems to want his *infinite intelligible extension*, provided it is unmoveable, to be able to be in God in a way in which extension which is moveable and moving could not be there, any more than sensible bodies which He also says cannot be in God. Now he cannot have denied that moveable and moving extension are, like sensible bodies, not in God *eminently*, i.e. in a wholly spiritual way and separated from all the imperfections which are always found in creatures, as he acknowledges elsewhere 'that the most material and terrestrial things are in God'. Thus he must either be contradicting himself or he must be claiming that *infinite intelligible extension* is not only in God *eminently* but also *formally*; or, rather, he has put this *infinite intelligible extension* outside God, just as Aristotle believed Plato put ideas outside God, not noticing that it was in God, and not outside Him, that he should have put it, since he only invoked it after failing to come up with some better way of making us see all things in God. Be this as it may, a cruder *formal* extension can hardly be conceived of than the one he proposes here, even though he calls it *intelligible*. He even wants – why I do not know – to get rid of one of the principal properties of extension that God has created, movability, and he has chosen to think of it like the space of the Gassendists, who also wish it to be unmovable. But, as I have just shown, I do not see that this makes it better able to be admitted into God; and I shall show in the next chapter that it renders it much less able to serve as a *representation* in which we see all bodies and all numbers.

Chapter 15

That infinite intelligible extension cannot be the means by which we see things that we do not know but wish to know.

We have just seen in the last chapter that there is nothing more unintelligible than this *infinite intelligible extension* that Malebranche has invented so as to provide us with a means of seeing things in God, being persuaded, on false grounds, that we cannot see objects outside us in any other way.

But it is no less strange that he is so mistaken in this alleged means of seeing things in God that, allowing him everything he assumes, it is impossible that this *infinite intelligible extension* in which he claims we ought to see everything could be a means by which we see any of those things that we do not know but wish to know.

I begin with numbers, for he puts these amongst the three things that we see in God, because 'we see them through illumination and a clear and distinct idea'. I would like to know what the number is which, when divided by 28 leaves 5 over, when divided by 19 leaves 6 over, and when divided by 15 leaves 7 over, i.e. I would like to know what year of the Julian period has the three characteristics of being 5 in the solar cycle, 6 in the lunar cycle, and 7 in the cycle of Indiction.[14] Now I ask what use an infinitely intelligible extension wholly united to my soul can be in finding this number. Am I being told that all the numbers are there because the mind can distinguish an infinite number of parts in it? This would mean that the numbers are there when my mind puts them there. But is their being there, as in a book where all the numbers are listed from one to ten million (for I am sure that the number I am seeking is not larger than that), of any great advantage to me in my search for it? Of course not. For even if I resolved to run through all these numbers until I got to it, this would be useless, for if I did not know it I would not know whether I had arrived at it or not. But perhaps this *infinite intelligible extension* only holds for bodies, and there is some other way of seeing numbers in God which he has not yet explained. Let us see, therefore, whether it will be of any more use in the case of bodies and shapes which I do not yet know but which I wish to know. We are assured that it is, and this is proved in three ways:

The first is that, since 'the mind can perceive a part of this intelligible extension that God contains, it can certainly perceive every shape in God; for every finite intelligible extension necessarily has a finite intelligible shape, since shape is only the limit of extension' [ST, 626].

The second is 'that this shape of intelligible, general extension becomes sensible and individual through colour or some other sensible quality that the soul attaches to it' [ST, 626].

The third

is that, if one conceives that a shape of intelligible extension made sensible by colour is taken successively from different parts of this infinite extension, or if one conceives a shape of intelligible extension turning on its centre or gradually approaching another shape, we would perceive the motion of a sensible or intelligible shape without there being any actual motion in intelligible extension. [ST, 627]

I cannot believe that it is not immediately clear that all these means, far from enabling me to know something I do not already know, necessarily presuppose that I already know it, and unless I know it, they can be of no use to me. But you will allow me, Sir, to make this clearer by the following tale, which we will take, if you like, as a story or parable.

A great painter, who had previously been a student, and was also skilful in sculpture, had such a great love for St Augustine that, talking one day with one of his friends, he admitted to him that one of the things he wished for most ardently was to find out, if he could, what this great saint really looked like. 'For you know', he said to him, 'that we painters like to have the faces of those whom we love as they actually were.' His friend, like him, found this a very laudable curiosity, and he promised to look for some way of satisfying his wish. And, whether it was to amuse himself or for some other reason, the next day he brought to the painter's house a large piece of marble, a great mass of good strong wax and a painting canvas (as for a palate of colours and brushes, he expected he would find them there). The astonished painter asked him what his aim was in bringing all these to his house. 'So that you might satisfy your desire,' he told him, 'to know what St Augustine looked like for here I give you the means by which to discover this.' 'And how do I do this?', asked the painter. 'The true face of the saint', his friend said, 'is surely in this block of marble, as well as in the piece of wax: you have only to get rid of what is superfluous, and what remains will give you the head of the real St Augustine, and it will be as easy for you to paint it on your canvas by applying the necessary colours.' 'You are mocking me,' says the painter, 'for I agree that the true face of St Augustine is in this block of marble and this piece of wax, but it is not there in a way which is any different from a hundred thousand others faces. How then do you think that, in hewing this marble, or working this wax, so as to make the face of a man, the face that I come up with at random will be that of the saint rather than that of one of the other hundred thousand which are in the marble and the wax just as much as his is? And if I do come up with his face by accident, which is outside the realm of moral possibility, I would be no better off, for since I have no idea what St Augstine looks like, I could not know whether the one I have come up with is St Augustine or not. And the same holds for the face you wish me to paint on the canvas. The means which you have provided me with in order that I might know what St Augustine looked like is thus quite absurd, for it is a means which presupposes that I know this, and which is of no use to me unless I know this.'

It would seem that the friend had no reply to this. But as the painter was very curious, he asked him whether he had a copy of *The Search after Truth*. He had, and went to fetch it, and putting it into the hands of his friend, the friend opened it at the [*Tenth Elucidation*, ST, 626] and spoke as follows:

You are surprised at the means I have given you of discovering the face of St Augustine as it really was. In doing this I have only done what the author of this book does in order to give you knowledge of material things, which, he claims, we do not know by themselves but only in God, and he says that the way we know them in God is by means of an *infinite intelligible extension* which is contained in God. Now I do not see that the means he gives me, by which to see in this extension a shape of which I have only heard the name and which I am not acquainted with, is different from that which I have proposed to you to give you the face of St Augustine as it really was. He says that, since our mind can perceive a part of this intelligible extension which is contained in God, it can perceive every shape in God, because every finite intelligible extension necessarily has an intelligible shape. This is just what I said to you: that there is no man's face which cannot be found in this block of marble by cutting it in the appropriate way. But is it any less necessary for me to know this shape (which I am supposing I do not know), in order to take a part of this intelligible extension and for my mind to limit it as required so that this shape forms its boundaries, than you rightly believed was necessary for one to know the true face of St Augustine, if we are to perceive it in this marble or this wax, where it is no less hidden than all the shapes in the intelligible extension? What then makes his suggestion any better than mine, which I do not doubt you have treated in your mind as if it were ridiculous, although you have not used this word?

We must also understand that my mind can see in this intelligible extension all the sensible bodies that I do not know, and which I need to know, by adding colour or some other sensible quality to a part of this intelligible extension.

But it would still be necessary, for this to work, that I know this sensible body if I am to apply a suitable colour to a part of extension; for if I applied a red colour to a given part of extension, that could not provide the means by which to see a sensible object which can only be green. This is just what I said to you: that you have only to apply the requisite colours to your canvas to form the face of St Augustine on it, and you need only do this to provide yourself with a portrait having a perfect likeness. For you were right to say to me that for this one needed to know what St Augustine's face looked like, and that your problem was that you did not know this.

Finally, since he must have known that the curves on which our knowledge of curvilinear figures depends can usually only be conceived by considering the motion from which they are generated,[15] he also wants us to be able to perceive motion in his *infinite intelligible extension*, because it is conceivable that an extended intelligible figure can turn on its centre, or gradually approach another. But as each curved figure of line is generated differently, and the motion by which the hyperbola is generated is different again from that by which an ellipse is generated, how could I see in this infinite intelligible extension the particular motion which I need in order to find an ellipse, by conceiving of it in terms of its parts gradually approaching one another in the requisite way, if I did not already know what an ellipse is or how it is generated? Must we not suppose, then, that I know in some way other than by this intelligible extension which it is claimed I cannot discover except in this intelligible extension? You must therefore decide either not to mock my means, or to accord no more standing to that of the author, however artful it be, than to mine.

The conversation finished with that, and the painter was not sorry that his eyes had been opened to this passage in *The Search after Truth*, which he had previously read with respect, and which he had not dared go into deeply, thinking it too mysterious and too lofty for him.

This is my story or parable. I have nothing to add to it, except that there is a passage in the same author on this very question of ideas which needs only to be applied to what he says about *intelligible extension* to confirm what I have just said – that it can only show us what one assumes we already know.

It occurs in Book 3, Part II, Chapter 3, where he argues against the opinion of those who say that the soul has the power to produce its own ideas: 'Even if the mind of man were granted a sovereign power to annihilate and create the ideas of things, still it would never use such a power to produce them' [ST, 223].

I maintain that the same holds for the mind in respect to finding ideas of things in his intelligible extension. Even though our mind can limit this intelligible extension as it pleases, it cannot find there the idea of any shape that it wishes to know and that it does not already know. And the arguments he adduces to prove his proposition prove mine even more strongly.

'For', he says:

just as the painter, no matter how good he is at his art, cannot represent an animal which he has never seen and of which he has no idea, so that the painting of it he would be required to produce could not resemble the unknown animal, so likewise a man could not form the idea of an object unless he knew it beforehand, i.e. unless he already had the idea of it, an idea which does not depend on his will. But if he already has an idea of it, he knows the object and there is no use in his forming another idea of it. There is therefore no use in attributing to the mind of man the power to produce its ideas. [ST, 223]

There is, therefore, also no use in attributing to the mind of man the power of limiting the *infinite intelligible extension* so as to discover there the idea of a shape which he needs to know; for, just as a painter, no matter how good he is at his art, cannot represent an animal which he has never seen and which he has no idea of, so that the painting of it that he needs to produce could not resemble this unknown animal, so a man could not limit intelligible extension in the way needed for it to be the idea of the shape he wishes to know – e.g. the shape a lens must have if it is to magnify objects – if he did not already know this shape, i.e. if he did not already have the idea of it. And if he already has the idea of it, he knows this object and there is no use in his forming another idea of it in this *infinite intelligible extension.*

He puts forward an objection to this, and his reply to it is the same as that which we should make to him when he puts forwards its counterpart:

It might be said that the mind has general and confused ideas which it does not produce, and that those which it does produce are clearer and more distinct individual ideas. But this amounts to the same thing, for just as the artist cannot draw the portrait of a particular man in such a way that he could be certain of having succeeded unless he had a distinct idea of that particular man, and indeed unless the man were there, so the mind that has, for example, only the idea of being, or animal in general, cannot represent a horse to itself, or form a very distinct idea of it, or be sure that it resembles a horse perfectly, unless it already has a prior idea with which it compares the second. Now if it has a prior idea, it is useless to form a second one, and therefore the same objection applies for the first idea . . . and so on. [ST, 223–4]

It is easy to see that the same thing can be said in reply to him: 'for, just as a painter' . . . and so on. Thus the mind, which only has the idea of a shape in general, could not limit intelligible extension in the way which would be required if it were to find there the idea of the shape of a lens designed to magnify objects, and be assured that this idea perfectly resembles what it seeks, unless it already has a prior idea of this shape with which to compare the second. Now if it has the prior idea, it is useless to seek a second in intelligible extension.

I would be very surprised, Sir, if someone could show me that what he says against his adversaries is conclusive but that what I say, following his example, is not even more conclusive against him.

Chapter 16

That what our author makes our mind do in order to discover its
ideas in his *infinite intelligible extension* is contrary to experience
and to the general laws that God has laid down for Himself in order
to provide us with knowledge of His works.

We have seen in Chapter 14 that this *infinite intelligible extension* is,
as Malebranche portrays it, completely unintelligible, and that it is
nothing more than a mass of contradictions, and in Chapter 15 that,
if it is understood as *he* wants to understand it, then the mind cannot
discover in it the ideas of things that it does not know but needs to
know. To overthrow this new philosophy of ideas completely, it only
remains for me to show that even if what he makes our mind do, in
order for it to be able to discover its ideas in this *infinite intelligible
extension*, could enable it to discover them there (which it can't, as
we have just shown), we should still reject everything he says on the
matter as chimerical because it is clearly contrary to what we know
with certainty to occur in our mind, and to the general laws God has
laid down for Himself in order to provide us with knowledge of His
works.

Two considerations suffice to show this. The first is that Malebranche does not undertake to explain how our mind could see
bodies in some extraordinary case such as that where we make the
fantastic assumption that God has not created them and that they
remain only possible. His aim has been rather to explain the common
and ordinary way in which our mind actually sees the bodies that
God has created, failing which it would be impossible for it to see
them. Now when one has an aim like this, it isn't enough to talk of
purely possible things and to pretend to subtlety by inventing imaginary systems. One must be careful above all to assume nothing
contrary to what is certainly the case, as nothing is more liable to lead
to the rejection of these ingenious reflections than our being able to
say: you torment yourself in vain trying to teach me how I do such a
thing, since I am convinced by incontrovertible experience that I do
not do it but the exact opposite.

The second consideration is that, when it is a case not of some
extraordinary and irrelevant effect but of a common, natural, ordinary effect which is a consequence of what God has willed to happen
in the world, according to the laws that He has established, one must

not imagine that it is enough to have shown (according to what we believe) that God is its creator to claim that it depends on His will to such an extent that one only has to suppose that He does this for no reason other than that He wishes it, without our needing to look for any other reason for it. Malebranche does not deny this for it is his first great maxim, one he sometimes takes further than he should, but which is incontestable when God acts according to the ordinary course of nature. What is at issue here is not what God does in the extraordinary and supernatural illuminating acts of grace, but what he does in respect to our more ordinary and natural perceptions of the most common objects.

These perceptions are of two kinds, according to the first chapter of Book 1 of *The Search after Truth*. The first represent to us something outside of us, such as a square or a house, etc. The second only represent to us what occurs in us, such as our sensations of light, of colours, and of sound. I will begin with the latter.

He wants God to be responsible for these, and we both agree about this. But it is necessary on his part that he acknowledge, as he does, that God does not bring them about in our soul haphazardly, but that He produces them only in a well-regulated way according to the intention He had when He joined our soul to our body. For, restricting ourselves to light and colours, he teaches, following Descartes, 'that the sensations of light and colours are only necessary in order that we might know objects more distinctly, and this is why our senses lead us to attribute them only to objects.' From this he concludes 'that the judgements to which our sense impressions lead us are quite correct if they are considered in relation to the preservation of the body' [ST, 60]

In the next chapter he adds that:

the reason why all sensations cannot be explained like other things, with words, is that attaching the ideas of things to such words as they please depends on men's will. But these same men do not attach their sensations to words, or to anything else, at will. They do not see colours, no matter how much one talks to them about them, unless they open their eyes. They do not taste flavours unless some change takes place in the arrangement of fibres in their tongue and brain. In short, some sensations do not depend upon the will of man, and only He who has made them keeps them in this mutual correspondance of modifications in their soul and body. [ST, 62]

Two things follow from this: first, that God only causes these sensations in our soul when some change occurs in the sense organs; second, that the function of these sensations, and above all those of light and colours, is only to enable us to know the bodies around us more distinctly for our own bodily self-preservation, and that this is why it is well for our soul to attribute them to bodies and to represent to itself the one as light and the others as coloured in such-and-such a way, according as the corpuscles which are reflected from these objects strike the fibres of the optic nerve differently and set them in motion in different ways. This is the common, ordinary way in which God causes these sensations in us.

But because Malebranche tries too hard to show that the ideas of all bodies that we see are in his *infinite intelligible extension* it makes him forget all these truths, which he had previously explained so well, so as to be able to persuade us that when our soul sees a block of white marble it does not see a square shape in this block, but it contemplates a part of infinite intelligible extension and conceives of it as limited in the appropriate way so as to have this shape, and also *that it does not attach the sensation of the colour white* to this marble, as we have believed up to now that it should on the basis of what the creator of the union of body and soul has instituted, but that it attaches it to some part or other of this same intelligible extension. I say 'some part or other' because this is what he teaches when he says that:

In order for us to be able to see the intelligible sun sometimes large and sometimes small it is enough that we see at one time a great part of intelligible extension and at another time a smaller part, and that we have a vivid sensation of light to attach to this extension. Therefore, as all the parts of this intelligible extension are of the same nature, all of them can represent any body whatever.

One example will suffice to show that one cannot more directly contradict the institution of the Author of Nature. I sell three different kinds of marble at different prices, because they are different colours: one is white, the other black, and the third mottled. Now in saying that these three different colours are only strictly speaking in my mind and not in the marble, it must not be imagined that there is nothing in any of them which causes it to appear to me to be of one colour rather than another. This is surely due to a different arrangement of the small parts of their surface, which is responsible for the corpuscles which are reflected from the marble towards our eyes stimulating the fibres of the optic nerve in different ways. But because our soul would find it too difficult to discern the difference in these stimulations, which is only one of degree, God has decided in this respect to give us the means to discern them more easily by those sensations of different colours, which He has willed be caused in our soul on the occasion of these various stimulations of the optic nerve, just as tapestry workers have a pattern, which they call a 'rough pattern', where the various shades of the same colour are indicated by completely different colours, so that they are less liable to mistake them.

But God's plan would be overturned if, on the pretext that none of these types of marbles is strictly white, or black, or mottled, the colours being only modifications of my soul, I could attach any colour I wish to them. For in that case the colours, far from enabling me to distinguish them, would only serve to confuse them. This is why God has not made it depend on my free will, and I am convinced of this by experience for I cannot freely ascribe the colour white to the marble that appears to me black, or black to that which appears to me white or mottled. This is not at all a choice I have, for I cannot prevent myself from attaching and applying, so to speak, white to the marble which strikes the organs of sight in a way which, according to the law that God has laid down for Himself, must be the cause of my soul having the sensation of whiteness.

We can be sure that Malebranche would contest none of this. Hence he must have given up what he knew best when, having to defend his new philosophy of ideas at any price, he finds himself reduced to attributing to our soul the illusory power to attach the sensation of green, red, blue, or any colour it likes to any part whatever of *intelligible extension*, which he cannot even claim has caused some motion in the organ of vision.

The way in which we perceive a body according to its size and shape is no less contrary to the claim he makes that, in order to have this perception, I must look for its idea in *infinite intelligible extension*. For in regard to individual bodies, this perception still necessarily depends on what occurs in our sense organs, there being no one who does not know that our soul usually perceives bodies as larger or smaller according as the images portrayed on the back of the eye are larger or smaller. It is not that these images cause our perceptions, but rather that, according to the institution of the Author of Nature, they are invariably formed in our mind when objects strike our senses and depending on how they strike them, whether it be God who causes these in us, together with perceptions of sensible qualities, or whether He has given our soul the faculty of producing them by itself, which falls under a completely different question from the one I am considering here. This being the case, and it cannot be doubted that it is, is it not evident that it is a pure fantasy, contrary to this institution of nature, not to maintain that but to want our soul to be able to have these perceptions only by applying itself to an *infinite intelligible extension*, in which it is forced to seek the ideas of the shapes of bodies that we think we see and which, according to this new philosophy of ideas, we do not see?

As for abstract shapes, which are the object of geometry, it is well known that those that are somewhat complex, and especially curvilinear ones, are not usually known at a glance, and we must consider the motions that generate them, and a long series of arguments is often necessary in order to know their principal properties: without these one cannot say, above all according to Malebranche, that one has a clear idea of them. Now is this at all like the alleged way of having the idea of them by going to find them in an *infinite intelligible extension* where they can only be found if one has put them there?

But the way Malebranche has found of reconciling his doctrine of ideas on this point with his other doctrine that God acts as a universal cause, whose general volitions must be directed to each effect by what he calls *occasional* causes, is even more inconsistent with our experience; for the occasional cause, which he believes is responsible for God giving each individual idea to us, is our desire for it. This is what he indicates in the *Second Elucidation:*

It should not be imagined that the will orders the understanding in any other way than by its desires and impulses, for the will acts in no other way. And the understanding should not be taken to obey the will by producing in itself the ideas of things that the soul desires, for the understanding does not act: it only receives illumination or ideas of things through the necessary union it has with Him who contains all beings in an intelligible fashion, as has been explained in the third Book. Here, then, is the whole mystery: man participates in sovereign reason, and the truth is revealed to him to the extent that he attends to it and beseeches it. Now the soul's desire is a natural prayer that never goes ungranted, for it is a law of nature that ideas are all the more present to the mind as the will desires them more fervently. [ST, 559]

It would be nice if this were true. But it is so contrary to experience that I cannot understand how someone can venture to put forward such things without first deliberating; and if one had done this one would not fail to recognise that there are many objects that displease us and that we do not want to see, the ideas of which we cannot help being forcefully present to our mind, and that we suffer painfully the troublesome representations that, far from desiring, we very much wish not to see.

But it is even more obvious that, in regard to the essences of things, and to extension and number, to which he sometimes limits what we can see in God, one cannot truthfully say that 'it is a law of nature that ideas are all the more present to the mind as the will desires them more fervently'. I only know in a confused way what a parabola is; I very much desire to have a clearer and more distinct idea of it, which would enable me to know its properties, and I am sure that if I only desire this, with however much fervour one likes, I will not experience what I am told with great confidence: 'that the desire of the soul that wishes to have the idea of an object is a natural prayer which never goes ungranted, and that experience teaches us that the idea of what we have desired to know is all the more present and clear as our desire is stronger'. For inasmuch as experience teaches me anything about this it surely teaches me exactly the opposite.

It is the same with numbers. I have very much desired for many years, with all possible fervour, to know the year of the *Julian period*, which I spoke of in the last chapter, which has as its three characteristics 5, 6 and 7. We can suppose as much as we like *that God is the author of our ideas*, but it is certain that I will find myself to be mistaken if I expect that my desire for it will be the occasional cause which will determine God to make the idea of this number present to my mind. But if, in order to find it, I use the method described in one of the *Journaux des Savants*,[16] I forget what year, then whether one's desire to know it is small or great, it will be the search carried out by this method that could be called 'a natural prayer which never goes ungranted'. Nevertheless, we are assured that the desire is this 'natural prayer that never goes ungranted', for in addition to what I have already quoted, a little further on it is stated that:

Whenever we wish to think about some object the idea of that object is present to us, and, as experience teaches us, this idea is clearer and more immediate as our desire is stronger . . . Thus when I said that the will orders the understanding to present some particular object to it, I only meant to say that the soul that wishes to consider this object carefully draws close to it through its desire because this desire, as a result of the efficacious wishes of God, which are inviolable laws of nature, is the cause of the presence and of the clarity of the idea representing the object. I could not have spoken in any other way, nor could I have explained myself as I am now doing, for I had not yet proved that God alone is the author of our ideas, and that our particular volitions are the occasional causes of it. [ST, 559]

It is difficult enough for two people to agree when each of them bases himself on contrary experiences. I fancy nevertheless that it will not be difficult to judge which of our two experiences conforms most to those of other men. I have, moreover, just found a passage in our friend which I cannot see how to reconcile with the maxim of the *Elucidations* that 'whenever we wish to think of some object the idea of that object is present to us', for I do not know if a proposition more directly contrary to this can be found than the following: 'It is absolutely false, in the state that we are in, that the ideas of things are present to our mind every time we wish to consider them' [ST, 249].

Chapter 17

Another discrepancy: the author says sometimes that we see God in seeing creatures in God, and at other times that we do not see Him but only His creatures.

Another discrepancy in this author, which I have touched on in passing but which I have not looked at sufficiently is that he says first that we see God in seeing material things and then that we do not see Him but only material things.

He says we see Him at [ST, 232] and he even claims that God could not have made things otherwise, by a strange argument which he calls a demonstration:

The last proof, which will perhaps be demonstrative for those accustomed to abstract reasoning, is this: It is impossible that God have any special end for His actions other than Himself, and thus it is necessary not only that our natural love – I mean the impulse that He produces in our mind – tends towards Him, but also that the knowledge and light He gives it must reveal to us something in Him, for everything that comes from God can be only for God. If God made a mind and gave it the sun as an idea or immediate object of knowledge, it seems to me that He would have made this mind and its idea for the sun and not for Himself. God can, therefore, make a mind so that it might know His works only if this mind sees God in some way in seeing His works. As a result, we might say, if we do not see God in some way or other, we do not see anything else. [ST, 232–3]

I have called this argument strange for that is what in fact it is, and because, far from being a demonstration, it is a pure sophism. For the author claims that our soul can know itself without seeing itself in God, and can know itself without seeing anything which is in God. However, this does not amount to saying that our soul exists for itself and not for God. Hence even though our mind has the sun as its immediate object of knowledge, it does not follow from this that our mind exists for the sun and not for God. And in fact there is no connection between this conclusion and the antecedent premiss; for, on the one hand, it is not so much what I do in regard to purely natural things as the end for which I ought to do them, so far as I am able, that must show that I have been created for God; and, on the other, it is through my will and not through my mind that I should be related to my final end. All we can say, then, in regard to the knowledge that I have of the sun is that, in order to satisfy the institution of my nature fully, I should not see the sun solely in order to see it, and in order to seek in it my own satisfaction, because it would then seem that I had been made for the sun. Rather, I should connect my knowledge of the sun with God, by praising Him for His works, and thanking Him for the use we receive from them. One can reasonably conclude from the general maxim, in this regard, that God has made us for Himself, but I do not know which minds accustomed to abstract reasoning would find that it must be concluded from this that 'if God, in revealing the sun to us, reveals something to us which is in Him, it would seem that He has made our mind for the sun, and not for Himself'.

Be that as it may, it does seem, from this alleged demonstration, whether it be sound or not, that his opinion is that: 'everything that comes from God can only be for God. He can, therefore, make a mind so that it might know His works only if this mind sees God in some way in seeing His works.' And: 'Since God can reveal everything to minds simply by willing that they see what is in their midst, i.e. what in Him is related to and represents these things, there is no likelihood of His doing otherwise' [ST, 231]. And a little further on: 'We see all created beings because God wishes us to discover what in

Him represents them' [ST, 231]. Now what in God represents created beings in God Himself, and hence we can only discover that by seeing Him; thus we see God in seeing created beings.

He says: 'We do not say we see God in seeing truths, but in seeing the ideas of these truths' [ST, 234]. Thus he claims that we see God in seeing the idea of the sun and the idea of the earth, but not exactly in seeing the truth that the sun is larger than the earth. A little further on he says: 'In our opinion, *we see God* when we see eternal truths, and not when we see that these truths are God because the ideas on which these truths depend are in God' [ST, 234]. Thus he maintains again that, when we say that every square is half of the square of the diagonal, we *see God* because we cannot affirm this unless our mind sees these two squares and it can see the two squares only in seeing God.

He continues: 'We also believe that changeable and corruptible things are known in God, although St Augustine speaks only of immutable and incorruptible things, because for this we need not put any imperfection in God, since it is enough, as we have already said, that God reveal to us what in Him is related to these things [ST, 234]. Now what in God is related to changeable and corruptible things is God Himself: thus we cannot see changeable and corruptible things unless we see God.

Nevertheless, at [ST, 231] he seems to say the complete opposite, after the first and immediately before the second of the two passages that I have quoted from this page. For in order that no one may conclude that we see the essence of God from the fact that we see all things in God, he says that: 'we do not so much see the ideas of things as the things themselves that are represented by ideas; for when we see a square, for example, we do not say that we see the idea of a square, which is joined to the mind, but only the square which is external to it'.

And in the [*Tenth Elucidation*], it being objected that it is said in John, 1:18 'that no one has ever seen God', he replies that: 'seeing His creatures in Him is not strictly seeing God. It is not seeing the essence of creatures in His substance just as merely seeing the objects a mirror represents is not seeing the mirror' [ST, 628].

But it should be noted that it is only because he is forced to, in order to escape an inconvenient objection, that he speaks in this latter way, i.e. that he appears to deny *that we see God in seeing creatures*; for everywhere else he makes it understood that we see

Him, and it is impossible for him to say otherwise if he is to follow his own principles. The comparison he draws with a mirror is thoroughly defective and does not prove that one can say, in accordance with his doctrine, *that in seeing things in God, it is not God we see but only His creatures.* For a mirror has nothing in it that represents objects; it only sends back images of them, on the common philosophical account, or, on Descartes' account, it is only that the corpuscles which are emitted from our face, on encountering the polished surface of the mirror, are reflected back to our eyes. Now this is not the way in which we see things in God, but he wants it to be in virtue of God showing us what in Him represents created beings. He explains himself in his own words. The mind, he says: 'can see in God the works of God, provided that He wills that *what in Him represents them* be revealed to the mind. Here are the arguments that seem to prove that He wills this' [ST, 230]. Thus he is claiming that we see things in God not as in a mirror but as in a picture which represents to us things which we cannot see by themselves because they are not present to us. For the argument he gives throughout for the necessity for our seeing material things in God is that they cannot be present to our mind, whereas God, who represents them, is intimately joined to it. Now it is inconceivable that one should see the things represented in a picture without seeing the picture: hence he cannot say, if he is to speak sincerely and remain within the principles of his philosophy of ideas, that in seeing things in God it is not strictly speaking God whom we see but only His creatures.

This can be shown by formal arguments, which are genuine demonstrations:

We cannot say that we do not strictly speaking see the immediate object of our mind.

Now when we see creatures, the immediate object of our mind is God, intimately joined to our soul.

Therefore, we cannot say that, in seeing creatures, it is not strictly speaking God that we see but only the creatures.

The minor premiss, which is the only one in need of proof, is to be found in several passages in the author. It is also the foundation of his whole philosophy of ideas. He says, in general terms, that: 'our soul does not perceive objects external to us by themselves, but the *immediate object* of our mind, when it sees the sun for example, is not the sun but something which is intimately joined to our soul' [ST,

217]. And, undertaking to prove *'that we see all things in God'* [ST, 230], he resolves that this something which *'is ultimately joined to our soul'*, which must be the immediate object of our mind when it perceives things which are outside of us, can only be God, because He also satisfies the two conditions necessary for this. The first condition is 'that He has in Him the ideas of all the beings that He has created, and He sees all these beings by considering the perfections, contained in Him, to which they are related'. The second condition is that 'He is very intimately joined to our minds through His presence.' From this he concludes 'that the mind can see what in God represents created beings, since it is quite spiritual, intelligible and present to the mind'. Thus it is clear that, in the sixth Chapter, he is applying to God in particular what he has said generally in the first Chapter, that 'when we see the sun it is not the sun that is the *immediate object* of our mind but something intimately joined to our soul'. Hence in this new philosophy of ideas, when one sees creatures in God it is God who is the immediate object of our mind: thus one cannot say, in this philosophy, that, when we see creatures, it is not strictly speaking God that we see but only the creatures, and if one does say this it is only in order to get around a difficult objection.

And here is another and equally compelling proof. He assumes throughout that there are two kinds of world, of sun, of space, and likewise for other corporeal things: a material world and an *intelligible world*, the material sun and the *intelligible sun*, material spaces and *intelligible spaces*. And what he understands by this word *intelligible* is that all these things, inasmuch as they are intelligible, are in God and even are God, for it is the ideas or perfections of God which represent these created beings. This is what leads him to say that 'God only sees the material world in the intelligible world that He contains' [ST, 573]. Now he says throughout that God only sees anything in Himself, and thus it is clear that according to him the *intelligible world*, and even the *intelligible sun* and *intelligible spaces*, are God Himself. For he says in this same passage that God does not see either the bodies or spaces that He created by themselves, but only through intelligible bodies and spaces.

Now he maintains in the same passage (as we have already said elsewhere) that 'the material body we animate is not the one we see when we look at it, i.e. when we turn our eyes towards it; rather, the body we see is an intelligible body, and it is also an intelligible sun that we see and not the material sun'. And he repeats this later: 'The sun we see is not the one that we look at; the soul can only see the sun to which it is immediately joined, i.e. the intelligible sun', which is God Himself according to Malebranche.

Hence, far from being able to say, in the new philosophy of ideas, that when we see creatures in God it is not God that we see but only the creatures, we must say the exact opposite: that when we see creatures in God it is God alone that we see and not the creatures. For, if someone who saw the sun in God did not see God but the sun that God had created, he would be seeing the material sun since it is the material sun that God has created. Now on Malebranche's account, someone who looks at the sun does not see the material sun but only the intelligible sun; thus he sees only God and not the sun that God has created.

Chapter 18

Concerning three prejudices which might prevent one conceding what has been said against the new philosophy of ideas so readily. The first is one's esteem for its author.

I am convinced that by now it will be seen that I was right not to waste time replying to the proofs this very ingenious and subtle author believes he has given of his opinion *that we see all things in God*. This would have been necessary had we put up only plausible arguments against him, for in that case we could only have decided between them by comparing them with one another. But this comparison is useless when I can show the falsity of the opinion I am opposing demonstratively, and I do not believe I am mistaken in daring to hope that everyone will find that I have done that here.

Nevertheless, I want to clarify three things which, it seems to me, could alone prevent one from conceding so readily what I have said up to now against this new philosophy of ideas.

The first is a prejudice that I forsee could hamper many people. The author of *The Search after Truth* has acquired such a great reputation in the world and rightly so (for there are a large number of things in his book which are very good), that there are many people who will find it hard to believe that so great and penetrating a mind could be justly reproached with having proposed so many things that are scarcely reasonable: and it is this that will make them suspect the demonstrations that I have put forward.

I could content myself with countering this prejudice by noting that common infirmity of human nature which makes the greatest men sometimes fall into the greatest errors. For that would be enough to prevent us ever weighing the authority of a man purely as a man against the evidence of truth. Consider as carefully as you can whether or not I am mistaken in taking arguments which are merely plausible as demonstrations; but consider this question independently of your and my esteem of the author I am refuting, for this has no bearing on the weakness or strength of my demonstrations.

I would only add that it is not as astonishing as one might think that I was able to find so many things which are scarcely reasonable in his philosophy of ideas, for his greatest mistake here is to have assumed as unquestionable a principle which is not peculiar to him, but which he has taken from everyday philosophy. It is this that led him, by an almost inevitable progression, into all the paradoxes that he derives from it by legitimate inferences and that he adopts with less caution in so far as they seem to establish in an admirable way the dependence of our minds on God, and their union with sovereign reason, which is the divine Word. Thus, in this project, one can say of him what St Ambrose said of the mother of the children of Zebedee – *Et si error est, pietatis tamen error est* [And if it is a mistake, nevertheless it is a mistake made out of respect].

The principle in question is *that our soul can only see what is intimately joined to it.* He took this as being beyond question, and he never took the trouble to prove it because he thought it couldn't be doubted. Now when a principle appears clear and evident to us, it is in some way encumbent on us to allow all its consequences, and we cannot believe they are false as long as we regard them as having a necessary connection with this principle. It is therefore not surprising that, letting himself be taken in by the common maxim *that only that which is present to, i.e. intimately joined to, the soul can be in a state where it can be seen*, he concludes from this all the following:
– That material things, since they cannot be intimately joined to our soul, cannot be perceived by themselves.
– That the sun, for example, is not visible or intelligible by itself.
– That in order to see the sun our mind needs a representation of the sun, otherwise called the *intelligible sun*, which is intimately joined to our soul.
– That when we look at the sun, i.e. when we turn our eyes towards

it, it is the material sun that we look at, but we only see the *intelligible sun*.

– That we must seek, where and how we can, this representation of the sun which must always be intimately joined to our soul. Now of all the ways in which this can be imagined to occur, there is none which involves less difficulty and is more probable than to say that this representation is God Himself, since it is easy to conceive *that the mind can see what there is in God that represents created beings, since this is completely spiritual, completely intelligible, and completely present to the mind.*

– That nothing conforms to reason more than to think that we see everything in God.

But in trying to explain how this comes about, he finds himself more perplexed than he had thought. For having first claimed that we see everything in the individual idea that God has of it, the material sun in the intelligible sun, he finds it difficult to explain why the sun, which, as an individual idea in God, is always the same, is seen by us larger when it is on the horizon than when it is in the south, and he is reduced to saying that we see everything in an *infinite intelligible extension*, any of whose parts can become the *intelligible sun* for us since they are all of the same nature.

Only this last view is particularly strange. As for the rest, there is no reason to be very surprised by what he takes to be the case, since such a lively and penetrating mind could hardly not have gone as far in following the road which he was forced to take by what he has supposed to be an indubitable principle, on the basis of which we are to judge what our mind can and cannot see. What Descartes says in his *Discourse on Method* is very true: 'Attempting to overcome all the difficulties and errors that prevent our arriving at knowledge of the truth is indeed a matter of fighting battles: we lose a battle whenever we accept some false opinion concerning an important question of general significance' [CSM I, 145], for it is scarcely possible that this will not lead us seriously astray.

Thus it seems that one can give as much pleasure to a man to whom this misfortune has fallen by exposing the falsity of a principle which has entangled him in many errors, as one can give pleasure to a lost traveller by putting him back on a road which he would not have abandoned had he not followed in the steps of many others who were mistaken before him.

This is why I have reason to hope that our friend will be grateful to me for having rendered this service, even if I have not been successful. But if he finds himself unable to reply to what I believe I have shown, I ask God with all my heart that he provide him with the grace to give our age an example of humility, which should be very common amongst Christians but which is so rare, by recognising in good faith that, having too readily embraced a false principle, he has thereby committed himself to untenable errors concerning the nature of ideas, and that he should not have put forward his novel view that 'we see everything in God' with so much confidence, as he can now see clearly that it is without substance.

Chapter 19

The second prejudice: that this new philosophy of ideas shows us better than any other how much minds are dependent on God, and the extent to which they should be united with Him.

One of the arguments that the author values most highly in corroborating his mysterious theory that we see everything in God, is that 'this opinion seems to [him] to agree with religion to such an extent that [he] believed it absolutely necessary to explain it and defend it as far as possible' [ST, 613]. These are his own words in the *Elucidation* entitled *On the Nature of Ideas, in which I explain how we see in God all things, eternal laws and truths*. And he shows his enthusiasm for the opinion even more vigorously in the following words:

I prefer to be called a visionary, or one of the Illuminati, or that people call me any of the lovely things with which the imagination, which is always sarcastic in the small-minded, usually answers arguments it does not understand and against which it is defenceless, than to agree that bodies can enlighten me, that I am my own master, my own reason and light, and that in order to be well-versed in anything I need only consult myself or other men who can perhaps fill my ears with noise, but who certainly cannot fill my mind with light. Here then are several more arguments for the opinion that I have proposed in the chapters which I am now considering. [ST, 613]

that is, arguments which corroborate this new opinion that we see all things in God.

He has already said much the same thing in Chapter 6 of Book 3, entitled *That we see all things in God:*

The second reason for thinking that we see beings because God wills that what in Him represents them should be revealed to us – and not because there are as many ideas created with us as there are things we can perceive – is that this view places created minds in a position of complete dependence on God, the most complete there can be. For, this being the case, not only could we see nothing but what He wills that we see, but we should see nothing except what God Himself makes us see: *Non sumus sufficientes cogitare aliquid a nobis, tanquam ex nobis; sed sufficientia nostra ex Deo est* [We are not sufficient to think anything of ourselves, as if from ourselves; but our sufficiency is from God (2 Cor. 3:5)]. It is God Himself who enlightens philosophers in the knowledge that ungrateful men call natural despite the fact that they receive it only from heaven: *Deus enim illis manifestavit* [God however revealed it to them (Rom. 1:19)]. He is truly the mind's light and the father of lights: *Pater luminum* [the father of lights (James 1:17)]. It is He who teaches men knowledge: *Qui docet hominem scientiam* [He who teaches man knowledge (Psalms 93:10)]. In a word, He is the true light that illuminates everyone who comes into the world: *Lux vera, quae illuminat omnem hominem venientem in hunc mundum* [The true light, which illuminates everyone who comes into the world] (John 1:19)]. [ST, 231]

Doubtless this can inspire in many people a kind of veneration for an opinion which is proposed with so much enthusiasm, and as being so advantageous to religion, that one is almost made to understand that it alone can make created minds completely dependent on God, and get them to understand that it is not bodies that illuminate them, nor are they their own proper light, but that they can get illumination from God alone.

If this were so then I confess that, however demonstrative they seemed to me, I would doubt the arguments with which I have challenged this mysterious opinion, and I would fear some illusion in them. But it is easy to show that the opinion that I have rejected has none of the advantages attributed to it. One only needs to take care not to be deceived in moving from one question to the other, which is what muddles up all disputes and introduces such confusion into them that after having argued at length one no longer knows what is at issue. When our only aim is the truth, we must endeavour above all to bring things out into the daylight, and to distinguish between questions properly, so as to avoid doubting what is evident in one because of what is obscure in another, and abusing the authority of great men by applying what they have said on one matter to a wholly different matter.

Before we do anything else, then, it is best to indicate what is not at issue, so that what is at issue might be grasped more easily.

1. The way in which God provides illumination through grace, how He provides us with good thoughts, how He instructs us internally on our duties: these are not at issue here. Now it is concerning good thoughts that St Paul says (2 Cor. 3:5), in speaking of the ministry of the New Testament, which is the ministry of grace: 'we are not sufficient to think anything of ourselves, as of ourselves, but our sufficiency is from God'. And thus this passage should not be cited in this question of ideas, where all ideas including the worst are considered. For we cannot think of anything without the idea of what we think about being present to the mind; consequently, if it *is* in this way that our minds depend on God – that we only find these ideas in Him – this dependence must apply equally to our good and our bad thoughts.

2. Certain moral truths, the knowledge of which God implanted in the first man, and which [original] sin has not completely effaced in the souls of his children, are not specifically at issue here. It is these truths that St Augustine often says we see in God. But as he himself does not explain the manner in which we see them, this cannot be of any use to Malebranche, who was sufficiently sincere not to take advantage of the authority of the saint, because he disagrees with him: 'for we do not say that we see God in seeing eternal truths, as St Augustine says, but in seeing the ideas of these truths. For the equality between the ideas, which is their truth, is only a relation which is not real' [ST, 234].

3. Neither is it a question of the way in which God has revealed His divinity to pagan philosophers, but of the source and of the means by which they came by the ideas on which they argued in the most natural of the sciences, and which, like those of mathematics, are less related to religion. Now these words of St Paul – 'God made it manifest to them' – do not concern these purely natural, abstract sciences, but the knowledge that they had of what can be discovered about God from His creatures. It is concerning this that St Paul says: 'GOD Himself made it manifest to them.' One should, therefore, not cite these words of the apostle in order to support the new system, according to which it is only in God that we see material things because it is only in Him that we find ideas in the *infinite intelligible extension* that He contains. This cannot have anything to do with the knowledge of God that these philosophers had, since Malebranche teaches that we see God without ideas, i.e. without *representations*

distinct from perceptions, which he claims we need in order to perceive all the other things that are external to us.

4. Nor is it a question of the cause of our perceptions, which he sometimes rightly calls ideas; for it has already been noted that, even if one agreed with him that our understanding is a purely passive faculty like matter, this has no bearing on the question of the necessity for ideas, understood as *representations*. And I add here that far from this lending support to what he says concerning the dependence of our minds on God – in that it is in Him alone that they find these *representations* in which, it is hoped, consists the illumination that our minds derive from Him – on the contrary, nothing undermines this opinion more than to propose another, which the author also holds, namely, that God is the sole cause of all our perceptions.

5. What is at issue is none of these, but our most natural and common knowledge: what is required if we are to perceive the sun, a horse, a tree; to have an idea of a cube, a cylinder, a square, a number. And even here it is not a question of knowing whether our mind should be illuminated by God but of the way in which it should be illuminated, and whether it is the way devised by Malebranche, which can be reduced to three points.

The first is that our mind cannot see material things by themselves, but only through *representations* distinct from our perceptions, which are prior to these and which he mistakenly calls ideas.

The second is that our mind can find these ideas or *representations* of material things only in God.

The third is that what provides our soul with the means of finding them in God is God's containing within Himself an *infinite intelligible extension*.

I have three things to say in response to these. First, even if we depend on God for this, this dependence is not so considerable that we need to make so much fuss about it. Second, it would not be of any use in attaching us to God; it would rather provide an occasion for us to become attached without hesitation to material things. Third, he cannot imagine this dependence being based on the necessity for *representations* distinct from perceptions without contradicting another maxim which he has taken such pains to establish, namely, that God does nothing in vain and thus that He never does in roundabout ways what He can do in simpler ways.

I say first, then, that even if our souls depended on God in that they found only in Him the *representations* he calls ideas, this dependence scarcely adds to that which we have as creatures, which makes us incapable of subsisting for a single moment unless, by a kind of continuous creation,[17] we are sustained by the same hand that drew us from nothing and brought us into existence, for these are things which are so necessarily dependent upon and consequent upon our nature that it is inconceivable that it was God's will to give us being without also giving us those dependencies; and this shows clearly, it seems to me, that the necessity with which we depend upon God in regard to the former adds nothing to the necessity with which we depend upon Him for our conservation, and this is, moreover, why God has connected them in such a way that they are almost inseparable, so that we must consider as one and the same act of will that which conserves us and that which provides us with whatever is required, because of our nature, for our conservation. An example of the latter, in regard to our body, is the faculty we have of moving its parts for the ordinary functions of life; and, in regard to our mind, that of thinking and being able at least to perceive our own body and those around it, by whichever of our senses.

Therefore we do not consider it a dependence we have on God which is distinct from the conservation of our existence, that we cannot make the least movement, either of the leg, arm, or tongue, unless God Himself moves the animal spirits which, for that to happen, must penetrate the nerves attached to our muscles – because in doing this He is only carrying out the general intentions He had when He created us, and it is through our will that this action of God determined each particular effect. So it would be the same in respect of our dependence on the *infinite intelligible extension* if we found there the idea of each of our thoughts having material things as their object. This would be a consequence of our nature, for we were made to think more than to walk or to move our hands, or our tongues. All God does in that case, as in the other example, is to implement the laws He has prescribed for Himself in instituting our nature: and our acts of will are no less the occasional causes of these ideas, according to Malebranche, than the movements of our legs and arms.

There is nothing here which we should be particularly surprised by. We have so many other reasons to be grateful to God, concerning our salvation and the state of grace and glory to which, by His infinite mercy, He calls us, which are infinitely more important than the fact that our mind is limited in such a way that if it applies itself very much to one object, it becomes incapable of intense application to others. Why then should we be so anxious to teach Christians to be grateful to God for this human illumination in which these philosophers and other children of the century have shared, in which God has only acted as the Author of Nature, instead of considering that it doesn't matter much to the children of the heavenly Jerusalem to know exactly what He does to them in this capacity, so long as they are not ignorant of how much they are indebted to Him for the truly divine illumination with which He enlightens their steps in order to make them walk in His path, and for all the good that He brings about in their hearts by the secret operation of His spirit, which breaks the hardness of their hearts and turns hearts of stone into hearts of flesh.

But the second thing that I promised to show is that, far from there being a reason for appreciating the spirituality of this new system of ideas, it seems to me to do more harm than good to those who accept it, for what does it teach us? That we see God in seeing bodies, the sun, a horse, a tree. That we see Him in philosophising about triangles and squares. And that women who idolise their beauty see God in looking at themselves in the mirror, because the face they see is not their own but an *intelligible face* which resembles it and which is part of the *infinite intelligible extension* contained in God. And it can be added that there is nothing in the whole of creation except our poor soul which, even though it is created in the image and likeness of God, does not have this privilege of seeing God in seeing itself. Do we have here a good way of inducing ourselves to leave our material bodies in order to go back into ourselves? Is it a way of making us have a little esteem for the purely human sciences, which it is not enough to spiritualise but which must be *divinised* in some way, by showing those who apply themselves to them that the objects of their sciences are something greater and nobler than they think. For if they seek the paths of the stars, the stars that they contemplate are not the material stars of the material world, but the *intelligible* stars of the *intelligible* world that is contained in God. And if they study the properties of figures, it is no longer the material shape they see but intelligible shapes which are only found in this *infinite intelligible extension* in which God Himself, who sees nothing except His own essence, sees them.

Does it not provide an opportunity for men to regard it no longer as being a blameworthy and shameful passion in a Christian to have this indefinite and restless curiosity, against which St Augustine speaks so often, which makes one seek to see and know all kinds of physical objects, merely to see them and to give demonstrations of them? Is this not to praise those who are sick in this way and give them cause to rejoice in their sickness, by persuading them that they see God when they think they see sensible objects?

But I cannot help saying something still stronger. We are given to believe that the principal aim of this philosophy of ideas is to teach us the extent to which our minds are joined to God. But we then see that, instead of being joined to God, they are supposed to be joined to an *infinite intelligible extension* which, it is claimed, is contained in God. And it is this that makes me say, without any fear, that I do not desire this union and renounce it with a clear conscience, for I do not recognise my God as being an *infinite intelligible extension* in which various parts can be distinguished, even if they are of the same nature. This is not the God that I worship. It is the idea that St. Augustine had of God when he was still a Manichaean. He testified in Chapter 1 of Book 7 of his *Confessions* that he 'was at that time only able to imagine God as an infinitely extended substance,' but he also says that 'this was because I could not at that time conceive of Him as being other than corporeal.' It will be said that he should not be understood so crudely, and I agree. But however one understands him, isn't it completely unworthy of God to understand Him as follows: that we must take seeing material things in God and in an *infinite intelligible extension*, in which we can distinguish various parts, to be the same thing and to approximate to one another? Is anything more likely to throw men into error and lead them to represent God as a corporeal substance which is only different from other bodies in that it is infinite?

I will not repeat what I have already said on this. I will add only that I do not see how this accords with what the same author says in the *Treatise on Nature and Grace* (First Discourse, Section 11):

When we claim to speak accurately about God, we must not deliberate or speak like the common run of men. One must raise the mind above all creatures, and deliberate with great attention and respect on the vast and immense idea of an infinitely perfect being; and as this idea represents to us the true God, who is very different from that which the majority of men imagine, one should not speak of Him in ordinary language. Everyone is allowed to say, with Scripture, that God *repented* for having created man, that He became *angry* with His people, that He delivered Israel from captivity by force *of arms*; but these and similar expressions are not allowed to theologians when they must speak precisely.

It is therefore even less allowable for them to say that, to see the sun in God is to see it in an 'infinite intelligible extension in which there are various parts, albeit all of the same nature, which may be thought of in such a way that one part gradually approaches or distances itself from the other'.

It is clear from these first two considerations that this dependence that we are forced to have on God, because of our alleged need for ideas taken as *representations*, would be hardly notable or useful for Christians even if it were properly founded. The final consideration will show us that it is very badly founded, according to this author's own principles, for I will restrict myself here to combatting him in his own terms.

He declares in the *Second Elucidation*, in the first Chapter of Book 1, that he had not yet explained the basis on which he was to demonstrate *that we see all things in God* in Chapter 6 of the second part of Book 3. Hence what he establishes in this first Chapter of the first Book is independent of this question.

Now what he establishes there is sufficient for the rest, for we are obliged to recognise that minds do not illuminate themselves, and are not their own light unto themselves, but that God Himself must illuminate them.

Thus it is not true that we have to believe everything he subsequently teaches concerning ideas taken as *representations* and the alleged necessity for us to see material things in God, in order to recognise that our mind does not provide its own illumination as regards knowledge of material things and that it must be God who illuminates it.

Only the minor premiss requires proof, and this is easy for I have already proved in Chapter 3 that, in the first Book, he takes the word 'idea' as 'perception', as is shown clearly by the fact that he takes 'notions' and 'ideas' as the same thing. 'It seems', he says, 'that the notions or ideas that we have of these two faculties are not sufficiently clear.' Now there can be no doubt that 'notion' and 'perception' are synonymous terms, and that here he is explaining 'receiving several ideas' as 'perceiving several things'. Now, taking the word 'idea' as 'perception', there cannot be a clearer demonstration that we are not our own light in regard to material things, and that there must be a God who enlightens us, than to show that we cannot provide ourselves with the idea or perception of material things; for active spiritual enlightenment, so to speak, just consists in this, that our mind is not capable of being enlightened in regard to an object unless it knows it, so that it is clear that if we are not able to provide ourselves with the perception of an object we cannot enlighten ourselves with regard to that object.

Thus what Malebranche teaches in the first Chapter of the first Book more than suffices to make us realise that our mind does not illuminate itself, and is not its own light in regard to material things, but that it needs God to enlighten it, if what he teaches there is that we cannot provide ourselves with the perceptions of material things.

This cannot be taught more clearly than he does, since he establishes there as something certain (I am not concerned here to examine whether it is as he says it is, having declared that my aim is solely to oppose him using only his arguments) 'that our understanding, or the faculty we have of receiving various ideas, i.e. of perceiving several things, is completely passive and contains no activity' [ST, 3].

Hence he has shown quite sufficiently in this chapter, where he takes ideas as *representations* and has not yet supposed *that we see all things in God*, that our mind is not capable of enlightening itself in regard to material things, nor of being its own light.

Thus he did not need, in order to establish this and to further his philosophy of ideas, to put forward this following paradox: that we cannot see the least body unless we see it in God, or rather, unless we see God, when we imagine we see the body.

Thus the enthusiasm he shows in stopping us believing that we are our own light should not serve to prejudice us into looking favourably on such strange views.

Chapter 20

The third prejudice: that in rejecting his philosophy of ideas we are reduced to saying that our soul thinks because that is its nature, and that God, in creating it, gave it the faculty of thinking.

What makes me believe that it is a prejudice of this philosophy of ideas that, if we do not accept it, we are reduced to saying 'that our soul thinks because that is its nature, and that God in creating it gave it the faculty of thinking', is the way in which our friend treats those who speak this way, because his confidence will convince some people that he is right. In reply to the first objection in the *Elucidations* he says that 'it is God alone who enlightens us, and we see all things in Him' [ST, 622].

But, professing to write for people 'who pride themselves with being very precise and rigorously exact', he would have done well not to run together two very different things: *that God alone enlightens us* and *that we see all things in Him.* For we have just shown that, on his own principles, one could perfectly well say that only God enlightens us without having to add the manifest falsehood *that we see all things in Him,* in the way in which he understands this. This is why he clearly side-tracks us in his reply to this objection, because he has only accepted the former – *that only God enlightens us* – and gives up the second – *that we see all things in God* – which is what the whole problem lies in.

Nevertheless, I shall not dwell on this. I claim only to justify, in its own right, the proposition that 'our soul thinks because this is its nature and because God, in creating it, gave it the faculty of thinking', and to show that there are a number of cases where this is the best response one can make; that it is because one is not content with it that one is thrown in a confusion from which one is only able to extricate oneself by the false philosophy of *representations,* and therefore that our friend is wrong to speak in the way he does.

He writes:

I am astonished that the Cartesian gentlemen who so rightly reject the general terms *nature* and *faculty* should so willingly employ them on this occasion. They criticise those who say that fire burns because of its *nature,* or that it changes certain bodies into glass through a natural *faculty,* and yet some of them have no hesitation in saying that man's mind produces in itself the ideas of all things because of its *nature,* and because it has the *faculty* of thinking. But, with all due respect, these terms are no more meaningful in their mouth than in that of the Peripatetics. [ST, 622]

I have already said that I only maintain this in its own right. Now in its own right it does not have the meaning that the author gives it in his reply to the objection: for to think of an object does not signify that one produces in oneself the perception of that object, but only that one has a perception of it, however one comes by it, whether from God or from oneself. Thus neither the truth of the proposition that 'our soul thinks because that is its nature, and because God, in creating it, gave it the faculty of thinking', nor its use in philosophising correctly, requires that our mind produce in itself, by its *nature*, the ideas of all things (for the term 'to think' does not involve this). But it is enough that this response be the right one on a number of occasions, and that we be satisfied with it. We have shown that this is the case in the second Chapter; for if it is asked, for example, how our soul can see material things, both its own body and those around it, even when they are far away from it, it is a perfectly good reply to say that 'it can see them because that is its nature, and because God has given it the faculty of thinking'. I maintain once again that this reply is a very good one, and that it is because one is not satisfied with it that one imagines that our soul can see material things only through *representations* which, being intimately joined to our soul, have been put in a state whereby they can be known by it. This gives rise to so many bizarre opinions that the author of *The Search after Truth* confutes them only by substituting for them another which is no better, and even more peculiar.

He says: 'But why do the Cartesian gentlemen have such an aversion to the general terms 'nature' and 'faculty' when the Peripatetics use them? Why do they think it wrong to say that fire burns because that is its nature, or that it changes certain things into glass through a natural faculty' [ST, 622].

The answer is not difficult. It is that these are words which can be used correctly or wrongly, and that the same person can rightly find good what is used correctly, and bad what is used wrongly. The word 'faculty' is used wrongly when one understands by it something distinct from the thing to which one attributes that faculty, as when one takes the understanding and the will as faculties which are really distinct from the soul. It is also used wrongly when one claims to have given an explanation of an effect which is unknown, or known very confusedly, by using the general term 'faculty' to describe its cause, as when one says that the magnet attracts iron because it has this faculty, or that fire changes certain bodies into glass through a natural faculty. For the abuse of the word in those cases consists principally in this: before knowing what is involved in iron being attracted to a magnet, or what is involved in ashes being changed into glass by fire, one is satisifed with saying that the magnet and the fire each have these faculties. But if, after having explained, as Descartes does, what vitrification is and what fire contributes to it, and what the attraction of iron by a magnet is and what the magnet contributes to it, one then asked anew how it comes about that fire has this violent motion which causes certain bodies to change into glass, and how it comes about that the magnet has screw-shaped pores, then it would be perfectly all right to reply by saying that it is because such is the nature of the bodies that we call fire and magnets.

Here is yet another example of the correct and the wrong uses of these terms. If I am asked why a stone, being suspended in the air from a thread, falls downwards as soon as I cut the thread, it is wrong to reply that it is because God, in creating it, has given it the faculty of tending to move to the centre, a faculty called heaviness. For the correct answer, see what Descartes says in his *Principles of Philosophy* [Part IV, 20–7]. But if one asks in general terms why matter is able to move, it is perfectly proper to reply by saying that this is its nature, and that God, in creating it, has given to its parts this faculty by which one of them can be moved closer to, or further from, another.

Now it is only in wholly similar cases that I use the words 'nature' and 'faculty' in regard to my soul's thoughts. In the case of my soul, I know that I see bodies, that I see the body I animate, that I see the sun, however distant it is from me; I know moreoever what seeing bodies consists in; and when I explain this to others all I need is to have a science which is certain. Finally, I know that it is unlikely that God would have joined me to a body without wishing that I know this body, and consequently He must have given me the faculty of knowing it, as well as those bodies that can help or hinder its conservation. Why then, if I am asked how it comes about that, although I am not corporeal, I can perceive bodies whether or not they are present, am I not right to reply as follows: since my nature is to think, I sense through my own experience that bodies number amongst those things that God has wished that I be able to think of, and having created me joined to a body it was fitting that He should have given me the faculty of thinking of material things as well as spiritual things? Anyone who is not content with this, and wants us to go beyond it and provide an explanation for what has no explanation other than the one he chooses not to be satisfied with, can only lose his way. Because, seeking what is not, he deserves because of his temerity not to find what is, as St Augustine says so well: *Compescat ergo se humana temeritas, et id quod non est non quaerat, ne id quod est non inveniat* [Stop, therefore, your human temerity, and do not seek that which is not, in case you do not find what is (*De Genesi contra Manichaeos*, Book 1, Chapter 2)].

I foresee that the author might say that he is not denying the proposition I am defending in the sense in which I take it and intend it. But I ask him whether or not he agrees with it in the sense in which I take it, which does not bear on the question whether God is or is not the author of my perceptions of material things. If he does not agree with it, I ask him why, for it is clear that nothing he says in his replies in the *Elucidations* deals with it. And if he agrees with it, I conclude from this that he has therefore only to cut out of his book everything he says on the nature of ideas, in the sense of *representations* distinct from perceptions, and all the consequences drawn from this, to convince us that we see material things only in God, or rather that we can turn our eyes towards material things, which we call 'looking', but that in looking at these it is only God that we see.

Chapter 21

When the author says there are things we see without ideas, what he understands by this is so impossible to make out, and is the cause of so much confusion, that one can have no clear notion of it.

Having explained his doctrine of the nature of ideas in the first six chapters of Book 3 [Part II] of *The Search after Truth*, the author distinguishes, in the seventh Chapter, four different ways in which he claims our mind knows things:

The first is to know them by themselves.
    The second is to know them through their ideas, i.e. as I mean it here, through something different from themselves.
    The third is to know them through *consciousness*, or inner sensation.
    The fourth is to know them through conjecture. [ST, 236]

He maintains that 'only God do we know by Himself'; that 'we only know bodies and their properties by ideas'; that 'we do not know our soul or its properties by means of its idea but only through consciousness or inner sensation'; and that 'we only know the souls of other men by conjecture'.

We need not detain ourselves here by looking at the first and the last: we shall discuss these below. Listen only to what he says specifically on the second and the third:

It cannot be doubted that we know bodies and their properties by means of ideas; for, since they are not intelligible by themselves, we can perceive them only in that Being which contains them in an intelligible way. Thus we perceive bodies and their properties by means of their ideas and in God, and for this reason the knowledge we have of them is completely perfect: I mean that the idea of extension is sufficient for us to know all the properties that extension can have, and we could not wish for an idea of extension, shape or motion more distinct or fruitful than that which God gives us. [ST, 237]

What is supposed here with great confidence to be such that 'it cannot be doubted' is something I believe I have shown conclusively to be such that, not only can it be doubted, but it must be rejected as absolutely false. Be that as it may, it must be noted that the notion he has when he says that 'we see bodies by their ideas' is not simply that of seeing them clearly, 'but that of seeing them in a Being who contains them in an intelligible way', i.e. in God. From this he infers, as a consequence of this way of seeing things, 'that the knowledge that we have of them is completely perfect', and it is not as if this way of seeing them only consisted in seeing them clearly. And this becomes clear from what he says about the way in which we know our soul:

It is different in the case of the soul, which we do not know by means of its idea. We *do not see it in God*, but know it only through *consciousness*, and because of this our knowledge of it is imperfect. We only know our soul through what we experience taking place in us. If we had never sensed pain, heat, light, etc., we would be unable to know whether our soul was capable of seeing these things, because we do not know it by means of its idea. But if we saw in God the idea corresponding to our soul we would, or at least could, then know all its possible properties, as we know all the possible properties of extension because we know extension through its idea. [ST, 237–8]

From this, it would seem once more that Malebranche takes 'seeing an object in God' and 'seeing it by means of an idea' to be the same thing. But he adds to this that this way of seeing things in God, by means of their ideas, is so perfect that it makes apparent, not just the thing known, but its properties and possible modifications as well.

Nevertheless, when it comes to the point where, more than anywhere else, he must rid the word 'idea' of the equivocation that he has allowed it in several places, he does this so inadequately that one is left still more uncertain of what he understands by the word when he declares in several passages that the soul does not know itself by means of its 'idea'. The relevant passage is in the *Third Elucidation:*

When I say that we have no idea of the mysteries of the faith, it is clear from what has been said and from what follows that I am speaking of clear ideas which produce enlightenment and evidence, and through which we have, so to speak, an understanding of the object. I agree that a peasant would be incapable of believing, for example, that the son of God was made man or that there are three persons in God, unless he had some idea of the Word's union with our humanity and some notion of a person. But if these ideas were clear, then by attending to them one could understand these mysteries perfectly and explain them to others, and they would no longer be ineffable mysteries. [ST, 561]

'Seeing things in God' is no longer mentioned in this passage in explaining what it is to see things by their ideas. That understanding of the word 'idea' is given up as if it had never been proposed and it is claimed only that to see something by means of its idea is to see it by means of 'a clear idea, which produces enlightenment and evidence, and through which we have, so to speak, an understanding of the object'. And it is maintained that we can say we have no idea of a thing when we do not have an idea of it of this kind, i.e. a clear idea, even though we may have some idea or notion of it.

And this is applied to something that he has often said about the soul, that 'we do not see it by means of an idea, and we do not have an idea of it':

I say here that we have no idea of our mysteries, as I have said elsewhere that we have no idea of our soul, because the idea we have of our soul is no clearer than the idea we have of our mysteries. Thus the word 'idea' is equivocal. Sometimes I take it as anything that represents some object to my mind, whether clearly or confusedly. More generally I take it as anything which is the immediate object of my mind. But I also take it as whatever represents things to the mind in a way which is so clear that one can discover in a simple inspection of it whether such and such modifications belong to them. For this reason I have sometimes said that one has an idea of the soul and at other times I have denied this. It is difficult and sometimes tiresome and ungratifying to preserve a too rigorous exactness of expression. When an author contradicts himself only in the mind of those who criticise him and hope that he will contradict himself, he should not be seriously concerned. And if he were concerned to satisfy, with tedious explanations, all the objections which the malice or ignorance of some people could raise against him, he would write a very poor book. [ST, 561–2]

I'll begin by examining the author's remark that, if one wants to preserve a too rigorous exactness of expression by avoiding equivocations that make it look as if one is contradicting oneself, then one is in danger of writing very poor books. I cannot agree with this in the case of scientific books, for as one writes only in order to make oneself understood, one cannot be too careful in avoiding whatever can hinder the proper understanding of one's thoughts. And nothing hinders this so much as when one takes essential and important words denoting what we especially want to clarify in very different senses, which form in the mind such contradictory notions that it turns out that we have not avoided the equivocations but are rather saying 'Yes' and 'No' to the same thing. Isn't it the first rule in dealing properly with a science to define its principal terms, so as to tie notions to single and univocal senses, however little reason one has to fear that they will be taken in different ways?

If one must be careful to make sure that the reader does not confuse and misunderstand the thought of the author, how much more must the author himself make sure that he does not let his own thoughts confuse him, and fall into apparent contradictions as a result of not being consistent because he has not given the principal terms of his discussion a constant meaning; at least he should change the meaning only after having warned everyone. What would we say, for example, of a geometer who said at one time that the diagonal of a square is oncommensurable with its side, and at others, that it can be commensurable with its side, and who replies, so as to save himself from contradiction, that he has taken the word 'square' in the first case as a rectangle having four equal sides, and in the other as a quadrilateral with four equal sides which are not at right angles to one another? Would one find this explanation to be reasonable in a dogmatic book and agree that he has taken to task those who complained of his lack of exactness as unjust critics with whom one should not trouble onself because one would only be able to produce poor books if one wanted to satisfy them?

I find myself all the more obliged to make the observation that it is not only the ambiguity of the word 'idea' that causes so much misunderstanding in the first work of this author, but that it is a fault to be found throughout his *Treatise on Nature and Grace*, where similar words which are taken in different sense seem to give rise to great mysteries, which disappear as soon as one gets rid of the equivocations.

Nevertheless, it is not this that I take most exception to here. I would excuse his taking the word 'idea' in *The Search after Truth* in a very different sense, if he had at least pointed this out clearly in the foreword to the fourth edition, and had separated out distinct notions. But, far from doing this, he merely confuses the meaning of. the word anew, and what he says does not accord with what he says in the third Book where he provides a detailed account of this matter. For the sole distinction between 'ideas' he makes in this third Preface is that between clarity and obscurity, providing no resolution of the contradiction that he has been criticised for, except to say that when he said we do not have an *idea* of our soul, he spoke in this way because we do not see it by means of 'those clear ideas which produce illumination and evidence, and by which one so to speak comprehends the object', and that when he said that we do not have an *idea* of the soul, he was taking this word generally to mean any kind of idea, clear or obscure.

But this explanation is throughly defective and does not enable us to understand his view of ideas any better. For the word 'idea' would not be *equivocal* but only *generic* if it only signified ideas of the same nature, some of which are obscure and others clear, and it would then be quite wrong to speak of denying the word 'idea' to one of its species, even the least of them. It is like saying that a trapezium is not a quadrilateral because it is its most imperfect species, or that a horse is not an animal because it is not a rational animal. It is also true that he hasn't fallen into this error, and that he could defend himself better against the contradiction that he is reproached with having fallen into in this Foreword. For he could say: the word 'idea' is equivocal because it signifies two quite different things which properly speaking do not share a common notion. And depending on whether I take it in one or the other of these ways, I can sometimes say that we have an idea of the soul and at other times that we do not. In the first Chapter of Book 1, I have taken 'the idea of an object' as 'the perception of an object', and in taking the word 'idea' in this sense I was able to say that we have an idea of our soul, since we could not know it – which we do – unless we have a perception of it. But in the second Part of Book 3, I took the word 'idea' as a *representation* of objects distinct from perceptions, which I have shown can only be found in God by taking the word 'idea' in this sense; I have said in many places that we have no idea of our soul, because my opinion is that we do not see it in God in the way that we see material things in Him, but we see it only *by consciousness and inner sensation*. And this shows me that we do not see it in God, and that what one sees in God, like extension, is seen more clearly and more perfectly than we see our soul.

This doctrine would have been more reasonable and would have conformed better with his doctrine of ideas than what he says in such a confused way in the third Preface. But whichever way one seeks to resolve the apparent contradiction, one cannot avoid being hampered by insurmountable difficulties, as we shall see in the following chapters.

Chapter 22

If it were true that we saw things by means of *representations* (which for the author is the same thing as seeing them in God), he would have no basis for his claim that we do not see our soul in this way.

Since I have claimed to have demonstrated that *representations* distinct from perceptions and objects are useless, and that we have little reason to infer from it the mysterious theory that *we see all material things in God*, you can take it that my aim is not to prove that we see the soul in this way. But so as to show even better how poorly this philosophy of ideas fits together, it is worth showing that if it were true that we see material things by means of *representations* (which for the author is the same thing as seeing them in God) then the author would not be able to maintain that we do not see our soul in this way.

To show this we need only apply to the soul the general arguments that the author puts forward to support his novel opinion *that we see all things in God*. This is the title of Chapter 6 of the second Part of Book 3.

(1) He assumes, correctly, that God contains the ideas of all things, and secondly that God is intimately joined to each soul by His presence. From this he concludes 'that the mind can see what in God represents created beings, since this is very spiritual, intelligible and present to the mind, and thus the mind can see His works in God, provided that God wishes it to discover what in Him represents them' [ST, 230].

Now isn't the idea of our soul in God as much as that of extension is? And whatever in God represents our soul, is it not as spiritual, intelligible and present to the mind as what represents bodies? And isn't it quite unproblematic that what in God represents our soul – which was created in His image and likeness because He willed that it be an intelligible nature like Himself – is better fitted to the soul being able to see itself in God than what in Him represents bodies; the latter can only be *eminently* and not *formally* extended, shaped, divisible, and mobile, and therefore cannot be suitable for our mind, which can only conceive them as extended, shaped, divisible, and mobile? Hence why, if our soul sees bodies in God, shouldn't it see itself there?

All the author can say is that God did not wish to reveal to our soul what in Him represents it, whereas He did wish to reveal what in Him represents bodies. And who has taught him that God wished to reveal the one but not the other? Does he not fear, in gratuitously positing these differences in God's conduct, something he shows he fears so much in other contexts, namely that it does not preserve sufficiently the characteristics which must always be present in the conduct of a perfect being: the characteristics of being *uniform*, *constant* and *regulated*? For is uniformity to be found here if God reveals, to the same soul to which He has willed that He be intimately joined, those of His perfections that represent the vilest of His creatures, namely material things, and hides from it the most noble, namely those that are spiritual? What uniformity can one find in this?

Another rule that the author makes a lot of is that the will of God always conforms to order. Now is it not orderly that our soul should at the very least be as enlightened by God in its knowledge of itself as it is in its knowledge of material things? And since the author takes divine illumination in the case of knowledge of natural things as God showing them to us in Himself, the will of God does not conform to order if He shows all material things in Himself but does not grant us the same grace by showing us our soul in Himself, even though (if what the author says is true) it is much more important for us to know it in this way than it is to know bodies.

(2)   The second reason why the author thinks 'that we see all beings because God wills that what in Him represents them should be revealed to us, is that this places created minds in a position of complete dependence on God, the most complete dependence possible' [ST, 231]. Why, then, if this is true of all beings, should it not be

true of our soul? Why exempt it from such a general proposition? Why should he want the created mind to be completely dependent on God for its knowledge of the sun, a horse, a tree, and a fly, and not have the same dependence in knowing itself?

(3) The proof he believes to be a 'demonstration for those accustomed to abstract arguments', which we discussed in Chapter 16, shows nothing in absolute terms, as I have shown. But if it were to show anything this would be in regard to the knowledge that the soul has of itself rather than in regard to its knowledge of other objects. 'Everything that comes from God,' he says

can only be for God; now if God made a mind which had the sun for the immediate object of its knowledge, it would seem that He has made the sun for this mind, and not for Himself: if this is not to be the case then God must, in making us see the sun, show us something which is in Him. [ST, 233].

How would he reply, then, to someone who argued in the same way but who substituted 'our soul' for 'the sun': 'Everything that comes from God can only be for God; now if the immediate object of our knowledge of the soul were the soul itself, it would seem that God had made the soul for itself and not for Himself: if this is not to be the case then God must, in showing us our soul, show us something which is in Him.' Hence we must be able to see our soul, just as with material things, only in God.

(4)   Moreover, it is only *a posteriori*, so to speak, that the author claims to show that we do not see our soul in God, or, what he maintains is the same thing, that we do not see it through an *idea* but only *through consciousness and inner sensation*. He argues as follows:

We see things in God in a completely perfect way [ST, 237], and we can discern in a simple inspection of [our idea] whether such-and-such modifications belong to it [ST, 218]. For since the idea of things which are in God contain all their properties [ST, 237], in seeing the ideas of them one sees the properties in turn.

Now our knowledge of our soul is very imperfect [ST, 237–8], and we do not know the properties it can have in the way we know all the properties of which extension is capable.

Therefore, we do not know our soul by means of an idea, and we do not see it in God.

But without even needing to examine whether knowledge of our soul is more imperfect than that we have of extension, in order to see immediately that the major premiss is false, we need only consider that, on his principles, everything created outside our own soul and the souls of others can be seen only in God and by means of ideas, and that this way of seeing material things – the sun, a tree, a horse – is not peculiar to philosophers or to those who have especially penetrating minds, but is common to the most ignorant and stupid. He says: 'We cannot doubt that we only see bodies and their properties by means of ideas because, not being intelligible by themselves, *we can only see them* in the being who contains them in an intelligible way. Thus it is in God and through ideas that we perceive bodies and their properties.' Thus there is no peasant who does not see the sun, his ass, the wheat that covers his fields, or the vine he cultivates, in God and through their ideas. 'Now the knowledge that we have of things in God and through their ideas', he says, 'is completely perfect.' Thus there is no peasant who does not or can not have, by means of the single inner perception that he has of these objects, a completely perfect knowledge of the sun, his ass, the wheat and his vine, and from which he knows, or can very easily tell, the properties of all these things.

Nothing is more untenable and contrary to experience than this. Thus it follows either that material things can be known by peasants in some way apart from in God and by means of their ideas, or that the fact that our soul knows itself only imperfectly does not amount to a proof that it does not know itself in God and by means of an idea: for one cannot doubt that the knowledge that a peasant or a child has of the sun is incomparably poorer than a philosopher's knowledge of his soul.

We don't even have to stop at peasants or infants to recognise that, if the major premiss were true, i.e. if it were true that the things that we know in God and through their ideas are known very perfectly, one would have to conclude not only that we do not see our soul in God, but that the ordinary way in which we see other things, to the extent that we do, in this life is not one of seeing them in God and is not due to God's revealing to us what in Him represents them. For if this were the case, how could it have come about that all the philosophers before Descartes did not share his notion of the sun, the stars, fire, water, salt, clouds, snow, hail, winds, and all the other works of God? If the others perceived these in God just as he did, they must have seen them as he did, 'since the ideas of things which are in God contain all their properties'. Now it is these ideas of created beings that I have just spoken about that God has revealed, according to Malebranche, to all the philosophers who have concerned themselves with knowing them. It follows from this that they did not see in these ideas all the properties of the sun, stars, water, fire and so on, since Malebranche puts it forward as a maxim 'that when one sees things as they are in God, one always sees them in a completely perfect way'.

Chapter 23

A reply to his arguments which try to show that we have no clear idea of the soul but that we have a clear idea of extension.

I believe I have said enough in the last chapter to convince any reasonable person that if we saw all things in God in the way in which the author understands this, then there would be no reason to exempt our soul from this, and hence one cannot conclude from it that *we have no idea of our soul*, and that we only know it through consciousness and by inner sensation.

But because he uses yet another way of showing this, which is to show that we have no *clear idea* of the soul, as we have of extension, I believe I must look at whether this way is any more secure than the first.

He recognises in one passage that we have ideas of both, i.e. of our soul and of extension. He speaks in the following way: 'I assume at the outset that one has reflected on two ideas that are found in our soul: one representing body and the other representing the mind; and that one can distinguish them easily because of the positive attributes that they contain; in a word, that one is convinced that extension is different from thought' [ST, 49].

It is true that at that point he took the word 'idea' as 'perception'. And he was right to take it in this way, for that is its true notion. But he has subsequently chosen to take this word only as a particular kind of *representation* distinct from *perception*, which he wanted to be located only in God and which, moreover, he distinguished from ideas taken generally as everything that represents some object to our mind, whether clearly or confusedly, in declaring that we should give the name 'idea' by preference to those 'clear ideas which produce illumination and evidence, and which enable one to comprehend an object, so to speak'. And it is owing to this disinction that he believes that, taking the word 'idea' in this latter sense, we have no idea of our soul but that we do have an idea of extension.

Now I want to confine myself to showing two things: first, that we cannot see extension by means of a *representation* any more than we can our soul; and secondly, that if the idea that we have of our soul were less clear than that we have of extension, then just as it would not follow from this that the two ideas are of totally different kinds, so also it does not follow that one would be right to say that we have no *idea* of our soul, but that we have an idea of extension; for varying degrees of clarity do not lead us to allow the name 'idea' only to our perception of extension and to withold it from our perception of our soul.

I could also refute him by showing the illusion that lies in his comparison between ideas of the soul and of extension. For he confines himself to extension in general, whereas if the proof is to be defensible he must show that the idea of our soul is not as clear as our idea of any body whatsoever. For assuming, as he does, that we see all material things in God, and that everything we see in God we see by means of our ideas, it would be enough if the 'idea' we have of our soul were at least as clear as that we have of an infinity of material things that, on his account, we see in God, and hence through clear ideas. This, I maintain, is enough to prevent him being right in saying that 'we have no idea of our soul' in the case where our idea of our soul is not as clear as that of extension in general. And if he does not agree with this, then it could be proved to him by the following demonstration.

The lack of clarity in our idea of our soul does not give us the right to say that we have no idea of it as long as it is at least as clear as that of very many things which, according to Malebranche, we see so clearly that we cannot say we have no idea of them. I have already shown that this is the case. For the stars, the sun, and fire have only ever been visible in God, on Malebranche's account, and according to him everything we see in God is seen by means of clear ideas.

Now the ideas that philosophers before Descartes had of the sun, the stars, and fire were not as clear as those we have of our soul. The author has, therefore, no right to claim that the idea we have of our soul is so unclear that it can be said absolutely that we have no idea of it.

But, pending his reply on these two points, I would like to examine whether he has as much reason as he believes to maintain that the idea that we have of our soul is so unclear, in comparison with what we have of extension in general, that he is right to say that we have absolutely no idea of our soul, and that we do have an idea of extension.

He is so sure of this that he finds it strange that some Cartesians were able to doubt it, and he can only attribute this to blind deference to the authority of Descartes. This is how he begins his *Elucidation* on this question:

> I have said in a number of places, and I even think I have proved it satisfactorily in Book 3 of *The Search after Truth*, that we have no clear idea of our soul, but only consciousness or inner sensation of it, and thus that we know it much less perfectly than we know extension. This seemed to me so evident that I did not think it necessary to show it at length. But the authority of Descartes, who clearly says that the nature of the mind is better known than the nature of anything else, has so taken hold of some of his disciples, that what I have written on it has only served to make me appear in their mind as someone weak who cannot grasp and hold fast to abstract truths . . . Yet the present question is so suited to the mind that I do not see the need for any great effort in order to resolve it, which is why I did not pause over it. [ST, 633]

Let us look at these arguments, which are very easy to find, and let us put at their head the one which is the basis of all the others, which will lead us to unravel what he has run together in his definition of a clear idea, which he takes as the basis for everything he says on this matter.

FIRST ARGUMENT:

> I take not having an idea of an object and not having a *clear idea* of it to be the same thing: and I call *clear ideas* only those ideas which produce illumination and evidence, and by means of which one (so to speak) understands an object, i.e. which are such that, in consulting them, one can perceive in a simple glance what they include and what they exclude, and thereby recognise all the properties of the object and its possible modifications. [cf. ST, 633 ff.]

Now we do not have such an idea in the case of our soul. We do not have a clear idea of it and this is sufficient for us to say that we have no idea of it.

REPLY: In order to be able to say what I think of the major

premiss, I must find out from him whether he is claiming that this definition which he gives of clear ideas must be accepted by everyone as being the true notion of the clarity of an idea, or whether he wishes only to compile his own dictionary by advising us, without troubling himself about the sense in which others take the term 'clear idea', that he has resolved to use this word only in the sense indicated.

If he claims the former, then I deny his major premiss, and I maintain that he is manifestly wrong if he has supposed that everyone is in agreement with his definition of a clear idea. It is at least certain that Descartes does not agree with it since he teaches in many places that we can have a clear and distinct idea of an object without knowing everything about that object. This is why he maintains throughout his work that we have a clear and distinct idea of God, even though it cannot be such that one could call it *adaequatam* [adequate] (this being the word he uses to indicate an idea which makes known all the properties of an object) *qualem nemo habet non modo de infinito, sed nec forte etiam de ulla alia re, quantumvis parva* [such as no one has, not only of the infinite but equally of any other thing, however small]. And, in the *Reply to the Fourth Set of Objections*, he says that the ideas that we have of the soul and the body can be clear and distinct, without either being *adequata*, i.e. without either being such that they comprise everything that can be known about either of these two substances.

It is thus certain that he does *not* believe that, for an idea to be clear, it must contain all the properties of the object.

And in fact can there be any doubt that there was a clear idea of a right-angled triangle before Pythagoras, even though it was he, we believe, who was the first to discover the marvellous property *that the square of its [hypotenuse] is equal to the sum of the squares of its sides*? And similarly, can it be doubted that there was a clear idea of an ellipse and a hyperbola before Descartes, even though it is perhaps he who was the first to discover the properties that he demonstrated in his *Dioptrics* in connection with the refraction of light?

If, not being able to claim that this definition of a clear idea is accepted by everyone, Malebranche is reduced to saying that the word may be taken in this sense, and if one describes an idea as clear only if it meets all the conditions he has indicated, one will also concede and agree that in taking the expression 'clear idea' in this sense, we have no clear idea of our soul. But one will also say that one no longer has a clear idea of extension, or perhaps anything else in the world, as Descartes noted. And thus everything in the other proofs will come down to showing that they are no more decisive against the clear idea of our soul than against the clear idea of extension.

SECOND ARGUMENT:

'I believe I can say that the ignorance of the majority of men in regard to their soul, to its distinctness from the body, to its spirituality, to its immortality and to its other properties, is enough to show clearly that they do not have a clear and distinct idea of it' [ST, 633].

REPLY: If the errors of men and the irrational doubts that they always have about absolutely certain things can be adduced to prove that we do not have clear ideas of the things they chose to doubt, there is no longer anything of which we can have a clear idea. For haven't sceptics and Pyrrhonists made a profession of doubting everything? One need only apply to them what he says in the *Eleventh Elucidation:* 'Let us do justice to everyone: those who are not of our opinion are as reasonable as us; they have the same ideas of things; they participate in the same reason. Why then have they doubted what seems to us to be most certain, even in geometry itself, if they have clear ideas of them?' [ST, 637–8].

Now if we descend from the general to the particular, isn't it clear that we have just as much reason to conclude from what he says that men have no clear and distinct idea of their bodies? For the Epicureans only denied the spirituality and immortality of the soul because they believed that their bodies were able to think. And there are still currently only too many impious people who hold the same opinion. Now if the one or the other had a clear idea of their body, they would not have held this belief for, according to Malebranche, 'when one has a clear idea of something, one sees directly and without any trouble what it includes and what it *excludes*'. Thus this argument proves nothing, or it proves as much against the clarity of the idea of body or extension as it does against the clarity of that of the soul.

THIRD ARGUMENT:

The idea of body or extension is so clear that everyone agrees on what it includes and excludes (for as regards those who wonder if the body is capable of sensation, they understand by body something other than extension, and they have no clear idea of body taken in that sense); whereas the idea of the soul is so confused that the Cartesians themselves constantly dispute as to whether the modifications of colours belong to it. [cf. ST, 634–5]

REPLY: I will examine the conclusion but I will give you a different reason for it. In so far as the clarity of the idea of extension is concerned, however, the argument is an amusing sophism. For he claims that everyone agrees with what it includes, while at the same time recognising that there are those who distinguish body from extension, since they do not know that body and extension are the same thing. Nevertheless, they do not deny that what they call body is extended, and hence they take body as an extended thing. How then can he say that 'everyone agrees on what the idea of an extended thing includes and what it excludes', since he agrees that there are some who consider that an extended thing is capable of sensation? But let us go on, and we will see the same illusion in the next argument.

FOURTH ARGUMENT:

One is never asked whether something does or does not pertain to extension without being able to reply easily, promptly, confidently, and solely by considering the idea that represents it. Everyone agrees on what one should think on this subject; for those who say that matter can think do not imagine that it has this faculty because it is extended; they continue to agree that extension, precisely as such, cannot think. [cf. ST, 633–4]

REPLY: This 'precisely as such' is a pure equivocation. For it is true that they do not believe that all extension can think, and in this sense one can say that they do not believe that extension as such can think (whatever does not belong to the genus cannot be attributed to the species when one considers it precisely according to its generic idea) but they believe that there are some extensions that do think. This is what seemed to be meant when it was said in the *Fifth Set of Objections* put forward against Descartes' *Second Meditation*:

Why, O Soul, is it not possible that you are the wind, are rather a very fine and subtle vapour, formed when the heart heats up the purest blood and diffused throughout the parts of the body, giving them life, which sees with the eye, hears with the ears, thinks with the brain and performs all the other functions commonly ascribed to you? If this is so, why should you not have the same shape as your body, just as air takes on the same shape as the vessel that contains it? For the coarse body to which you are joined has an infinite number of small pores through which you are diffused, in such a way that you have no reason to say that there is nothing in you which appertains to the nature of body. [CSM II, 181–2]

Isn't this to claim that there is an extended substance that can think and have different sensations, namely something which, being very subtle, is distributed throughout the pores of the substance of the brain and the organs of sense? I agree that there is nothing more unreasonable and shocking to good sense than these impious thoughts. But Malebranche does not merely say this: on his account it is impossible for anyone ever to think this. For he claims that the idea we have of extension is so clear 'that women and infants, the wise and the ignorant, the most enlightened and the most stupid, easily conceive, by the idea that they have of it, what does and what does not belong to it' [ST, 635]. Thus it is necessary that they agree that there is no extended substance that can think and have sensations. Now those of whom I have just spoken, whose views Gassendi puts forward, far from agreeing with this, maintain that the extended substance which is in the pores and in the substance of our brain has the ability to think. Thus it appears that Malebranche rests his new views solely on manifestly false hypotheses which he considers as indubitable.

FIFTH ARGUMENT:

In order to determine whether sensible qualities are or are not modes of existence of the mind, we do not consult the alleged idea of the soul; even the Cartesians consult rather the idea of extension, and they argue as follows. Heat, pain, and colour cannot be modifications of extension, for extension can only have various shapes and motions. Thus pain, heat, colour, and all the other sensible qualities belong to the mind. Now there are only two kinds of beings, mind and body. Since we have to consult our idea of extension in order to discover whether the sensible qualities are modes of existence of our soul, is it not evident that we have no clear idea of the soul? Would we have taken such a detour otherwise? [ST, 634]

REPLY: I do not know who these Cartesians are who argue as they are made to here, and I find it hard to believe that there are any. I do know at least that Descartes never argued in this way. One need only look at what he says in *The Principles of Philosophy*, Part I, Sections 68 and 70:

But in order to distinguish here what is clear from what is obscure in our sensations, we must be careful to note in the first place that we clearly and distinctly perceive pain, colour, and other sensations when they are regarded merely as thoughts. But when we wish to judge that colour, pain, etc., are things existing outside our thought, there is no way we can understand what colour, pain, etc., are. When someone tells us that he sees colour in a body or feels pain in one of his limbs, this is the same as saying that he sees or feels something there but is completely ignorant of its nature – or, rather, that he does not know what he is seeing or feeling. For, when he fails to pay sufficient attention to his thoughts he may perhaps convince himself that he has some knowledge of what he sees or feels, because he may suppose that the colour he believes he sees in the object is similar to the sensation he has in himself. But if he examines what is represented by the colour, or the pain, in so far as they exist in the coloured body or in the wound, he will realise that he does not know them . . . Thus it is clear that when we say to someone that we perceive colours in objects, this is just the same as saying that we perceive something or other in the objects whose nature we do not know, but which produces in us a certain very clear and vivid sensation which we call the sensation of colour. But there is a great difference in our judgements. For to the extent that we merely judge that there is something or other in objects (i.e. in the things themselves) which causes us to have the confused thoughts that we call sensations, we are less likely to be mistaken; rather we avoid the puzzlement which could make us misunderstand, because we are not so ready to make rash judgements about a thing when we realize that we do not know it well. But when we believe we perceive a certain colour in an object, even though we have no distinct knowledge of what it is that we are calling by this name, and cannot find any resemblance between the colour we suppose to be in this object and that which is in our sense, nevertheless, because we do not take account of this, and we notice in these same objects several other properties such as size, shape, number, etc., which exist in it, in the same way as our sense or, preferably, our understanding makes us perceive them, we easily let ourselves be convinced that what is called colour in objects exactly resembles the colour which is in our thought; and consequently we think we clearly perceive in this thing something we do not perceive in any way as belonging to its nature. [CSM I, 217–18]

We can see, then, from something that everyone can recognise in himself, as Descartes did, that no one ever needed to consult his idea of extension in order to determine whether the sensations of colours and pains are modifications of our soul. For no one has ever been able to doubt it, since these are things of which everyone is internally convinced by his own experience. What, then, have people doubted, and what are so many people still doubtful about? Is it that what we already know to be a modification of our soul is also a modification of our body, or of those we look at, i.e. whether there is something in objects that we see which is similar to the colours red and green of which we have sensations, and whether there is in our arm, when it is cut, something similar to the unpleasant sensation we call pain, which our soul senses on the occasion of our arm being cut – these are all questions on which we had to consult our idea of extension in order to convince ourselves and others that the colours and the pain are not modifications of it, for extension is only capable of different shapes and motions. Thus the greater detour that the author makes the Cartesians take in order to prove that colours and pains are modifications of our soul is a figment of his imagination, and the argument he ascribes to them, and which he appears to approve of, would be ridiculous, and would presuppose what, it is claimed, is being sought. For it would require as its major premiss:

Colours and pains must be modifications either of my body or of my mind.
    They cannot be modifications of my body.
    Therefore, they must be modifications of my mind.

As a counter-example to the major premiss here is a similar argument with a conclusion which Malebranche considers false:

The ability to send animal spirits along the nerves and muscles of my legs, so as to make me walk, must belong to my body or to my mind.
    Now it does not belong to my body; for the body is able to receive all sorts of motion, but it cannot give rise to any.
    Therefore, it must belong to my mind.

And yet it belongs neither to one nor the other according to Malebranche, for it must be God alone who causes this motion in the animal spirits, albeit on the occasion of various impulses of our will.

But, without dwelling on this, I ask whether, supposing I had never sensed colours or pains, I would ever have been right to say that they must be modifications of my body or of my soul? And then I can ask the question – which of these two parts of myself are they modifications of? – only because I have sensations of them, i.e. only because I perceive them with my mind. Now this could only have been possible if I already knew that they were modifications of my mind; consequently that is not what I should have tried to show but only whether, besides being modifications of my mind, they are also modifications of my body.

There was, then, never anything less appropriate to convincing us that we have no clear idea of our soul, than the false supposition that it is necessary that we consult the idea of extension in order to show whether colours or pains are modifications of our soul.

SIXTH ARGUMENT:

How can it be maintained that one knows the nature of the soul more clearly than one does that of body, since the idea of body or extension is so clear that everybody agrees what it includes and what it excludes, whereas the idea of the soul is so confused that the Cartesians themselves constantly dispute whether modifications of colour belong to it? One even makes oneself ridiculous among some Cartesians if one maintains that the soul actually becomes red, blue, or yellow, or that when one smells a carcass the soul becomes formally putrid. [ST, 634]

REPLY: I am surprised that he has not seen that this argument is far more effective against the clarity of the idea of extension than against the clarity of the idea of the soul. For those who think that sensible qualities do not belong to the soul believe that they belong to the body. Hence they do not have a clear idea of the body since, according to Malebranche, in order for an idea to be clear one must be able to perceive in a simple vision 'what it includes and what it excludes'. Now they do not see that the idea of body excludes colour. Hence the idea that they have of body is not clear, and, availing myself of his own terms, 'thus the idea of extension is so confused that there are countless people who do not see that the modifications of colours cannot belong to it'.

But this could prove nothing against the clarity of the idea of the soul, for there is no one whom one cannot easily make understand that the sensation of colour belongs to the soul. But it is much harder to disabuse people of the opinion, held by almost everyone, that other than the sensation of colour, which it cannot be doubted is a modification of the soul, there is something in those objects which are called 'coloured' which is like the colour of which we have the sensation. If, then, this doubt must derive from the fact that one or the other of these ideas is unclear, the lack of clarity must certainly be in the idea of extension rather than in the idea of our soul, since the doubt concerns the body and not the soul.

As for those Cartesians who do not wish to acknowledge that 'our soul is green, or yellow, or putrid', I do not know what Malebranche means by this. For if those of whom he speaks claim that sensible qualities are modifications of extension and not of our soul, then to this extent they are not Cartesians. But if, acknowledging that they are modifications of our soul and not of extension, they maintain only that this does not mean that our soul should be called either 'green', or 'yellow', or 'putrid', this will only be a question of nomenclature, in which, I believe, they are not as wrong as the author imagines. All we need to do is to understand properly what is at issue.

Two Cartesians are walking together. 'Do you know', says one of them, 'why snow is white, why charcoal is black, and why corpses are putrid?' 'These are foolish questions', the other replies, 'for snow is not white, nor charcoal black, nor corpses putrid; it is your soul that is white when you look at snow, and which is black when you look at charcoal, and which is putrid when you are near a corpse.' I assume they both agree on the essentials of the doctrine; but I ask who expresses it better, and I maintain that the former does, for the reproach of the latter is unwarranted. For, first, there are infinitely many *names* which suppose no modification in the thing to which they are given. Is it to speak wrongly to say that the statue of Diana was worshipped by the Ephesians? Yet the hommage that these idolators paid to this statue was not a modification of the statue but only of the idolators. It is clear, moreover, that of the two kinds of language, the former should be regarded as the more reasonable and correct, and as conforming better with the institution of nature. It is not for our soul's sake that God gives us the sensation of colours or putridness, but in order to provide us with an easier means of distinguishing the bodies that we look at, or of removing ourselves from those whose presence would harm us. Thus it was due to our making language match the intentions of the Author of Nature that we call bodies white, black, or putrid, since it is in relation to bodies and not in relation to itself that our soul takes on different modifications. Another consideration which shows that we should speak in this way, and that one should not say that 'the soul is green, yellow, or putrid' is that the signification of our words depends on the will of men. Now it is certain that men never intended to call anything green or yellow except those things which our soul sensed and on whose surfaces, it believed, were spread the colours green or yellow. But, it will be said, it is in this that they are mistaken. All right, do not use these words if you do not want to. But you must not give them bizarre meanings which usage has never provided them with, as is done when it is said that the soul is yellow or green, for that would imply that the soul is something whose surface is covered with the colour green or the colour yellow, something that would be a far greater error than the one we are trying to avoid, since this would suggest that the soul is corporeal. And, what is more, men are only partly mistaken when they regard colours as being spread over objects. For while they are not really spread over them, nevertheless the intention of the Author of Nature is that our soul attach colours to them and apply them to bodies in some way, in order to distinguish between them more easily. And this is enough to sanction the usage of those who wish that it be bodies, and not our soul, that are called 'green' or 'yellow'.

There are, then, insufficient grounds for complaint against the Cartesians, who are against introducing another language and claiming to find useful bizarre ways of speaking which can only serve to discredit the truth and make it ridiculous.

SEVENTH ARGUMENT:

'Although I see or sense colours, flavours, odours, I can say that I do not know them by a clear and distinct idea, since I am unable to discover their relations clearly. We do not therefore have a clear idea either of the soul or of its modifications' [ST, 636].

REPLY: This argument can be conclusive only in virtue of the completely false major premiss, that 'we only have clear ideas of those things whose relations to other things we know'. He must himself recognise that this major premiss is completely false, for he acknowledges that we have a clear idea of the square and the circle and yet no one has so far been able to discover their relation. Moreover, I have no doubt that there are infinitely many curved lines whose relation to the straight line, or to the other curves, we do not know. From this new condition which he adds to his notion of clear ideas, we must therefore conclude that we have no ideas of the majority of modifications of extension any more than we do of the modifications of our soul.

Moreover, it is certain that relations apply strictly only to quantities, extension, numbers, time, and motion; and sensible qualities are not quantities. Why then does he think we should know their relations in order to be able to say that we have clear ideas of them?

EIGHTH ARGUMENT:

Although musicians distinguish very well between the different consonances, this is not because they distinguish their relations [i.e. intervals] by clear ideas. It is the ear alone that judges the difference in sounds for them, and their reason knows nothing of it. But one cannot say that the ear judges by a clear idea, or in any way other than by sensation. Thus musicians have no clear idea of sounds taken as sensations or modifications of the soul. Consequently, neither the soul nor its modifications are known by a clear idea, but only through consciousness or internal sensations. [ST, 636]

REPLY: This argument is as confused as can be. To give it some shape, we must resolve it into two arguments. The first of these is:

We do not know by a clear idea what we only know by the ear and not by reason.

Although musicians distinguish very well between the different consonances, it is only by means of the ear that they judge, and not by reason.

Therefore, we do not know sounds by clear ideas.

The second argument is:

The soul does not know by a clear idea what it only knows by internal sensation.

The soul only knows its own modifications by internal sensation.

Therefore, it does not know them by clear ideas.

I deny both major premisses. And I maintain that in both cases we are led to think that two things are contrary, whereas they are not contrary at all.

For in the major premiss of the first argument, as well as in the minor premiss, it is assumed that it is the ear alone that judges sounds, and that reason does not know them, although there is nothing falser in Malebranche's whole philosophy than the idea proposed here, that the ear alone judges consonances, reason playing no part in this judgement. We know that he teaches throughout his work that the senses judge nothing, and that it is reason alone that judges what is reported by the senses. Thus it is futile for him to contrast the ear and reason in something that can occur only through the reason, albeit via the mediation of the ear. Thus he must speak more clearly and more philosophically, and confine himself to saying that although it is our reason that perceives sounds, and judges them together with other sensible qualities, nevertheless it must be accepted that it can only perceive through the agency of the senses and this is an indication that it does not perceive them by clear ideas. I could be content with saying I deny this and wait for someone to show me that I was wrong, for I do not believe that one should venture to propose this maxim as a first principle which one could not in good faith doubt. Nevertheless, I wish to do more than this and show, as much by what anyone can know through his own consciousness as by the authority of a great man, that there is no incompatibility between knowing something solely through the agency of the senses and having a clear idea of it.

But first of all it must be noted that the problem generally is not with the *idea* but only with the property of *clarity*, for since he acknowledges that he has recognised in one passage that we have an idea of our soul, even though he has said in others that we do not, he resolved the apparent contradiction only through this distinction: in saying we had such an idea, he was taking the word 'idea' as 'anything that represents something to the mind, whether clearly or obscurely', and when he says that we do not have such an idea he is restricting the word 'idea' to a clear idea. Thus it is not a question of showing that the idea we have of sensible qualities like colours, sounds, and odours, inasmuch as these are modifications of our soul, is a clear idea. And for this he only has to show that we know them clearly: for since we know them by an idea, taking the word in the general sense recognised by him, if this idea only represents them to us confusedly then it will be a confused idea, but if it represents them to us clearly and distinctly, then it will be a clear idea.

I call everyone's attention to this. Let them deliberate and tell me whether it is not true that they believe they know clearly the different colours that they see and the various sounds they hear. In fact, Malebranche even recognises this, although he appears to have some difficulty with it, and this is why he trivialises it, having perhaps foreseen that it will not accord at all with other of his maxims. The passage occurs in Book 1, Chapter 13:

There are always innumerable people who are at a loss to know what pain, pleasure and the other sensations are . . . Such people are surely remarkable in wishing to be taught what they cannot be ignorant of. Someone who burns his hand, for example, distinguishes well enough the pain he feels from light, colour, sound, tastes, odours, pleasure, and from all pains other than the one that he feels. He distinguishes it very easily from wonder, desire, love; he distinguishes it from a square, a circle, motion; in short, he recognises it to be very different from everything other than the pain he feels. Now I would like to know how, if he had no knowledge of pain, he could realize clearly and with certainty that what he senses is none of these things. [ST, 61]

He is content to say that this shows that we have some knowledge of pain. But it is clear that it shows more than this, and that one must conclude that we know it clearly, for if we only had an obscure knowledge of it we would only know with some doubt, and not *with evidence and clarity*, that what we sense is none of all the other things we have noticed.

And in fact Descartes assures us that we perceive sensible qualities clearly when we consider them merely as modifications of our mind, even though he was the most careful man in the world about taking something as clear which was not clear. It cannot be put more positively than it is in the passage that we have already quoted from Section 68 of Part I of the *Principles*:

In order to distinguish here what is clear from what is obscure in our sensation, we must be careful to note in the first place that we *clearly and distinctly* perceive pain, colour, and other sensations when they are regarded merely as thoughts. But this is not the case when we judge them to be things existing outside our thought. [CSM I, 217]

I draw two conclusions from this. The first is that there is nothing falser than the major premiss of the second argument, which is an assumption that the author makes throughout, wanting us to take 'seeing a thing by a clear idea' and 'seeing it only by an internal sensation' as two contrary things. For we perceive pain, colour, and other sensible things only through *internal sensation*, and yet Descartes maintains that they are seen clearly and distinctly when they are conceived merely as sensations and thoughts.

The second is that it follows from the second argument that since pain, colour, and other similar things are only known obscurely and confusedly when we wrongly consider them to be outside the soul, the ideas of these sensible qualities are only obscure and confused when one connects them with bodies, as if they were modifications of it. And consequently one cannot reasonably argue from their obscurity against the clarity of the idea of the soul; rather, one is led to doubt the clarity of the idea of extension.

I could stop at this point, but since he places so much weight on the question of sensations in showing that we do not have a *clear idea* of our soul, it seemed to me a good idea to show that, without leaving the question of sensations, one could easily convince him, by an argument similar to his own, that we have no clear idea of extension, or at least that the idea of our soul is clearer than that of extension.

For this we need only note that our different sensations depend on different occasional causes which are modifications not of our soul but of matter. For example, if I have a sensation of the colour red when looking at an object, and of green when looking at another object, this is due to the particles on the surfaces of these two objects being arranged differently, which is the reason why the corpuscles by which the action of light is communicated are reflected in different ways from the two objects towards our eyes, and why they subsequently cause different motions in the strands of the optic nerve. Now there is nothing in these three things that does not pertain to extension rather than our soul. Taking this as given, I argue as follows.

I know my sensations clearly and distinctly when I consider them merely as modifications of my soul. This I have just shown. On the other hand, I do not know at all, or know only obscurely or confusedly, the occasional causes of my different sensations, even though it is certain that there is nothing in the occasional cause that does not pertain to extension. For who can boast that he knows clearly how the particles on the surface of a body have to be arranged so as to be the occasional cause of my sensation of the colour red, and thus of the two other things, namely the motion of corpuscles and the motion of the strands in the optic nerve?

Now according to Malebranche, we are supposed to have a clear idea of an object to the extent that we know clearly the modifications of which it is capable, and we are supposed to know this by considering the idea. This is his principle, although I dispute it.

Consequently, if the knowledge – clear or obscure – that we have of what is involved in our sensations can be adduced as proof of the clarity or obscurity of the ideas of our soul and extension, it can only serve to make us conclude, contrary to Malebranche's claims, that the idea we have of our soul is clearer than that we have of extension.

NINTH ARGUMENT:

As we have a clear idea of order, if we also had a clear idea of the soul by the inner sensation that we have of ourselves, we would know clearly whether the soul conformed to order; we would know whether we were righteous or not. We would even be able to know exactly all its inner dispositions towards good and evil when we sensed them. But if we could know ourselves as we are, we would not be so liable to presumption. [ST, 637]

REPLY: All this is based merely on the incorrect definition of a clear idea, which I have already discussed in the reply to the first argument, for I acknowledge that if the only *clear idea* were one which provided us with the means of knowing an object so perfectly that we could never be ignorant not only of its principal properties but generally of all its modifications, I acknowledge, I say, that if we take the expression 'clear idea' in this sense, then we have no clear idea of our soul. But I also maintain that we do not have a clear idea in this sense of anything, and above all Malebranche should not have supposed that we have it in the case of *order* and *extension* while denying we have it in the case of our soul.

For, to begin with the case of order, if we were to have a clear idea of order which satisfied his definition, we would have to know everything that conforms to order. And as clear ideas are common to everyone, according to him, there could not be anyone who did not know what does or does not conform to order. Now if this were the case, how does it come about that pagans, and even the most enlightened amongst them, have so many wrong moral rules? How does it come about that, even amongst Christians, there are so many people who are sure that they do nothing contrary to order when they violate it in a million ways? Thus we must either have no clear idea of order, or else we have one even though we do not know everything that conforms to it. Consequently I could have a clear idea of my soul even though I did not know it in such a perfect way that everything in it is always evident to me. For some strange reason Malebranche appears to have assumed that our clear idea of order provides us with the means of knowing clearly what conforms to order. Otherwise, he would not have been able to conclude 'that as we have a clear idea of order, if we also had a clear idea of our soul, we would know clearly whether it conforms to order'. For if I can be mistaken in believing that something conforms to order which does not do so, I could have prefect knowledge of the state of my soul without thereby knowing clearly whether this conformed to order. An example will make this clear. When St Paul persecuted the Christians, he was not ignorant of the state of his soul on this, for he knew full well his plan of eradicating the religion that the disciples of Jesus of Nazareth wanted to establish. Thus there was nothing, in respect to the knowledge of his soul, that prevented him from knowing clearly whether or not it was in conformity with order. And yet he did not know this, and he was certainly mistaken in believing it did conform to order. His error came, then, not from not knowing his soul well, but from not knowing what conforms to order. Consequently it would be just as correct for us to conclude from this that we do not have a clear idea of order, as it would be to conclude that we do not have a clear idea of our soul.

It is the same with the idea of extension. There are infinitely many things of which we never know whether or not they belong to extension unless we have grasped it in experience. Who would ever have imagined all the effects of gunpowder unless he had accidentally discovered them? And it is accident again that has led us to recognise that effects that were attributed to the void should be attributed to the weight of air.[18] And there are very few people who can believe that what animals do they do unknowingly, merely by modifications of extension. But if men were born on a desert island where there were no animals, it is still more certain that they would never find in the idea of extension even the possibility of such automata. It is much the same with plants. If we had never seen them, the clarity of the idea of extension would not be sufficient to enable us to have the least thought of them. Yet Malebranche cannot help but believe that we have a completely clear idea of extension. Why then does he want it to be a proof that we have no clear idea of our soul, that we often need experience to know the inner dispositions of virtue or to gauge its strength, in order for it to remain firm in its duty?

TENTH ARGUMENT:

We need very strong arguments to prevent the soul being confused with the body. But if we had a clear idea of the soul, as we do of the body, we certainly would not have to take all these roundabout ways of distinguishing it from the body. We could do so at a single glance, as easily as we see that a square is not a circle. [ST, 638]

REPLY: This passage and numerous similar ones show that Malebranche believes that we do not know by a clear idea anything that we do not discover at a single glance but know only by reasoning. We find a similar view in the *Third Set of Objections* made against Descartes by an Englishman called Hobbes, for this philosopher also claims that we do not have an idea of what we know only by reasoning. In the third objection to the *Third Meditation* he says:

I have already frequently pointed out that we do not have an idea of God, or of the soul. I add now that we do not have an idea of substance either. For we know it solely through reasoning, and it is therefore something that is not conceived, or which we are presented with an idea of. [CSM II, 130]

Descartes replies curtly: 'I too have frequently pointed out that I use the term "idea" for the perception we have of anything we know by reasoning just as much as anything we know in any other way' [CSM II, 130].

The same holds for clear ideas. An idea should be called 'clear' if it is the perception of anything which we know clearly by reasoning, however lengthy, provided our reasoning is demonstrative, or of anything else that we know clearly in some other way.

And Malebranche must grant this, because he wants us to know all the properties of extension by means of clear ideas; will he deny that there are infinitely many of these which are not perceived in a single glance but can be discovered only by lengthy reasonings? Did Pythagoras only have to consult the ideas of the right-angled triangle and the square to discover at a single glance that the square of the [hypotenuse] must be equal to the sum of the squares of the other two sides? Did Archimedes have only to consult the idea of the sphere to discover at a single glance that its surface area is four times the area of one of its greater circles? Were all the properties of conic sections likewise discovered at a single glance? He has proclaimed himself the patron of the *clear idea* of extension too loudly not to want all of these to be seen by a clear idea. He is, then, using double standards when, in order to support his position that we do not have a clear idea of our soul, he maintains that we see by a clear idea only what we see at a single glance, without the need for reasoning.

Chapter 24

Conclusions of the author's arguments against the clarity of the idea of the soul. How it comes about that he cannot find this in himself.

I believe I've covered all Malebranche's arguments against the clarity of the idea of the soul. I do not know whether he will be satisfied with what I have said in showing that they are not at all sound, for, from the way in which he arrives at them, it seems he has no doubt that everyone will be convinced by them. He writes:

I shall not pause to give further proof that we do not know the soul or its modifications by clear ideas. No matter how we look at ourselves, we recognise this fully. And I add this to what I have already said in *The Search after Truth* only because of the way in which certain Cartesians have criticised it. If this does not satisfy them, then I am waiting for them to show me this clear idea which I cannot find in myself, however much effort I make to discover it. [ST, 638]

It is not surprising that since, as we saw in the last chapter, he has tied the notion of a clear idea to so many conditions, he wasn't able to find in himself the clear idea of the soul he is after, and which satisfied the definition he gave of it. It is by the same reasoning that the Stoics believed that there was no man on earth whom one could call a good man; for they included so many things in this quality of being a good man that they should have clearly foreseen that they would never find anyone in whom they could discover the quality. But what is surprising is that he did not imitate these philosophers in also pushing the consequences of his definition of a clear idea as far as they should go. On the contrary it seems that his sole aim was to apply the definition to the soul, so as to persuade us that it is so obscure that we must rather say that we have no idea of it all: whereas in the case of everything else he either readily forgets the conditions he has imposed on an idea if it is to be clear, or else he imagines in some passages that these conditions are satisfied and in others that they are not. For is it possible to maintain more surely that the idea of extension is given to us by means of knowing all the modifications of which it is capable than to say, as he does in Book 3, Part II, Chapter 7 of *The Search after Truth*, that 'Our idea of extension suffices to enable us to know all the properties which extension can have; and we could not wish for a more distinct and fruitful idea of extension, shape, or motion, than that which God has given us?' [ST, 237]. And is it possible to recognise more clearly that this is not so, than to acknowledge, as he does in Book 3, Part I, Chapter 1, that: 'the least part of wax is capable of an infinite number, or rather an infinitely infinite number, of different modifications that no mind can comprehend?' [ST, 199]. For since this is undoubtedly what we know of the modifications of matter by this idea which is 'so distinct and fruitful', which he says elsewhere God has given us, it is nothing in comparison with what we do not know, and with what God could have revealed to us had He wished. And thus it is a curious overstatement to declare that 'our idea of extension suffices to enable us to know *all* the properties of which extension is capable, and we could not wish for a more distinct and *fruitful* idea of extension'.

But let us return to the idea of our soul. It will not be difficult to teach him how to find this in himself. One only has to remove various ill-founded prejudices from one's mind, as he himself could easily recognise by considering closely the ideas he believes to be clear. For he would either have to cease taking them as clear ideas, or acknowledge that what does not agree with these ideas will not be necessary for an idea's clarity.

The first of these prejudices is 'that the idea of an object cannot be clear if it does not provide us with a means of knowing clearly all the modifications of which this object is capable'. This is to confuse a clear idea with a *comprehensive idea*, and revives Pyrrhonism for, as Descartes rightly noted, we would not be able to convince ourselves that we had a clear idea of anything if we have a clear idea of something only when it provides us with such a complete knowledge of an object that there would be nothing that escaped it, not only as regards its essential attributes but even as regards its simple modifications.

The second is 'that we know two things by clear ideas only if we know the relations between them'. I have already shown this to be baseless by two examples which, I believe, it is impossible to reply to. The first is that we have very clear ideas of the circle and the square, of the sphere and the cube, although we do not know the relation between the circle and the square, nor that between the sphere and the cube. The second is that relations properly speaking belong only to quantities, and consequently things which are not quantities can be known by clear ideas without knowing their relations.

The third is 'that we know something by a clear idea only if we discover it in a single glance, and if we know it as easily as we recognise that the square is not a circle'. To want this is to want us to have no *clear ideas* in the most certain sciences, such as algebra, geometry, and arithmetic. For other than first principles and the simplest definitions, which are discovered at a single glance, all the rest can be known only by demonstrations which often consist in very long chains of reasoning.

The fourth is 'that we do not know by clear ideas what we know only by consciousness and by sensation'. Exactly the opposite is the case, at least as far as things we know in this life are concerned. For nothing is clearer to us than what we know in this way, as St

Augustine teaches us in the thirteenth Book of *On The Trinity*, Chapter 1, where he says that we know our own faith (and it is the same for all our other thoughts) *certissima scientia, et clamante conscientia* – by a most certain science and with a proclamation by our conscience [/consciousness]. Now as Augustine says, what we know by this inner sensation we can be so certain of only because it is clear and evident. For in natural knowledge, only clarity and evidence can make us certain. If we wish to question whether the perception we have of our thought, known as it is by itself and without express reflection, is really an idea, at least we cannot deny that it would be easy for us to know it by an idea, for in order to do this we only have to reflect on our thought expressly. Then, since this second thought will have the first as its object, it will be a formal perception of it, and consequently an idea; and this idea will be clear since it will reveal to us very evidently what it is the idea of. And consequently it is indubitable that we see by clear ideas what we see by sensation and consciousness, wholly contrary to Malebranche's view, which is that we must regard these two ways of knowing as opposed.

When Malebranche comes to rid himself of these four prejudices, then, it will be easy for him to find a clear idea of the soul on himself: and there is even enough in his own book to help him discover this.

What he says about the soul in the first Chapter of the third Book would be enough to enable him to understand that we have a clear idea of our soul if he were content with the true notion of a clear idea, without adding to it lots of conditions which the clarity of an idea does not require.

He says: 'Having given it serious thought, one cannot doubt that the essence of mind consists only in thought, just as the essence of matter consists in extension' [ST, 198]. Can one say with certainty what the essence of something which one does not have an idea of consists in, and can one say of it, as he does later on, 'that it is the one thing in the world that one knows best as regards its existence and least as regards its essence' [cf. ST, 238]?

He adds in the same context that:

it is not possible to conceive of a mind that does not think, though it is possible to conceive of one which does not sense or imagine, or even will . . . But the power of willing is inseparable from the will, although it is not essential to it: as the capacity for being moved is inseparable from the material, although it is not essential to it. [ST, 198–9]

At the same place there are many similar things which clearly show either that he pushes forward recklessly without knowing what he is saying, or that he knows the nature of his soul better than he admits.

In this chapter, however, he says something which contradicts what he gives elsewhere as the principal condition for something's being the *clear idea of an object,* namely its providing us with a means of knowing all the modifications which it may have. He says:

It must be agreed that the soul's capacity for receiving different modifications is seemingly greater than its capacity for conception. By this I mean that, just as the mind cannot exhaust or comprehend all the shapes of which matter is capable, so also it cannot comprehend all the different modifications the mighty hand of God can produce in the soul, even if the mind knew the soul's capacity as distinctly as it knows that of matter. [ST, 200]

We can extract from this two demonstrative arguments against his definition of a *clear idea.* The first is:

Our mind cannot understand all the shapes that matter can have.
    This does not prevent our mind knowing matter by a clear idea.
    Therefore, if we are to know an object by a clear idea, it is not necessary that we understand all the modifications of which it is capable.

The second is:

If our soul were to know itself as distinctly as it knows matter, there is nothing to stop one saying that it knows itself by a clear idea.
    If it knew itself as clearly as it knows matter, it would not be able to understand all the modifications that the mighty hand of God can produce in it.
    Therefore, the proposition that it does not know all the modifications of which it is capable cannot prove that it does not know itself by a clear idea.

In Book 3, Part II, Chapter 7, he says that 'our knowledge of our soul is sufficient to demonstrate its immorality, spirituality, freedom, and several other attributes that it is necessary for us to know' [ST, 239]. Now it is contradictory to argue that one can demonstrate nothing from what one only knows confusedly and obscurely. I wish for no other proof of this than the one Malebranche has given us, for he will certainly acknowledge that to demonstrate is to prove *with evidence,* and he tells us in Book 1, Chapter 2 'that evidence consists only in the clear and distinct perception of all the parts and of all the relations of the object that are necessary to support a well-founded judgement' [ST, 10]. Thus we can demonstrate nothing about an object unless we have *a clear and distinct perception* of it. Consequently, if we did not have a clear and distinct perception of our soul, we would be able to demonstrate neither its immortality, its spirituality, nor its freedom. Now to have a clear and distinct idea of an object, and to know an object by a clear idea, are clearly the same thing: hence it is not true that we have no clear and distinct idea of our soul.

Finally, he has only to do what he counsels others to do, in order to find this idea, which he says he has not been able to find in himself. In Chapter 10 of the first book, he refers his readers to various books of St Augustine, Descartes, and de Cordemoy,[19] in order to learn how to distinguish better the ideas of the soul and the body. Now these writers, and especially the first two, maintain that our idea of our soul is clearer and more distinct than that of our body. Why then does he refer us to these, if we are bound to find there something he believes is contrary to truth?

Nothing is finer than what St Augustine says on this in Book 10, Chapter 10 of *On The Trinity:*

For, having shown that the philosophers have many opinions concerning the nature of our soul, some have believed it is made of air, others that it is made of fire, and others of this and that; but they have agreed that whatever it is in them that they called 'soul' lives, remembers, conceives various things clearly, wills, thinks, knows and judges. That is something that no one was able to doubt. For the doubt itself would reveal all those things in him, since he can say to himself: if I doubt, I exist and I live. If I doubt, I remember whatever I doubt. If I doubt, I see clearly that I doubt. If I doubt, I wish to be certain of what it is that I doubt. If I doubt, I think. If I doubt, I know that I do not know. If I doubt, I judge that I ought to resolve not to assent rashly. And thus, whoever doubts, whatever he may doubt, he cannot doubt all these things that he finds in his soul, since if they were not there he would not be able to doubt anything.

And he continues a little further on:

These philosophers who have had so many different opinions on the soul, have not noticed that our soul knows itself when it seeks to know itself. Now one cannot be said to know that one knows something when its nature and substance are not known. Thus when our soul knows itself, it knows its substance and its nature as well. Now its knowledge of itself is certain, as we have shown: thus it knows its nature with certainty. Now it is not certain that it is made of air or fire, or of some other body, or a mode of existence of body; hence it is made of none of these.

Is this the language of a man who believed we have no clear idea of the soul, and that we know it only confusedly and obscurely?

He refers us again to Descartes' *Meditations*, and above all to what he says when proving the distinction between mind and body. But this is precisely where one finds that this distinction is based on clear ideas of the soul and the body. In the *Sixth Meditation* he gives the following rule: 'It is enough that I be able to conceive one thing without another *clearly* and distinctly to be certain that they are not the same' [CSM II, 54]. And when he is challenged on this in the *Second Set of Objections*, he reaffirms it even more strongly in his response:

Can you deny that it is enough for us to be able to conceive one thing without another *clearly* and distinctly in order for us to judge that they are really distinct? Give me a more certain criterion of a real distinction. I am confident that you can provide none. Do you say that you derive this knowledge from the senses, since you can see one thing without the other? But the evidence of the senses is much less reliable than that of the mind. Besides, properly speaking, it is through the mind and not through the senses that we know things: so having a sensation of one thing without the other is to have the idea of one thing and to know by the mind that the idea of this thing is not that of something else; that is to say, to conceive of one thing apart from another, and we cannot conceive of it with certainty unless the idea that we have of each is *clear* and distinct: *nec potest id certo intelligi, nisi utriusque rei idea sit* clara *et distincta.* [cf. CSM II, 95 ff.]

Thus he believes that the idea of the soul has to be as clear as that of the body if we are to establish firmly the distinction between the soul and the body.

And it is the soul above all that he does not doubt is distinct. For, far from thinking that our knowing our soul by consciousness is a sign that we do not know it by a clear idea, he even infers from this that we cannot doubt that we know it by a clear idea. He states this in a few precise words at the end of his *Reply to the Sixth Set of Objections: Non dubitavi quin claram haberem ideam mentis meae, utpote cujus mihi intime conscius eram* [I did not doubt that I have a *clear idea* of my mind since I had a close inner awareness of it].

I would have offered no objection at all to *The Search after Truth* if its author had not referred to Descartes' *Meditations* on the question of ideas of the soul and the body, for I know very well that he does not believe he should hold the same opinion on this. He even reproaches the disciples of Descartes for being weak in letting themselves be so taken with the authority of their master that they can believe him when he says 'that the nature of the mind is better known than anything else'.

But because these Cartesians could complain that they are being wrongly accused of blind deference to the authority of one man, when they are only following his arguments, he tries to remove this ground for complaint by showing them that there is nothing feebler than what they have been persuaded of. This is what he undertakes to show in the *Elucidations*, when he says:

These philosophers, following Descartes, say that we know the nature of a substance more distinctly as we know more of its attributes. Now there is nothing of which we know more attributes than our mind, because as many attributes as we know in other things can be counted in the mind, by the fact that it knows them. And consequently its nature is better known than that of anything else. [ST, 635]

There are indeed many people for whom this argument has appeared as strong as it is subtle and ingenious; but for Malebranche, it is easily rebutted by his prejudices. 'Who does not see', he says, 'that there is indeed a difference between knowing by a clear idea and knowing by consciousness?'

REPLY: This is his fourth prejudice. For he does not just wish to say that there are many things that one knows by clear ideas and does not know through consciousness. That is indubitable, but it does not count against the argument to which he planned to reply. He wants to say more, namely, that one does not know by a clear idea what one knows by consciousness. Now I have just shown the contrary by arguing that what one knows by consciousness one knows *certissima scientia*, as St Augustine says – by a most certain science. There is certainty in naturally acquired knowledge only through clarity and evidence; thus one knows clearly what one knows by consciousness. We shall now see that, as a consequence of his response, he takes 'knowing clearly' and 'knowing by a clear idea' to be the same thing.

'When I know that two times two is four', he says, 'I know it very clearly; but I do not know *clearly* what it is in me that knows it' [cf. ST, 635].

REPLY: I deny this. These are empty words which lack any basis. For I know clearly that it is me who knows it. Now I cannot doubt, even if I were to doubt everything, that I am a substance that thinks, as we have just seen St. Augustine prove in a remarkable way. Thus I know clearly that it is me, a substance that thinks, who knows that two times two is four. Nevertheless, note that he takes 'knowing clearly' and 'knowing by a clear idea' as the same thing.

Malebranche says: 'I sense it, it is true. I know it by consciousness or by internal sensation, but I have no clear idea of it, as I have of numbers, the relations between which I can clearly discover' [ST, 635].

REPLY: This is the second prejudice, which I have already refuted several times.

He says:

I can *count* three properties in my mind: that of knowing that two times two is four, that of knowing that three times three is nine, and that of knowing that four times four is sixteen. And, if you wish, these three properties are different from each other, and hence I can count in me an infinite number of properties; but I deny that the nature of the things that can be *counted* can be known *clearly*. [ST, 635–6]

It seems, then, that he agrees with the strong claim of Descartes' argument, namely 'that there is nothing of which I know more attributes than my soul, for to the extent that one knows the attributes of other things in those things, one can count an equivalent number of attributes in the mind because it knows them' [CSM II, 249]. They agree on this. But Malebranche is reduced to saying that we do not know them *clearly*, his only argument for this being that 'it does not follow that the nature of things which can thus be *counted* can be known *clearly*' [ST, 636], as if it had been supposed that we know them *clearly* because we can count them. This never entered Descartes' mind. All he said was that we can count as many modifications of the mind as our mind knows in other things, in order to show that there is nothing of which one knows as many attributes as of our mind. But he did not envisage that the absence of clarity would halt the soul in its knowledge of its own modifications because, like St Augustine, he supposed that there was nothing clearer to us. And, as I maintain I have shown that Malebranche has no reason to deny this, I maintain also that he has not refuted the argument by which Descartes hoped to show 'that the nature of mind is better known than anything else'. For one has only to suppose this distinction, by taking as true (which it is) what he tries to call into doubt, namely, that we know the nature of a thing all the more distinctly as we know its attributes, *provided we know them clearly*. This conclusion makes the major premiss undeniable by Malebranche.

Our mind knows clearly more attributes or properties of itself than of anything else. For I cannot know the attribute or property of anything else unless I know the perception that I have of it clearly, and this perception is an attribute or property of my mind. From this it follows, by the author's own admission, that, putting to one side whether the mind knows its own perceptions clearly and distinctly, it can count in itself an infinite number of properties, if it has an infinite number of perceptions.

Thus it knows more of its own properties than it does those of anything else. And provided it knows its own properties clearly, which no one can doubt, we cannot doubt either that we know the nature of our mind better than that of anything else.

Chapter 25
Whether we know the souls of others without ideas.

I will only say a word on the way in which he claims we know the souls of others. He says that 'we do not know them in themselves, because we only see God by an immediate and direct vision' [ST, 236–7]

He says that 'we do not know them by their ideas', without providing specific arguments for this, no doubt because he believed that we have only to apply those he has given to show that we have no idea of our own soul.

We do not know them by consciousness because they are different from us, and one does not know by consciousness what is different from oneself. From this he concludes 'that we know them by conjecture, i.e. we conjecture that the souls of other men are the same sort as our own' [ST, 239].

I do not need to go into detail on this. For, first, everything that I have said when showing that, if it were true that we see things in God, which he takes to be the same thing as seeing them by clear ideas, then there could be no reason to exempt our soul from this, is still more powerful in showing that, if we are unable to see the souls of other men by consciousness, as each sees his own, then it would be even more contrary to the uniformity of God's conduct not to reveal to us the souls of others in the same way in which, according to

Malebranche, He gets us to see material things, i.e. 'shows us what it is in Him that represents them'.

Secondly, if we can perceive by clear ideas individual things like the sun, fire, water, a horse, a tree, I do not understand why we cannot see in the same way the souls of other men by clear ideas. For I do not see the substance of the sun in a single glance, but by judgements that I make on the reports of my senses, which make me perceive something very high in the sky, very bright and very hot. I judge in the same way from the report of my senses that bodies like mine approach me, and this leads me to believe that they are human bodies. However, when I speak to them and they reply to me, and when I see them perform a large number of actions which are infallible signs of mind and reason, I conclude from this very much more clearly that these bodies which are like mine are animated by souls similar to mine, i.e. by intelligent substances really distinct from these bodies, than I conclude that there is a sun and what the sun is. And hence I know this with at least as much certainty as everything I know about the sun, whether through the observations of astronomers or by Descartes' speculations.

Now I am convinced, as I have said in earlier chapters, that in the case of knowledge of natural things, *knowing an object with certainty* is the same thing as *knowing it by a clear idea*, whether it be known at a single glance or only through argument, since otherwise geometers could never perceive by clear ideas, since they hardly ever have knowledge except by reasoning.

And thus I find nothing wrong with saying that we only know the souls of other men by conjecture, providing that, on the one hand, the word 'conjecture' is taken generally as whatever is not known *at a single glance*, and is extended to everything one knows by reasoning, and even by the most certain demonstrations; and on the other hand that we will not imagine that we do not perceive by clear ideas what we know by reasoning, as some critics of Descartes have unjustifiably wished to claim, so as to have more means of weakening his demonstrations of the existence of God and the immortality of the soul, which are based on ideas of God and of the soul.

Chapter 26

Whether we see God in Himself and without ideas

It is difficult to glean Malebranche's actual views concerning the idea of God, for on the one hand he accepts such an idea in many passages, even making it the principle of the best proof of His existence, and on the other he denies it so strongly, and maintains so explicitly that we do not know God by an *idea* and that nothing created can represent Him, that it is impossible to know how he can put forward such things without contradicting himself.

In the *Elucidations,* he writes:

Men sometimes say that they have no idea of God, nor any knowledge of His will, and often they even think this as they say it, but this is because they think they do not know something which perhaps they know best. For where is the man who hesitates to answer whether God is wise, just, and powerful, whether or not he is triangular, divisible, mobile, or subject to whatever changes? Yet one cannot answer without fear of error whether or not certain qualities belong to some subject if one has no idea of the subject. [ST, 568]

And later he says:

If we did not have within us the idea of the infinite, and if we did not see everything through the natural union of our mind with infinite and universal reason, then it seems evident to me that we would not be able to think about all such things. He recognises, therefore, that we have in our minds the idea of the infinite, i.e. of God. [ST, 616]

And later still:

There is always a pure idea and a confused sensation in the knowledge that we have of things that currently exist, the knowledge of God and the soul excepted. I make an exception for the existence of God, because we know it through a pure idea and without sensation, His existence depending on no cause and being contained in the idea of an infinite and necessary Being, just as the equality of the diameter is contained in the idea of a circle. [ST, 621]

This is to recognise the idea of God in the way in which Descartes took the expression, for it is to accept the demonstration he gave of the existence of God based on the necessity of His existence being contained in the idea of a perfect Being, just as it is contained in the idea of a triangle that it has three angles equal to two right angles, or, what is the same thing, that the equality of the diameter is contained in the idea of a circle [ST, 621].

He speaks more in conformity with this thought of Descartes' when he says in Book 3, Part II, Chapter 6: 'Finally, the best proof of God's existence is the idea we have of the infinite; for it is certain that the mind perceives the infinite, though it does not understand it, and that it has a *very distinct idea of God*' [ST, 232]. And he is still following Descartes when he says in the same passage:

Not only does the mind have an idea of the infinite, it even has it before that of the finite; for we conceive of infinite Being simply in conceiving of Being, without thinking whether it is finite or infinite. But in order for us to conceive of a finite being, something must necessarily be eliminated from this general notion of being, which consequently must be prior to it.

Hence there are plenty of passages where he recognises that we have an idea of God. But there are others where he denies this and where he seems at the same time to undermine his conclusion that the best proof of God's existence is based on this idea of God.

For in the same Book 3, Chapter 7, he claims that it is characteristic of God to be known by Himself and without any idea. He says:

We know things by themselves and *without ideas* when, being intelligible, they can enter the mind and reveal themselves to it . . . Now only God do we know by Himself, for though there are other spiritual beings besides Him which seem intelligible by their nature, only He can enter our mind and reveal Himself to us; thus we perceive God alone by an immediate and distinct perception. [ST, 236]

I would like to believe that the contradiction here is only apparent, and I would even try to disentangle it; but what prevents me from doing this is that I do not see that it would be of any help in its resolution, given what he says in the *Third Elucidation* in resolving a similar problem concerning the soul, which in several places he says we have an idea of, and in others that we do not. His solution is that

the word 'idea' is equivocal in that sometimes it is taken as anything that represents an object to the mind, whether it be clearly or confusedly; more generally it is taken as anything that is the immediate object of our mind; but I also take it as anything that represents things to the mind in such a clear way that we can discover at a single glance whether such-and-such modifications belong to them. [ST, 561]

Applying this to the soul, he states that he has said 'that we have no idea of it, because the idea we have of it is not clear'. Now there is no indication here that he wishes to use the same solution in reconciling

those passages where he says that we have an idea of God with those
where he says that we perceive God without an idea; for whatever it
is that he has understood by the idea of God when he says that it is
certain that we have a very distinct idea of God, he has certainly not
denied that this idea is clear, for in his *Treatise on Nature and on
Grace* he recommends very carefully 'consulting, with great attention, the vast and immense idea of a perfect infinite Being when one
claims to speak of God with some exactness'. And he adds in the
same passage 'that in order to judge the expression one uses in
speaking of God better, one must not look for whether they are the
common ones but whether they are *clear*, and whether they accord
exactly with the idea everyone has of an infinitely perfect Being'.

Thus the idea that everyone has of God is a clear idea, since it is this
idea that they must consult in order to speak of God exactly – which
one could not say if it were obscure and confused.

How is this to be reconciled with what he lays down as one of the
principal doctrines of his philosophy of ideas, namely 'that, of all the
things we know, it is only God that we know by Himself and without
ideas'? This can only be because of another equivocation on the
word 'idea' which I noted at the beginning of this treatise.

From the very beginning of *The Search after Truth*, he takes the
word 'idea' in its correct sense, as the perception of an object, and he
recognises there that this perception of an object is a modification of
our mind. Now it is clearly undeniable that, taking the word 'idea' to
have this meaning, we have an idea of God. It is also in this sense that
he acknowledges that we have one, as is clear from the third Book
[ST, 232], where he takes the *idea* of the infinite to be the same thing
as the *notion* of the infinite; for the word 'notion' is not equivocal
and never means anything other than 'perception'.

But in the second Book, he gives the word 'idea' another sense
altogether; for he understands by this word a *representation* distinct
from perceptions, which he imagines to be necessary to put objects
which he thinks are not intelligible in themselves in a state whereby
they are known by our soul. In this way there are, according to him,
three things that should be distinguished in the knowledge of these
kinds of objects: the object which must be known and which is not
intelligible by itself; the representation, which puts it in a state of
being known; and the perception of our mind, by which it is actually
known. Now taking the word 'idea' in this sense, he should have
said, according to his system, that we perceive God by Himself and

without any idea. For this means only that God, being intelligible by Himself and being intimately present to our soul, does not need to be put in a state of being known by a *representation* distinct from Himself. This means that we cannot distinguish three things in our knowledge of God, as we can in our knowledge of corporeal things, but only two: the object, which is God, who is intelligible by Himself, and the perception by which we know Him, without needing a representation distinct from the perception of the object. And this is what is indicated when he says 'that it is inconceivable that one should perceive Being that is without restriction, immense and universal, by an idea, i.e. through a particular being different from universal and infinite Being' [ST, 237].

But he could not have meant by this that one should know God without *perception*. First, because this would be a manifest contradiction, since to know God and to have a perception of God are exactly the same thing. Second, the perception is only a modification of our soul and cannot be called 'a being', 'a particular being', 'a being different from universal and infinite Being'. Third, what does it mean to say that 'one cannot conceive universal Being being perceived by an idea', taking the word 'idea' here as 'perception'? Could one rather conceive of Universal Being being perceived without one's having a perception of it? Fourth, since he speaks in so many passages of the 'idea of God', of the 'vast and immense idea of a perfect Being', and since he declares that everyone has this idea, there must be a sense of the word 'idea' according to which he believes that this is indubitable. No sense is to be found other than that which he gives to the word at the beginning of his work, where he takes it as 'perception'. Hence he has no other means of reconciling the passages where he says that we have an idea of God with those where he says that we know God without an idea, except to assume that in the first he takes the word 'idea' as 'perception' and that in the second he takes it as that *representation* which he mistakenly supposes we need in order to know everything other than God and our soul.

To the other proofs that I have used to show that this latter notion of the word 'idea' lacks any rational foundation, one can add the following: it only serves to muddle up the clearest and most natural notions that we would otherwise have of our own knowledge, and that it is almost impossible for those influenced by it not to fall, without noticing it, into several contradictions. For when a word has an ordinary meaning which is clear and distinct, if one erroneously gives it another meaning which is not only not clearer but is very obscure and confused, it is almost impossible to be consistent in always taking the word in this new sense; it constantly breaks free in various places where one takes it in its common sense, and one cannot banish it from one's mind without it constantly returning. We have seen that this is what has happened to this author in the case of the word 'idea', which is assuredly the cause of much confusion and obscurity in dogmatic discourses on very abstract matters which one cannot be too careful to make clear.

Here is another example. In the one sentence, he must at the beginning have taken the word 'idea' as *perception* and, in this sense, what he says is very true; but at the end of the sentence he took it as *representation*, which confuses everything he has said previously. He says:

Finally, the proof of God which is the best, the loftiest, the most solid and the primary one, or the one which assumed the least, is the idea that we have of the infinite; for it is certain that the mind perceives the infinite though it does not understand it, and that it has a very distinct idea of God. [ST, 232]

So far so good. But it is undeniable that the word 'idea' should be taken as 'perception', as Descartes takes it in this demonstration of the existence of God, which is what this author has in mind when he calls it 'the best, the loftiest, the most solid, and that which assumes the least'. But what he goes on to say no longer has any sense if we remain with this notion of *idea*: 'it is certain that the mind has a very distinct idea of God, which it can have only through its union with Him, since it is inconceivable that the idea of an infinitely perfect Being, which is what we have of God, should be something created' [ST, 232]. Isn't it clear that he has imperceptibly, and without warning, shifted from one notion of 'idea' to another, and that he is no longer taking 'the idea of God' as 'the perception of God', for if he were taking it in this sense how could he say that 'it is not something created'? Can we have uncreated perceptions? And aren't our perceptions essentially representations of their objects? Thus it must necessarily be the case either that we have no perception of God, so that when we speak of Him we speak as parrots do, not knowing what we are speaking of, or that, if we do have perceptions of Him, and it cannot be doubted that we do, then they represent infinite Being, contrary to his claim 'that we cannot conceive how something created can represent the infinite' [ST, 237]. But what makes him say this, as I have already noted, is that he has suddenly lost sight of 'ideas' taken as 'perceptions', and has carelessly substituted for this word his bizarre notion of *representations*, which he imagines to be like pictures and images which our mind must envisage before it forms perceptions. We can give some meaning to his statement that 'one cannot perceive the idea of an infinitely perfect Being by something created' by substituting the word 'representation' for the word *idea*, since it is clearly difficult to conceive how one could have a *representation* distinct from God if this is like a picture or image which our mind must contemplate before it can form a perception of the infinitely perfect Being. This is all one can say in mitigation of this proposition, which would be a very dangerous one if the word 'idea' were taken in the same sense at the beginning and at the end of the sentence. For if we take it in the same sense at the end as at the beginning, it would be necessary either that the perception we have of God not be a mode or attribute of our mind but something uncreated, which is inconceivable, or that we have no perception of God, which would completely destroy the proof of His existence from our idea of the infinite, and which is completely inconsistent with his statement that it is the best proof of it.

And in fact we see that all those critics of Descartes who have disagreed on the soundness of his proofs of the existence of God from the idea of a perfect Being, always stubbornly deny that we have any idea of God. One of the objections in Gassendi's large book of *Instances*[20] is that *omnes homines Dei in se ideam non animadvertere* – it is not true that all men can find the idea of God in themselves. Descartes replies that:

If we take the word 'idea' in the way I took it in my demonstrations, as the perception we have of an object, no-one can deny that he has in himself the idea of God, at least so long as he does not say that he does not understand the meaning of the phrase 'the most perfect thing which we can conceive of', for this is what everyone understands by the word 'God'. Now to say that one does not understand words as clear as these is to prefer to go to extreme lengths rather than admit that one had been wrong in rejecting another's view. To which I may add that one can hardly imagine a more impious confession than that of a man who says that he has no idea of God in the sense in which I take the word 'idea'; for this is to profess not to know Him either by natural reason, or by faith, or in any other way at all; since if we have no perception which corresponds to the meaning of the word 'God', then there is no difference between saying that God exists and saying that one believes that nothing exists. [CSM II, 273]

And in the same passage he adds something which may serve as a reply to Malebranche's claim – 'that nothing created can represent infinite Being' – for these philosophers insisted that *we would understand God if we had a clear idea of Him*. Descartes replies that:

this objection is baseless. Since the word 'understand' implies some limitation, it is impossible for a finite mind to understand God, who is infinite. But that does not prevent one being able to have an idea of the infinite, i.e. a perception of it; just as one can touch a mountain without being able to put one's arms around it. [CSM II, 273–4]

And Malebranche also recognises this, in the passage I have looked at, where he says that 'it is given that the mind perceives the infinite, even though it does not understand it'.

I believe that even Malebranche will not be able to find anything more plausible to reconcile the different things he says about the idea of God, whether allowing it or denying it. But I hope that he will himself conclude from this that it would have been better to have taken the notion in the way Descartes proposed, which is the only clear and distinct sense it can have, rather than to have formed a new sense which we have shown throughout this treatise is based merely on a false assumption that he shares with the scholastics, but which is fraught with many greater absurdities because he pushes it further than they did.

Chapter 27

On the origin of ideas. There is no reason to believe that our soul is purely passive in regard to all its perceptions, and it is more likely that it has received the faculty of forming many of them from God.

There is nothing of which one should take more care, in dealing with a scientific matter, than to avoid the muddle and confusion which results from running together different questions. This has required me to distinguish, in a number of places in this treatise, between what concerns the nature of ideas and what concerns their origin, and to put off dealing with the latter point until the end.

But to clarify things and anticipate objections which are not relevant, I must point out two things. The first is that I take the word *idea* to mean 'perception', in the same way as the author of *The Search after Truth* does in the first Chapter of his work. The second is that we are concerned here only with purely natural knowledge, and not with the way in which the Holy Ghost illuminates us in the order of grace.

Given this, the question is to determine whether all our ideas or perceptions come from God, or whether there can be some which we provide ourselves.

Malebranche is of the former opinion in *The Search after Truth*, and he advances it with great zeal in many places in his book. He assumes from the beginning:

that the first and principal agreement found between the faculty that matter has of receiving different *shapes* and *configurations*, and that which the soul has of receiving different *ideas* and *modifications* is that, just as the faculty of receiving different shapes and configurations in bodies is entirely passive and involves no action, so the faculty of receiving different ideas and modifications in the mind is entirely passive and involves no action. [ST, 3]

And this is how he distinguishes the understanding, i.e. that faculty which can receive many perceptions, and the will, i.e. that faculty which can receive many inclinations, by the fact that the latter is not purely passive as the former is:

For just as the Author of Nature is the universal cause of all the *motions* which occur in matter, so too is He the general cause of all the natural *inclinations* which occur in minds ... But there is a very significant difference between the impression of motion that the Author of Nature produces in matter and the impression of motion towards the general good that the same Author of Nature continually impresses in the mind. For matter is altogether without action; it can exert no force to arrest its motion or to direct it and turn it in one direction rather than another . . . But such is not the case with the will which can in one sense be said to be active, because it has within itself the force to direct in various ways the inclination or impression that God gives it. For although it cannot stop this impression, it can in a sense turn it in the direction that it wants, and thus cause all the disorder found in its inclinations. [ST, 4–5]

And this is what he says in the *Elucidations*: 'If it is maintained that to decide different things is to give oneself different modifications, then I agree that in this sense the mind can modify itself differently through the action that God puts into it' [ST, 551].

This is what he claims in respect to the will and its inclinations. But as regards perceptions, he always maintains that our understanding does not act, and that all it does is to receive them from God. He repeats this in the *Second Elucidation*: 'It must not be thought that the understanding obeys the will by producing in itself the ideas of things that the soul desires. For the understanding does not act: it only receives illumination or the ideas of things' [ST, 559].

I do not claim to refute what he claims, in all these passages dealing with the origin of ideas taken as perceptions, in as convincing a way as, I believe, I have destroyed his teachings in the same book concerning the nature of ideas taken as *representations*. For there is a great difference between what can be taken exception to in each of these two kinds of views.

I shall content myself with showing that there is no good argument to show that our soul is purely passive in respect to all its perceptions, and that it is much more likely that it received the ability to form them from God. And in showing this I shall only make use of things which are agreed upon.

(I) I do not know why he appears to want only to acknowledge conditionally something which he cannot avoid acknowledging absolutely. 'If it is maintained', he says, 'that to will different things is to give oneself different modifications, then I agree that in this sense the mind can modify itself differently'. The 'if' here is completely otiose; for he agrees in this same passage that the inclinations of the soul, i.e. its volitions, are *modes of being* of the soul. And a *modification* is undeniably the same thing as a *mode of being*. Thus it is indisputable that if a soul can will different things (as is appropriate to it) by directing the impression it receives from God towards the general good however it pleases, it can also provide itself with different modifications. And this is what is established absolutely, without the 'if', in the *First Elucidation* in these terms:

I answer that faith, reason, and the inner sensation I have of myself force me to abandon the comparison of the soul with matter where I do. For I am completely convinced that I have within myself a principle of my determinations, and I have reasons for believing that matter has no comparable principle. [ST, 547]

He thus acknowledges that our soul can be given, and can in fact give itself, new modifications at almost every moment in respect to its determinations and volitions. And I maintain that by this admission he loses all means of showing what at the same time he wants to show, namely that it can give itself no new modification in respect to its perceptions. For why would the soul be purely passive in respect to its perceptions and not in respect to its inclinations?

The reason cannot lie in the fact that it is a creature, as if it were impossible for creatures to perform any action and absolutely necessary that God perform them all, *the creature contributing nothing to it except passively.* For if that were the case, then since our soul is no less a creature in regard to its inclinations than in regard to its perceptions, it would have to be the case that it had no power to direct itself, which Malebranche declares to be contrary to faith and reason, and to the internal sensation we have of ourselves.

Nor could the comparison of the soul with matter make one believe that the faculty which our soul has of receiving different ideas must be completely passive, because the faculty which matter has of receiving different shapes is completely passive and contains no action. For since this comparison is wrong in regard to the faculty by which matter can be given different motions compared with the faculty that the soul has of receiving different inclinations, there is no necessary reason why it should be true in regard to shapes on the one hand and perceptions on the other. And conversely it is easy to use the comparison to show that the soul can be active in regard to its perceptions just as much as in regard to its inclinations.

For it should be noted that our soul and matter are two simple beings (i.e. they are not composed of two different natures, as man is) and above all the different faculties that we predicate of the soul are not actually distinct things but only the same reality considered in different ways. To allow, then, that the soul is active in respect of one of its faculties, namely the will, is to allow that it is active absolutely and by nature; and hence it is wrong to compare it with a simple being such as matter, which is by nature purely passive. Nothing, then, can be concluded from this comparison which should play no part in any reasonable demonstration.

I may even add that, if one is to conclude anything from this, it would be the opposite of what Malebranche concludes. For matter is unable to give itself different shapes only because it is unable to give itself different motions, since it is certain that it cannot give itself shape if it cannot move itself. Now inclinations are to the soul, according to Malebranche, what motions are to matter, so the power the soul has to give itself different inclinations should at least provide a probable argument that it also has the power to give itself different perceptions; since if matter had the power to give itself motions, it would also have the power to give itself different shapes.

(II) Unless what is active in the soul is extended to cover not just its inclinations but its perceptions as well, I do not see how Malebranche can explain what he believes to be necessary if we are to be free. In this respect, we need only understand what he says in Book 1, Chapter 1:

The mind, in so far as it is thrust towards the good in general, cannot direct its impulse towards a particular good (which is what its freedom consists in), unless that same mind, insofar as it is capable of ideas, knows that particular good. By this I mean, in plain language, that the will is a blind power that can proceed only towards those things that the understanding represents to it. As a result, the will can direct its tendency towards the good and all its natural inclinations in various ways, only by ordering the understanding to represent some object to it. The power that the will has of directing its inclinations therefore necessarily includes the power of being able to convey the understanding towards the objects that please it. [ST, 5]

It would clearly follow from this that our mind, in order to act freely, can give itself new perceptions. This can be proved by the following demonstration.

According to Malebranche, the mind considered as being thrust towards the good in general can only direct its impulse towards the particular good, which is what its freedom consists in, through the power it has to do this; and it is because it is able to have ideas, i.e. perceptions, that it comes to know the particular good which it did not previously know.

It is impossible for our mind to come to know an object which it did not previously know, except through a perception that it did not previously have.

It follows from this, therefore, that the mind cannot be free on his account unless it has the power to give itself new perceptions as well as new inclinations.

I don't know if he believes he has been able to avoid this difficulty in what he says about this passage in the *Elucidations*:

It should not be imagined that the will orders the understanding in any way other than by its desires and its impulses. Nor should the understanding be taken to obey the will by producing in itself the ideas of the thing the soul desires. The whole mystery is that the desire that my soul has to know an object is a natural prayer which is always answered. And thus this desire, as a result of the efficacious decrees of God, is the cause of the presence of the clarity of the idea representing the object. [ST, 559]

But he hasn't noticed that the only gain from this is to change the word 'order' to the word 'desire', which is of no help to him in extricating himself from the difficulty he is faced with in explaining the freedom of the will in the way he wants; for he has not retracted the general proposition that 'the mind, in so far as it is considered as being thrust towards the good in general (i.e. as the will), *cannot* direct its impulse towards a particular good (which is what freedom consists in) unless that same mind, in so far as it is capable of ideas, knows that particular good'. Nor has he retracted the consequence he draws from it, namely that

the power that the will has of directing its inclinations *therefore necessarily* includes the power of being able to convey the understanding towards the objects that please it, i.e. the power of being able to bring it about, through its desires and as a result of the efficacious decrees of God, that the understanding represent to it the objects which please it.

Now one can only maintain this by arguing in an endless circle. For he says in the same passage 'that the will is a blind power that can proceed only towards those things that the understanding represents to it'.

– Thus, in so far as an object pleases it, the understanding must represent that object to it.

– Thus in so far as it can desire the understanding to represent to it the objects that please it, the understanding must have represented them to it.

– Thus, it follows that what it wishes to be done must already have been done.

The same would hold if we removed the words 'which please it', which are perhaps only there inadvertently, from the proposition, and concentrated only on the desire that he supposes the soul must have to know the particular good that we will call A, if it is to be able to direct the impulse which God has given it towards the good in general towards this good A.

For the soul, in the form of the will, cannot desire to know the good A unless, in the form of the understanding, it has the perception of A, since the will, *being a blind power, can only convey itself to those objects that the understanding represents to it*. Hence it must have a perception of the good A in order to desire it. Now it is its desire that makes it have this, according to our friend, so it must have

what it desires to have if it is to be in a state in which it desires to have
it.

Now suppose it is said that this perception of A which it already
has is only an obscure perception of it contained in the desire, and
that it wants a more perfect perception of it; this desire, on Malebranche's account, depends on us and is a modification which the
soul can give itself, and hence the soul must be able to give itself what
is essentially contained in this desire, and without which one could
not say without manifest contradiction that it had the desire. Now
this desire necessarily contains a perception, if only an imperfect one,
of A, since it clearly would not be possible for me to have any will or
desire in regard to A if I had no perception of it at all: *ignoti nulla
cupido* [I desire nothing of which I am ignorant]. It is clear then that
one cannot reasonably say that I give myself the desire to know A,
and that my freedom consists in this, unless at the same time one
recognises that I can give myself a perception of A.

Perhaps it will be said that this only shows that I must already have
an obscure and confused perception of A before my soul can desire to
know it more perfectly.

But how are we to understand this obscure and confused perception of the particular good I have called A? Is it an idea or a
perception which represents A so confusedly that it could just as
easily be representing to our soul the goods B, C, D, or an infinity of
other particular goods to which my soul can direct the impulse it has
from God towards the good in general; or does this idea, although
called obscure and confused, only represent A to my soul?

If one maintains the former, it will follow that this idea will not
give my soul the power to desire A any more than the power to desire
B, C, D, and an infinity of other similar things, unless, out of this
confusion, it chooses A. But it can only do this if it has a perception of
A which is more distinct and less confused than those of the other
goods, and consequently it would have to provide itself with this
before it could desire to know A more perfectly.

If one maintains the latter, then either our soul would have to have
all the infinitely many obscure and imperfect notions of each one of
the particular goods together, in order to desire to know one rather
than another of them more perfectly, or else its turning the impulse
that it has from God towards the general good in the direction of
whatever particular goods it wants would not depend on its freedom,
but it would only be able to turn it towards the particular good of

which it already has an obscure idea. Otherwise we would have to explain how it comes about that God has given it, independently of its freedom, the obscure idea of one particular good rather than another, without our being able to connect this to its desires as the occasional causes that determined the general decrees of God, for this would lead to an infinite regress. Hence I cannot see that the way in which Malebranche has claimed to explain freedom can be sustained unless he recognises that our soul can provide itself with new modifications in respect to its ideas as well as in respect to its inclinations.

(III) I do not know whether I should respond to the arguments that he puts forward in Book 3, Part II, Chapter 3, to show that the soul does not have *the power to produce ideas*. For I have already noted on several occasions that in the third Book it is not *perceptions* but *representations* that he understands by the word 'idea'. I do not believe at all that our soul has the power to produce these *representations*; in my opinion they are only chimeras.

Nevertheless, if one wanted to apply these same arguments to perceptions, it would be very easy to see their weakness.

'No one', he says, 'can doubt that ideas are real beings, since they have real properties, they are different from one another, and they represent quite different things' [ST, 222]. And I agree, provided that by the word 'being' we understand 'modes of being' as well as substances.

'One cannot reasonably doubt that they are spiritual and are quite different from the bodies they represent' [ST, 222]. This again is true.

'And this seems sufficient to make one wonder whether the ideas by which bodies are seen are not more noble than the bodies themselves' [ST, 222]. This is true in one sense, because they are spiritual. But in another sense it is not true, because ideas taken as perceptions are only modes of being whereas bodies are substances.

'Thus, when it is claimed that men have the power to form such ideas as please them, one runs the risk of claiming that men have the power to create beings which are worthier and more perfect than the world God has created' [ST, 222]. I deny this inference; for ideas, taken as perceptions, are not 'beings' properly speaking, but only modes of being.

But even if it were true that ideas were only lesser and insignificant beings, they are still beings, and spiritual beings; and given that men do not have the power of creation, it follows that they are unable to produce them: for the production of ideas in the way they explain is a genuine creation. [ST, 223]

I shall not go to the trouble of explaining in what way others explain the production of ideas, nor what they understand by the word 'ideas'. But taking ideas as *perceptions*, as one must if one is to speak precisely, and as Malebranche himself takes them at the beginning of his work, it is not correct to say that the soul would have to have the power to create them if it had the power to provide itself with some ideas, i.e. perceptions. For creation is the production of a substance: and one never says, if one is speaking exactly, that giving a new mode to a substance is *creating*. This is all right in figurative language, as when David asks God 'to create a new heart in him', or when St Paul says 'that we have been created in Jesus Christ in good works'. But speaking exactly and philosophically, creation, as I have said, is the creation of a substance, whereas our perceptions are not substances but only *modes of being* of our soul. Thus it is not true that the soul cannot provide itself with new perceptions unless it has the power to create.

And Malebranche must agree with this, for he cannot deny that our particular inclinations and volitions are *modes of being* of our soul any more than that our perceptions are. Now he agrees that our soul can give itself new modes in the case of its inclinations and volitions without it thereby having the power to create. It is therefore not necessary that it have the power to create in order to give itself new modes in the case of ideas.

(IV) It is enough for me to have shown that one has no grounds for believing that our soul, not being purely passive in regard to its inclinations, should be so in regard to its perceptions. This does not prevent us being able to say that our soul is perhaps active only in so far as it functions as a will, for it is perhaps only in willing that we are able to give ourselves different perceptions.

I could stop here, for I am not sufficiently enlightened to be able to determine which perceptions we necessarily receive from God and which our soul is able to provide itself with. I shall nevertheless say something about this, but only by proposing what seems to me most likely, without settling anything absolutely.

(1) There are grounds for believing that God, in creating the soul, gave it the idea of itself, and that it is perhaps this thought of itself that constitutes its essence; for as I have already said elsewhere,

nothing seems more essential to the soul than to have consciousness and inner sensation of itself, which the Romans more appropriately called *esse sui consciam* [knowing oneself].

(2) The same can be said of the idea of infinity, or of a perfect Being. It is inconceivable that we could have formed it ourselves, and we must get it from God. And provided Malebranche understands only *perception* by the word *idea*, I would have no difficulty agreeing with him when he says:

> It is certain that the mind perceives the infinite though it does not understand it fully, and that it has a very distinct idea of God, which it can have only through its union with Him (i.e., as I understand him, it can only be derived from God). We even have the idea of the infinite before that of the finite, for we can conceive of infinite Being simply in conceiving of being, without considering whether it is finite or infinite. But in order to conceive of a finite being, something must necessarily be omitted from the general notion of being, which consequently must be prior to the former. [ST, 232]

But on this account, instead of his analogy between mind and matter, which he had to abandon half-way, he could have chosen a better one, between the will and the understanding, saying that just as God is content to give the will an impulse towards the good in general which it can direct through its different inclinations towards particular goods, He may have been satisfied to give the understanding the idea of infinite Being by giving it the power to form from this idea the ideas of finite beings. I do not say that I agree with this, only that it agrees well enough with his principles.

(3) It can hardly be doubted that it is God who gives us perceptions of light, sound and other sensible qualities, as well as perceptions of sadness, hunger, and thirst, albeit on the occasion of what occurs in our sense organs or in the constitution of our body.

(4) There is also every indication that God provides us with our perception of very simple objects such as extension, the straight line, prime numbers, motion, time, and those very simple relations which enable us to see clearly the truth of first principles, such as 'the whole is greater than the part'.

(5) On the other hand, there is every indication that our soul provides itself with the ideas or perceptions of things that it can know only by reasoning, such as almost all curves.

But however we come by ideas, we are always indebted to God for them, as much because it is He who has given our soul the faculty of producing them as because, in a thousand ways which are hidden from us, according to His plans for us for all eternity, he arranges by the secret orders of His providence all the events of our life. On this depends our knowing an infinity of things that we would not have known had He arranged them differently.

Chapter 28

Various thoughts on the claims of the author of *The Search after Truth* that one cannot be entirely assured of the existence of bodies except by faith.

I had intended to stop at this point, but, having toiled over another passage in *The Search after Truth* which is clearly related to his philosophy of ideas, since consideration of *the intelligible world, the intelligible sun,* and *intelligible spaces* make up one of the principal proofs of what he tries to establish, I think I should add here the arguments which have always prevented me from being able to agree with him.

It is a question of knowing whether, in the passage that I wish to examine, we can be convinced by reason of the existence of bodies, or whether we can only be convinced of this by faith.

He deals with this question in one of the *Elucidations*, entitled: 'That it is very difficult to prove that there are bodies, and what we should think of the proofs of their existence' [ST, 568].

He first praises Descartes, in that:

wanting to establish his philosophy on unshakable foundations, he did not believe he could assume that there are bodies, nor that he ought to prove their existence on the basis of sensation, even though these [arguments] seem very persuasive to the ordinary man. Clearly he knew as well as we do that he had only to open his eyes to see bodies, and that we can approach them and touch them to ascertain whether our eyes deceive us in what they report. He knew the mind of man well enough to judge that such proofs were not rejected. [ST, 572]

Our friend could have stopped here, and he would have done well to do so. But he goes further, for he claims that this cannot be demonstrated by argument, even when one has recourse to Descartes' statement that God is not a deceiver and that He would be had He given us so many different sensations of the bodies around us, including that which we believe is joined to our soul, and if there were nothing in the world except God and our mind. He claims that, even with this, we could and should not maintain that bodies exist, but rather that we can only be completely assured of their existence through faith:

But although Descartes has given us the strongest proofs that reason on its own can furnish for the existence of bodies, and although it is evident that God is no deceiver and that He could really be said to deceive us if we deceived ourselves in making use of the mind and the other faculties which He created in the way we should. Notwithstanding this, we can still say that the existence of matter is still not perfectly demonstrated. For in the area of philosophy we must not believe anything until the evidence compels us. We use our freedom as much as possible; and our judgements should not go beyond what we perceive. Thus when we see bodies, let us judge only that we see them and that these perceptible or intelligible bodies actually exist. But why should we judge for certain that there is an external world like the intelligible one that we see? (ST, 572]

And a little further on:

For us to be fully convinced that there are bodies, we must have demonstrated not only that there is a God, and that God is no deceiver, but also that He has assured us that He has really created such a world, and I have found no proof of this in Descartes' writings. *God* speaks to the mind and obliges it to believe in only two ways: through evidence and through faith. I agree that faith obliges us to believe that there are bodies: but, as for evidence, it seems to me that it is incomplete and that we are not inescapably led to believe that there is something other than God and our own mind. It is true that we have a very strong propensity to believe that there are bodies around us. Here I agree with Descartes. But this propensity, however natural it is, does not force us to believe in bodies through evidence; it merely inclines us towards belief by impression. Now our free judgements should follow only light and evidence, and if we let ourselves be led by sense impressions we shall almost always err. [ST, 573]

And having gone through an argument to prove the existence of bodies, he adds:

This argument is perhaps sound enough. Nevertheless, it must be agreed that it should not be taken as a conclusive demonstration of the existence of bodies. For God does not make us yield to it inescapably. If we consent to it, we do so freely: we are able not to consent to it. If the argument I have given is sound, we should believe it entirely probable that there are bodies, but we should not be completely convinced by this single argument. Otherwise it would be we who acted, and not God in us. It is by a free act, and consequently one liable to error, that we consent, and not by an invincible power; for we believe because we freely will to do so, and not because we perceive it to be evident. Surely only faith can persuade us that there really are bodies. There can be no exact demonstration of the existence of anything except that of a necessary being. And if you pay close attention, you will see that it is not even possible to know in a completely evident way whether or not God is truly the creator of the material and sensible world. For such evidence is found only in necessary relations, and there is no necessary relation between God and such a world. He was able not to create it, and if He has created it it is because He has willed to do so and willed to do so freely. [ST, 573]

In what follows, Sir, I offer three or four reflections on his claims to have proved that it is only faith that can assure us that there are bodies, and on the proofs he employs.

First reflection

It is very strange that he has not noticed that, if he keeps within the principles he has set out here, it is impossible for him to *demonstrate* anything from anything he puts forward in his *Treatise on Nature and Grace*. For he does not say that he has learned, by revelation from God, the great maxims on which the whole of the treatise turns, namely 'that if God wishes to act externally, it is because He wishes to obtain for Himself an honour worthy of Him; that He acts by the simplest means; that He does not act through particular volitions but through general ones which are determined by occasional causes'. He has not undertaken to prove this from Scripture, and if he believed he could do so, he should have said that he knows it by faith, and not that he *demonstrated* it.

Now he couldn't say that there was a more necessary relation between God and these ways of acting than between God and the creation of the world. For although he says on a number of occasions (e.g. Discourse 1, Part 1, Section 18) that the laws of nature are constant and immutable, he is obliged to recognise in other passages (e.g. *ibid.*, Section 20) that the law of impact

is not essential to God but arbitrary, that there are occasions when these general laws must cease to produce their effect, and that it is inappropriate that men know that God is master of nature in the sense that, if He submits

Himself to the laws that He has established it is because He wants to rather than because of any absolute necessity.

Thus he is able to demonstrate nothing from all these maxims, which are the foundation of everything that is distinctive in his treatise, if it is true, as he claims in the passage we have just quoted, that it is not possible to know in a completely evident way whether or not God is truly the creator of the material and sensible world because such evidence is only appropriate to necessary relations, and there is no necessary relation between God and such a world, which He was able not to create. For He was also able not to act through general volitions directed by occasional causes, and consequently there is no necessary relation between God and this mode of action. On this account, then, one could have neither complete evidence nor exact demonstrations on this question.

It might be said that it is enough that it is sufficient that what he has said on these things has a great appearance of truth, and that it is not necessary that he prove them by completely exact demonstrations. However, as far as he is concerned, it is very obvious that he cannot say anything like that, after what we have just looked at; for he didn't write about such important questions in order not to convince anyone. Now he has told us very directly that we are not to acquiesce in his arguments, however correct they seem, if they are not demonstrative,

because it would be we who acted, and not God in us, and it would be by a free act, and consequently one liable to error, that we would embrace its judgements, and not because of an indubitable conviction; for we believe it because we freely will to do so, and not because we perceive it to be evident.

Thus there is nothing new done in this book, either for the Church in general or for those in particular who are singled out as 'priding themselves in their great fairness and rigorous exactness', if what has been provided has only a great appearance of the truth, for on his principles he should at least have *evidently demonstrated* his basic foundations. However, it wouldn't take me long, Sir, to show you that is very far even from saying nothing which is not very close to the truth.

Second reflection

Nothing is less true than Malebranche's statement that:

in order to be convinced that there are bodies, we must demonstrate not only that there is a God, and that God is no deceiver, but also that God has assured us that He has really created them; and if we did not have the faith which obliged us to believe that there are bodies, we would not be inescapably led to believe that there are any.

For I maintain, on the contrary, that the very principle that is the foundation of faith, which does not presuppose it but is prior to it, necessarily shows that there are bodies and other beings as well as God and my mind.

This is the principle that one should take as true what could only be taken as false on the pain of allowing in God things wholly contrary to divine nature, such as His being a deceiver, or being subject to other imperfections which the light of nature shows us evidently not to be in God. In holding this principle, neither faith nor particular revelation concerning the existence of bodies is assumed. Hence what evidently follows from the principle, when one adds to it only those things which I can no more doubt than I can my own existence, should be taken as completely demonstrated, and consequently I have reason to take the following arguments as genuine demonstrations.

First argument

There is a certain argument from [the fact of] our speaking for the existence of bodies, if we add to it the principle that God is not a deceiver. For I cannot doubt that I have believed myself to speak ever since I have known myself, i.e. that I joined my thoughts to certain sounds which I believe are formed by the body to which I have supposed I am joined, in order to make them understood to others similar to me whom I supposed to be around me and who, as far as I can tell, are able on their part to show, either by other words which I imagine I hear or by signs I believe I see, that they have understood what I wished to say to them.

Now if I had no body and there were no men other than myself, it would be necessary for God to deceive me on an infinite number of occasions, by forming in my mind directly, by his own agency – and without being able to say that he used the occasion of the motions which occur in my body, for we are assuming that I have none – all the thoughts I have from so many different sounds, as if these were formed in the organs of my body, and by replying to me Himself internally, whenever it is appropriate, so that I could not doubt that it was the people to whom I thought I spoke who were responding, and this would occur not once or twice but on an infinite number of occasions.

Thus, since God is not a deceiver, it must necessarily be the case that I have a body, and that other men similar to me attach their thoughts to sounds just as I do so as to make them known to me.

Second argument
I have learned several languages so that I might understand different people. I am completely certain that I have not invented them; and I have judged these languages quite differently, some appearing to me more beautiful than others, and I believe I know with great certainty that some are newer and some older. And I have noticed that, believing myself to speak to particular people, they understand me properly when I speak in one of these languages, but not when I speak in another.

Now we would have to attribute to God behaviour completely unworthy of Him if only He and my mind existed; for it would be necessary that He be the author of all these different languages, without our being able to conceive of any point in this apart from His wish to amuse Himself and to deceive me, and that, making me believe that I speak now one language and now another, He also wants to make me believe, by mimicking the characters of those to whom I believe I am speaking, that there were some that did not understand and some that did.

I cannot suppose, therefore, without believing unworthy things of God, that there are no men outside me, or that there are no beings other than God and my mind.

Third argument
I believe that I have heard men speaking to me on countless occasions, some of them saying, it seemed to me, good things and others very bad things which would have made me offend God greatly if I had followed the impressions that their words could have given me, for they were such as to lead me to believe that there is no God. Now I am quite sure that these thoughts did not come from me, since I am horrified by them; thus they must have come from God, who has

spoken to me internally instead of these people who I believe were speaking to me externally. Now the idea that I have of a perfect Being does not allow me to attribute to Him a conduct unworthy of His goodness; thus I must treat the supposition that only God and my mind exist as being impossible.

Fourth argument
Still stronger arguments can be had from the art of writing, i.e. forming certain visible characters which can awaken in the mind of those who see them the ideas of their sounds, which have already been taken as signs of thoughts. I am sure I have not invented this art, and when I learned it I imagined that it was from other people similar to me. It would again be necessary that this be done by God, who took the place of all those people by fantasies He put in my mind, as if to amuse Himself with me. Can one think this and not believe that He is a deceiver? But since I have understood that the greatest use of this art is to make oneself understood to people who are absent and who can by the same means reply to what we have written to them – on many occasions only after a long delay, when they are far away – I have used it with this aim on countless occasions, and I have never failed to receive a reply at the time I thought. If both of these, i.e. the letter and the reply, had only been fantasies which God had Himself placed directly in my mind, could there be any doubt that He had taken pleasure in misleading me? Now this would have to be the case if only God and my mind existed. Hence this hypothesis, which contains so many things unworthy of God, should be rejected as impossible.

Fifth argument
I believe that the art of writing has produced countless books, that I myself have read many of them, that they have been on different topics, and that I did not produce these books. There were amongst them different histories, written in several languages, some of which seemed to me true, some doubtful, and some false. I took to be true, at least as far as the main incidents were concerned, those which related things which occurred in their own time, and were seen and known by everyone, or which were related in the same way by several other authors whom one could not reasonably believe to have conspired together in order to lie. I took as doubtful those which were not so well attested, and as false those which were manifestly

contrary to the facts, or which had been constructed only to provide stories, like poems or novels. What could I say about this on the hypothesis that only God and my mind exist? Being quite certain that I have not composed these histories myself, God would have to be their author, and to have impressed them in my mind and my spiritual memory when I imagined I read them in books, and I would no longer know how to assess them. For, being in God, they all become true, even the most false of them, which is a ridiculous contradiction. And the most true would become false, since if only God and my mind exist then nothing they tell us actually occurred in the past. Do we need anything else to show the absurdity of this supposition, when we know God?

Sixth argument

It has been my belief that I read other books on all kinds of subject. Some of these deny the greatest truths, even that of God's existence; others, such as those I thought to be by pagan poets, are full of things completely contrary to decency and modesty. Could I believe without impiety that God produces both these, imprinting them directly in my mind? I would have to believe this if there were only me and God, for I am sure that I haven't produced them.

Seventh argument

The sensations of pain, hunger, and thirst can, if you want, prove nothing concerning the existence of my body, taken alone; but when we consider God along with these, they prove it demonstratively.

When I have believed myself to get too close to a fire, I felt a smarting pain, which I call burning, and which made me draw back from it. And since this pain ceased or lessened considerably as soon as I believed I moved away from the fire, I was led to believe that God had given me this sensation of pain for the conservation of my body, which would have been quite pointless and unworthy of Him if I hadn't had a body. Thus I do have a body.

From time to time I believed I needed to eat and drink, i.e. to take food and drink, which I believed to be bodies, into that body that I believed was united to my mind. And I was informed of this need by a sensation which I call hunger, and by another I call thirst. When these sensations were strong, I felt uncomfortable and I imagined that my heart languished. But after I ate and drank I felt better. Would it not be to accuse God of nothing short of deluding me if He had given me these sensations, with everything that follows, always in the same way on countless occasions during my life, if I did not have a body which needed all of these things?

Eighth argument

The same holds for other sensations. If it had pleased God to give me sensations of light, colours, sounds, odours, cold, and warmth without reference to anything, I would be less surprised, and I am sure He could have done this if I had no body. But why, if He did not wish to deceive me, did He give me sensations of light and colours, and vivid ones at that, only when I believe I open my eyes, if I have no eyes? For if I have no eyes, my imagining that I open my eyes can have no bearing on these sensations of light and colours. Why does He never, or almost never, give me the sensation of a brilliant light which dazzles me except when I believe I am facing the body I call the sun, if that body does not exist? Why, taking great pleasure in hearing harmonious sounds, does He only ever give me this pleasure when I imagine that bodies around me are agitated, and when I imagine that their motion is at least the occasional cause of my experiencing these sounds? If there were no bodies, could it be in God that we would find this invariable rule of accompanying almost all our vivid sensations by the images of those bodies to which I am naturally led to attribute them? And wouldn't He at least have had to have given us some means of avoiding error where it was impossible that this would not throw us into it?

Third reflection

This reflection concerns the objection he tries to forestall in *The Search after Truth*, and which it was easy to foresee. It is that one must be convinced that there are bodies before having faith, since faith presupposes that there are bodies: prophets, apostles, holy Scripture, miracles. He replies to this as follows:

But if you attend closely you will see that, even if one only assumes the appearance of men, prophets, apostles, sacred Scripture, miracles, etc., what we have learned from these supposed appearances is absolutely undeniable; for as I have proved in several places in this work, only God can represent these appearances to the mind, and God is no deceiver, for faith itself assumed all this. Now through the appearance of Sacred Scripture and miracles we learn that God has created a heaven and an earth, that the Word was made flesh, and other such truths which assume the existence of a created world. Thus it is certain through faith that there are bodies, and that by faith all these appearances become realities. [ST, 575]

I don't know whether I am mistaken, Sir, but I don't believe that there has ever been a more vicious circle; for we must decide whether, having assumed that there are no bodies and that only God and my mind exist, I can hold onto this assumption until I have faith and abandon it only through faith. I maintain that this is impossible and that Malebranche's argument does not establish it at all. For as long as I make the assumption, I must believe that only God could have represented to my mind everything good or bad that I have ever read in books which I know I have not written. Hence He must have represented to me what I imagine I read in the Koran just as much as what I believe I read in the book called the Bible. Thus on the hypothesis that there is only me and my mind, if the argument that 'God is no deceiver and only He could have represented to my mind what I imagine I have seen in the Bible, therefore this must be held to be unquestionable' holds good for the Bible, I do not see why it does not also hold good of the Koran. And thus I am sure that I can only resolve this difficulty by using the maxim that God cannot be a deceiver to convince myself of the evident falsity of the supposition that there are no bodies apart from God and my mind, and not to conclude from it that, even before recognising the absurdity of this hypothesis, a few appearances of prophets, apostles, sacred Scriptures and miracles might be enough to get us to put our faith in the Scriptures and thereby change these appearances into realities.

If I could be shown that there is no contradiction in this, I would admit that I am stupid, for I believe I see it clearly.

Fourth reflection

I do not know whether he has noticed that, if the principles he laid down in his *Treatise on Nature and Grace* were true, he would have to retract what he positively asserts in *The Search after Truth* – that before faith I cannot be completely convinced that there is something other than God and my mind – for he did not claim to have taken these principles from divine revelation but from the idea of a perfect Being, and yet I can evidently conclude from that that it is impossible that there should only be me and my mind. Thus if they were true and necessary, as principles should be, we could be certain of the falsity of the supposition without recourse to faith. I shall limit myself to two or three examples.

(1) *If God wishes to act externally, this is because He wishes to obtain a worthy honour for Himself.* On the one hand, I am sure that God wishes to act externally, since I cannot doubt that I am His work: and on the other, I am very conscious of not being able to render Him an honour worthy of Him.

Thus in acting externally He must have in view something other than me, something which can render Him an honour worthy of Him: thus, I cannot believe that only God and my mind exist.

(2) *It is unworthy of the perfect Being to act in the ordinary course of events through particular acts of will: it is more worthy of Him to act as a universal cause, whose acts of will are directed to particular effects by occasional causes.*

Now if I had no body and if my mind were the only creation, then since God would have created me by a particular act of will, He would also create in me thousands and thousands of things by particular acts of will, without occasional causes, above all in everything that seems to me to concern the body that I would not have and other bodies that would not be there either.

Thus it is not true that I have no body and that my mind is the sole creation of God.

(3) *God acts in the simplest ways and according to general laws.* This would not be so if I had no body and He acted only in relation to me. Thus it is not true . . ., etc.

I do not accept these demonstrations because I do not accept that the principles from which they are derived are sufficiently general or necessary to demonstrate a disputable proposition. But I believe the conclusion is derived correctly, and consequently he must recognise either that these maxims are not as he believes them to be, or that he was mistaken in saying that it is only faith that can assure us that there are bodies.

Conclusion

Here, Sir, are the first difficulties I have had with the particular opinions of our friend. They still don't cover those in the *Treatise on Nature and Grace*. But he himself believes that they are closely related, since he asked that one study them before studying those of his *Treatise*, and he refers to them explicitly in the first Chapter of his third Discourse. Hence the best approach I could have taken when dealing with the new views of the latter work, was to begin with *The Search after Truth*.

I found this to be more advantageous both for him and for me. It means I don't have to contrast the two, something which often foists on us very annoying questions of fact, nor do I have to combat it with old rules and principles of a philosophy that he does not accept. More usually, I have only had to oppose his own statements to one another, to ask that he take more care in his thoughts, to warn him, as he does so many others, to take more notice of reason than prejudice, and to make him remember the maxims he has established for properly seeking after truth.

If I have succeeded in this, I do not claim to take the glory, for I cannot say how all this has come into my mind, since I myself have never formed any opinions on the matter until now; so if it is thought that I have thrown some light on it, I would freely acknowledge that it must have been more luck than skill.

But if, on the other hand, I have been mistaken, and have blinded myself when I imagined myself to have discovered blindness in others, it would be right that I should bear the shame. And it seems to me, as far as I can plumb the depths of my heart, that I would not complain, and I would not think ill of it if I were treated as I deserved if I have been unwise enough to speak with so much confidence without being right: for it is a human and pardonable fault to fall innocently into some error which does not have evil consequences. But in any discussion whatever, we will scarcely excuse a man who is not content with attacking what he should accept, but who does it with so much presumption that he undertakes to pass off the aberrations of his mind as true demonstrations.

But I shall say, furthermore, Sir, that if everything I have written on this question of ideas is sound (and I admit to you in good faith that it is impossible for me to believe otherwise so long as I have no enlightenment other than that which I have presently) I would be very glad, if our friend were not persuaded by it and continued to hold the first views he had, that he would defend them as best he can without sparing me, and that he would use whatever words he judges most appropriate to show that he was not wrong; and that it was I who have fought poorly against that beautiful maxim which is so worthy of God: *that we see all things in God*.

Translator's notes

1 The book is addressed to the Marquis de Rouey, as is much of Arnauld's later correspondence on Malebranche.

2 The doctrine of substantial forms derives from Aristotle, and was the most widely ridiculed feature of scholastic natural philosophy in the seventeenth century. The thrust of the doctrine is that physical bodies are comprised of matter and form, the latter providing the body with all its features and qualities. Those features of a body which are essential to it, i.e. constitutive of it, make up its substantial (as opposed to its accidental) form, the medieval paradigm for which was the soul as the substantial form of the human body. Aristotle explicitly opposes the doctrine of substantial forms to the Atomist belief that only matter need be invoked in explaining the properties of physical bodies. Late scholastic natural philosophy – whose most important sources in the seventeenth century were Johannes Magirus' *Physiologia Peripatica* (Frankfurt, 1597) and Scipion du Pleix's *Corps de Philosophie* (Geneva, 1645) – takes over this doctrine, but focuses on the imposition of form on an original propertyless substratum called 'prime matter', an imposition which differentiates the prime matter into four elements (secondary matter). These four elements then do all the explanatory work, and in some respects what results resembles some of the newer corpuscularian philosophies of the seventeenth century.

3 I have translated the expression '*être représentatif*' as 'representation' throughout, and not literally as 'representative being/entity'. It is crucial to Malebranche's theory, and to Arnauld's criticism of this theory, that the *êtres représentatifs* are actual entities distinct both from what they represent and what they represent it to. This is obvious from the context, and in any case the term 'representation' in the British philosophy from the late seventeenth century onwards usually has this connotation.

4 Malebranche's *Conversations chrétiennes* first appeared in 1676 and Erastus is one of its interlocutors.

5 Giovanni Domenico Cassini (1625–1712) was *de facto* director of the Paris Observatory from 1669 onwards. In 1672 he collaborated with

Jean Richer in measuring the distance of Mars from the Earth by the method of parallax. Richer took observations of Mars from Cayenne in French Guiana, and Cassini took observations from Paris. Each noted the position of Mars in the sky at a fixed time. They compared their results, and calculated the parallax against the 'fixed stars'. Knowing this, which gave them the base angles of a triangle, and the distance from Cayenne to Paris, which gave them the length, the distance of Mars could be calculated by elementary trigonometry. They were then able to use Kepler's laws to calculate the distance from Mars to the Sun, and from the Earth to the Sun. They came up with a figure of 140 million kilometres, which stood until 1901, when it was revised upwards to 150 million kilometres.

6   The word Arnauld uses here (and elsewhere in the treatise) is '*machine*' – literally, 'machine'. The idea of the human body as being merely a machine animated by a soul is a radical consequence of Descartes' dualism. How far Arnauld is committed to the 'automaton' account is unclear: he expresses some reservations about the related Cartesian doctrine that animals are mere machines in his Objections to the *Meditations* (CSM II, 144).

7   The reference here is to the late scholastic textbooks that dominated the teaching of natural philosophy in the schools and universities up until the last decades of the seventeenth century. There is a good summary of this obscure literature in P. Reif, 'The textbook tradition in natural philosophy, 1600–1650', *Journal of the History of Ideas* XXX (1969), 17–32.

8   This is perhaps a reference to Simon Foucher, whose *Critique de la Recherche de la Vérité* appeared in 1675. Foucher criticises *The Search after Truth* from a sceptical standpoint and he denies that we can have indubitable grounds for supposing that the mind perceives material things.

9   This is a crucial passage for Malebranche, and he quotes it in full in the Preface to his *Conversations on Metaphysics and Religion*.

10   Plato's theory of ideas was initially developed in the context of moral considerations, as a way of securing moral objectivity by supplying an unchanging idea or Form of 'the good', but it almost immediately became a general epistemological doctrine. In the later dialogues, however, Plato raised a number of difficulties with the general doctrine, and in the first part of the *Parmenides* he effectively denies that there are Forms of individual material things. A second point is worth bearing in mind here. It must always be remembered that, in medieval discussions of Plato, it is some form of Neoplatonism that is being considered, and not necessarily doctrines that we would now ascribe to Plato himself. In the present context, for example, neither Augustine nor Aquinas thinks of Plato's Forms as having a completely independent existence, but rather consider them as existing in the mind of God as archetypes on which He modelled His creation. This is a distinctively Neoplatonist doctrine, although it draws on Plato's account of the demiurge in the *Timeaus*.

11 The stone is objectively in my mind because the idea I have of it represents the stone, but the actual form (i.e essence) of the stone is not there.

12 Arnauld accepts the Cartesian premiss that the extended world is a plenum. In such a world, one region of material extension is distinct from another contiguous region of extension only when it is moving with respect to it. In other words, boundaries of bodies are created by relative motion and have no existence otherwise.

13 There was a lively debate in the second half of the seventeenth century between the advocates of the traditional epigenetic theory of embryonic development, according to which organs are formed out of the indifferent matter making up the eggs from which all living creatures evolve, and advocates of the preformation theory, which Swammerdam did much to establish, according to which embryonic development is to be seen in terms of the growth of previously created parts. Malebranche explicitly advocates the preformation theory. Arnauld does not indicate which he accepts, but the preformation theory was well on the way to becoming the generally accepted account by this time.

14 The significance of this problem is very obscure. The solar cycle is a 28 year cycle (the return of the pattern of successive week-days for a given year), and the lunar cycle is a 19 year cycle (235 lunar synodic months). Both were used in determining the date of Easter from the sixth century onwards. The two cycles did not correspond exactly, however, and a number of writers on calendar reform had sought matches between different cycles plus or minus days or fractions of days in their attempts to calculate the date of Easter, an operation known as *computus*. (For details see W. M. O'Neill, *Time and the Calendars*, Sydney, 1975.) What is obscure is why Arnauld should want to include the cycle of Indication in the calculation. This is a fiscal 15 year cycle, introduced after Diocletian's reconquest of Egypt in AD 297, and beginning on 1 September. It plays no role in calendar reform.

15 Curves can be thought of as being 'generated' from the motion of points. A circle, for example, is generated from a point moving at a fixed distance from a fixed point, a quadratrix is generated by following a fixed point on a circle as it 'rolls over' a straight line, and so on.

16 The *Journal des Savants* was one of the principal scientific journals of the period, and indeed one of the first scientific journals. Arnauld and Malebranche were to reply to one another in the pages of the *Journal* in 1694.

17 Arnauld is accepting here Descartes' doctrine that God must effectively recreate the world at each instant if it is to persist. The doctrine is a consequence of Descartes' extreme interpretation of what a fully mechanical philosophy requires, namely, that there are no active principles or powers residing in nature. He denies, in particular, that a body has any power to conserve itself in existence from instant to instant, and hence God is required to recreate the world (both as regards existence and essence) from instant to instant if it is to persist. The doctrine is not developed in any detail in Descartes, which is just as well as it would cause havoc in other parts of his physical theory. Since there is no motion within the instant, for example, change of position can only be a result of God's having recreated some region of matter (i.e. a body) at a slightly different place at each instant. But this surely presupposes that we can identify bodies prior to what we experience as their motion (which is actually only their discontinuous change of place from instant to instant), whereas Descartes elsewhere denies this: see note 12 above. Arnauld, in accepting both doctrines, gets himself into the same problem. See, however, J. M. Beyssade, *La Philosophie prémière de Descartes* (Paris, 1979) for an argument that the instants are not quite instantaneous.

18   This is a reference to the 1643 experiment of Torricelli, repeated and made famous in 1646 by Pierre Petit and Etienne and Blaise Pascal. The interpretation of the experiment was hotly disputed in the seventeenth century. Arnauld clearly accepts the most obvious (and correct) interpretation: the air has weight and is capable of supporting a column of mercury 76 centimetres high.

19   Géraud de Cordemoy (1620–1684) was a historian and philosopher who developed Cartesian dualism in the direction of occasionalism, and he was in many respects the precursor of Malebranche. He argued, in particular, that motion cannot be part of the essence of matter and must be due to something spiritual, and that there can be no interaction between mind and body. See the account of Cordemoy in A. Balz, *Cartesian Studies* (New York, 1951), Ch. 1.

20   The reference is to Gassendi's *Disquisitio Metaphysica sive Dubitationes et Instantiae* (1644), which contains both Gassendi's original objections to the *Meditations* and his counter-objections to Descartes' replies.

Appendix

A list of subsequent exchanges between Malebranche and Arnauld with a summary of Malebranche's 1684 reply

The debate between Malebranche and Arnauld by no means comes to an end with *On True and False Ideas*. The question of ideas dominated the dispute until 1685, after which time the central question became that of grace, although the origin and nature of ideas still figured occasionally.

Below is a list of the exchanges between Malebranche and Arnauld after the publication of *On True and False Ideas*, together with date and place of first publication. Pierre Bayle gets caught up in the debate at one point, so his defence of Malebranche against Arnauld is included. Malebranche's replies were collected in *Receuil de toutes les réponses du P. Malebranche à M. Arnauld* (4 vols., Paris, 1709). Malebranche's contributions can all be found in volumes 6 to 9 of Robinet's edition (OC), and Arnauld's contributions can all be found in volumes 38 to 40 of the *Oeuvres de Messire Antoine Arnauld* (43 vols., Paris, 1773–83).

Malebranche, *Réponse de l'Auteur de la Recherche de la Vérité au livre de M. Arnauld, Des vraies et de fausses idées* (Rotterdam, 1684).

Arnauld, *Défense de M. Arnauld, docteur de Sorbonne, contre la Réponse au livre Des vraies et des fausses idées* (Cologne, 1684).

Malebranche, *Trois lettres de l'Auteur de la Recherce de la Vérité, touchant la Défense de M. Arnauld, contre la Réponse au livre Des vraies et des fausses idées* (Rotterdam, 1685).

Arnauld, *Neuf lettres de M. Arnauld au Père Malebranche* (Cologne, 1685).

Malebranche, *Quartième et dernier éclaircissement de Traité de la Nature et de la Grâce. Les miracles fréquents de l'ancienne loi ne marquent null-ement que Dieu agisse souvent par des volontés particulières*. Appended to the 1684 edition of the *Traité de la Nature et de la Grâce*.

Arnauld, *Dissertation de M. Arnauld sur la manière dont Dieu a fait les miracles de l'ancienne loi par le ministère de Anges, pour servir de réponse aux nouvelles pensées de l'Auteur du Traité de la Nature et de la Grâce, dans un éclaircissement qui a pour titre: Les miracles fréquents de l'ancienne loi . . .* (Cologne, 1685).

Malebranche, *Réponse à une Dissertation de M. Arnauld contre un éclaircissement du Traité de la Nature et de la Grâce, dans laquelle on établit les principes nécessaires à l'intelligence de ce même traité* (Rotterdam, 1685).

Arnauld, *Quatre lettres de M. Arnauld au P. Malebranche pour servir de réplique à la réponse à la Dissertation sur les miracles de l'ancienne loi* (Cologne, 1685).

Arnauld, *Réflexions philosophiques et théologiques sur le nouveau système de la Nature et de la Grâce. Livre I touchant l'ordre de la Nature* (Cologne, 1685).

Malebranche, *Trois lettres du P. Malebranche à un de ses amis dans lesquelles il répond aux Réflexions philosophiques et théologiques de M. Arnauld touchant le Traité de la Nature et de la Grâce* (Rotterdam, 1686).

Arnauld, *Réflexions philosophiques et théologiques sur le nouveau système de la Nature et de la Grâce. Livre II touchant l'ordre de la Grâce* (Cologne, 1686).

Arnauld, *Réflexions philosophique et théologiques. Livre III touchent Jésus-Christ comme cause occasionnelle* (Cologne, 1686).

Malebranche, *Deux Lettres du P. Malebranche touchant le IIe et le IIIe volume des Réflexions philosophiques et théologiques* (Rotterdam, 1687).

Malebranche, *Quatre lettres du P. Malebranche touchant celles de M. Arnauld* (Rotterdam, 1687).

Arnauld, *Avis à l'Auteur des nouvelles de la Republique des lettres* (Delft, 1685).

Bayle, Pierre, *Réponse de l'Auteur des nouvelles de la République des lettres à l'Avis qui lui a été donné sur ce qu'il a dit en faveur du P. Malebranche touchant les plaisirs des sens* (Rotterdam, 1686).

Arnauld, *Dissertation sur le prétendu bonheur des plaisirs des sens, pour servir de réplique à la Réponse qu'a faite M. Bayle* (Cologne, 1687).

Arnauld, *Première lettre de M. Arnauld, docteur de Sorbonne, au R. P. Malebranche, prêtre de la l'Oratoire (30 avril, 1694)* in *Journal des Savants*, 28 June 1694, 291–9.

Arnauld, *Seconde lettre de M. Arnauld, etc., au R. P. Malebranche, prêtre de l'Oratoire (4 mai, 1694)* in *Journal des Savants*, 4 July 1694, 302–9.

Malebranche, *Premiére lettre du P. Malebranche, prêtre de l'Oratoire, à M. Arnauld, docteur de Sorbonne (1 juillet, 1694)* in *Journal des Savants*, 12 July 1694, 326–36.

Malebranche, *Seconde lettre du P. Malebranche, prêtre de l'Oratoire, à M. Arnauld, docteur de Sorbonne (7 juillet, 1694)* in *Journal des Savants*, 19 July 1694, 326–36.

Arnauld, *Troisième lettre de M. Arnauld au P. Malebranche sur deux de ses plus insoutenables opinions (24 mai, 1694)*. This and the next letter, together with the first two, can be found in the *Recueil de plusieurs lettres de M. Arnauld, docteur de Sorbonne* (Liége, 1698).

Arnauld, *Quartième lettre de M. Arnauld au R. P. Malebranche (25 juillet, 1694)*.

Malebranche, *Réponse du P. Malebranche à la troisième lettre de M. Arnauld, docteur de Sorbonne* (Amsterdam, 1704).

Malebranche, *Contre la prévention* (Amsterdam, 1704).

There is not a great deal to be learned from the long dispute between Arnauld and Malebranche. It was always acrimonious – Malebranche did not hesitate to point to the heretical aspects of Arnauld's Jansenism, even when they were not strictly relevant to the argument, and Arnauld himself was instrumental in getting Malebranche's *Treatise on Nature and Grace* placed in the Index of Prohibited Books at the end of 1689 – and it quickly degenerated into abuse. Malebranche's 1684 *Reply* is worth summarising, however, for it brings out clearly the differences between his view of what the central issues are and what Arnauld takes to be the central issues. Moreover, although it is really little more than a restatement of his position, it does bring to light the crucial distinctions he must make if his position is to be protected from at least some of the criticisms Arnauld makes.

In what follows, I have aimed only to report, in summary form, Malebranche's response to Arnauld. I have, however, tried to put things in a broader perspective where this has seemed to be necessary for an understanding of what is at issue.

The *Reply* is a work of nearly 200 pages, divided into twenty-six chapters, and it must have been completed within four months at the outside. It shows evidence of haste, and Malebranche does not explore any of the issues in more detail, confining himself in the main either to restating his own position or responding directly to Arnauld's objections, or at least those that he sees fit to reply to. The first three chapters summarise his own general position, and tend to play down the role of his theory or ideas. He points out, in Chapter 2, that Arnauld misrepresents him when he claims that we need to understand the doctrine that we see all things in God, as set out in *The Search after Truth*, if we are to understand his *Treatise on Nature and Grace*. In fact, what Malebranche has maintained is that, if we are to understand the latter, there are four doctrines that we must first grasp. These are: his doctrine of original sin, his doctrine of the nature of ideas, his denial of the independent action of second or occasional causes, and his doctrine that God acts in the simplest ways. The two latter doctrines, he tells us, are the really crucial ones. It is of interest to note in this connection that Malebranche does manage to move the issue away from the doctrine of ideas in later exchanges with Arnauld, and it cannot be denied that this is not the most central of Malebranche's doctrines as far as the *Treatise* is concerned, as Arnauld makes out. Malebranche hints in Chapter 3, somewhat mischievously, that the reason why Arnauld steers clear of the other questions, and why he does not take on the *Treatise* itself if he believes it to be so mistaken (something Arnauld will in fact do in 1685), is that his own doctrines, e.g. on grace and predestination, are in fact closer to the heresy of the Pelagianism than to the teachings of the Fathers of the Church.

In Chapter 4, Malebranche sets out his own position in a very general and traditional way: in terms of the relation between God and His creation. Such a broad conception of the issue clearly includes the questions of grace, ideas, causation, and the Divine mode of acting in the world, but it also enables him to make causation and God's mode of acting very much the central questions. Basically, he presents us with three choices: (1) the world is regulated by a blind nature; (2) it is regulated by particular acts of God's will; (3) it is regulated by general acts of God's will. The first, as might be expected, is rejected out of hand as a pagan doctrine, and it is the third that Malebranche undertakes to defend. In his defence, the doctrines that only God can initiate any action and that He always acts by the simplest means play a crucial role. He begins by explaining the difference between God's general acts of will and His particular acts of will. God acts through general manifestations of His will when He acts in accord with general laws which He has established, and through particular manifestations of His will when He acts independently of any such laws. For example, He acts in the former way when He makes me feel pain on my being wounded, since this comes about as a consequence of His establishing the union of mind and body in the way He did; if, on the other hand, He were to make me feel pain without any of the physical or neurological concomitants, which are the second or occasional causes, then He would be acting through a particular manifestation of His will. Again, God acts in the former way when, having determined that the motion and direction of bodies are to be regulated by general laws, He causes bodies to behave in specific ways in impact; and He would act in the latter way were He to initiate motion in a body without that body being affected in any way by any other body or act of will. That He never acts in the latter way (even in the case of miracles) Malebranche then demonstrates from the nature of God. Since God is a Perfect Being, this perfection must be manifested in His attributes, and in turn in His mode of action. To act through general manifestations of His will is the simplest and most fruitful way of acting, whereas acting through particular manifestations of will is a sign of limited intelligence.

Having shown how God must act through general manifestations of His will, Malebranche next proceeds to show how these general acts of will take effect in the world. The overall picture is one where God is the source of all action, which is regulated by His general acts of will, but where this action is channelled in different ways by different occasional causes. It is, for example, a combination of God's action, regulated by His laws and sets of occasional causes, that brings about the evils that befall people, as well as the good that befalls them. If God acted only through particular manifestations of will, we would have to say He intended the evils to occur. But in fact He does not. He is concerned only with Himself when He acts, and His sole aim is to manifest His attributes. Now He provides the soul with all the thoughts it has, and with all its sensations. Whereas Arnauld sees God's behaviour here as manifesting a direct concern for the human being – we see colours for instance so that we can distinguish bodies more easily, and we feel pain so that we can conserve ourselves – Malebranche denies God has any such concern. How could the sensation of pain a man still has a month after he has suffered a wound possibly be of use to him in serving his body, he asks, and he points out that many of the sensations we receive from God – such as dreams – are completely useless to us. God has not, of course, *intended* dreams to be useless, any more than He has intended the pain experienced on the infliction of a wound to be useful. Such questions simply fall outside the interest of a being who acts only for Himself.

In Chapter 5, Malebranche finally turns to the doctrine of ideas, and presents the crux of the difference between Arnauld and himself. Arnauld claims that the modes of the soul are essentially representative of objects whereas Malebranche maintains that these modes are only sensations which represent the soul to itself. The difference arises, Malebranche says, because whereas he assumes that God is our sole source of illumination, Arnauld assumes that man is his own light. It is not explained here what the connection is between the nature of ideas, on the one hand, and the source of intellectual illumination, on the other. But the differences that Malebranche draws attention to are both connected with a deeper contrast, which is surely what he has in mind here. This is the contrast between that traditional Cartesian view of ideas as images of some kind, and Malebranche's conception of ideas as being more like Platonic archetypes: as being divine and existing independently of the mind.

The next chapter is a crucial one, and we are taken through a number of arguments put forward in *The Search after Truth* aimed at establishing the difference between sensation and knowledge. The crux of Malebranche's argument is that sensation is essentially direct and non-representational, whereas knowledge is essentially representational. Some states of mind just involve sensation, some involve just knowledge, and some involve both sensation and knowledge. Malebranche's point is that Arnauld has failed to come to terms with his argument because he has ignored these crucial distinctions. When I sense pain, for example, sensation alone is involved: I do not represent the pain to myself in any way, I am simply aware of it 'by an inner sensation'. It is therefore merely a 'modification of my mind'. My knowledge of geometry and arithmetic, on the other hand, involves nothing but representation, for I cannot grasp abstract numbers and geometrical figures by sensation. Finally, we come to sensible objects. Our grasp of these is both by inner sensation, since we distinguish them by the fact of their colour, and colour, as Arnauld himself points out, is a modification of the soul; but we must also grasp them in a 'pure idea', namely that of extension (or intelligible extension), for when I perceive a physical object such as the sun I perceive something with definite extension. (It is crucial for this last argument that both Arnauld and Malebranche accept a representational account of colour, so that colours are always in the mind and never in the object.)

Malebranche's claim is that representation requires ideas, and that anything we see that requires ideas we see in God. Whereas Arnauld maintains that all our perceptions are 'representative modalities', Malebranche argues that reflection on the different kinds of perception we have shows us that some involve representation and some do not, and that there are, in any case, many things that the soul's modifications cannot represent. Modifications of the soul cannot represent bodies, for example, but only their mode of existence: they can represent the fact that something is round, or coarse, etc., but they cannot represent the thing itself (i.e. as pure extension). But the thing itself *is* represented to us, for I cannot see something circular without seeing the extension of which this circularity is the mode. So something over and above the soul's modifications must be involved.

Now of course Malebranche thinks that what is represented to us in perception exists in God. Arnauld argues that this means that God contains within Himself toads, mosquitoes, gnats, etc., and that this would be demeaning to God. Malebranche replies that God only contains extension within Himself. He has, of course, arranged a part of this extension into the body of a toad, and He knows this is a toad because He knows His own creation. But it is not the coloured, foul-smelling, vile creature that we sense it to be, for colours, smells, etc., exist only for us, not in nature itself and certainly not for God. This is a perfectly good Cartesian response, and one Arnauld cannot legitimately quarrel with.

The main focus of the next two chapters – 7 and 8 – is the Augustinian orthodoxy of Malebranche's position, and here a staunchly anti-Cartesian line is taken up. Malebranche quotes a long passage from *The Search after Truth* (ST, 228–9) where he argues that there are some who want to transfer the intelligible world, which he considers exists in God, into the soul. Arnauld, in wanting to make all perceptions just a modification of the soul, falls into this category. The discussion does not then turn, as one might expect, to the apparently solipsistic position this argument tries to force Arnauld's reasonably orthodox Cartesian view into, but focuses instead on the related issue of what the source of our intellectual illumination is. Arnauld is claiming that he is the sole source of his own intellectual illumination (a distinctive feature of the Cartesian doctrine of method), whereas Malebranche is maintaining the traditional Augustinian view that God is our sole source of intellectual illumination. Malebranche then proceeds to provide support for his position in St Augustine, and in Chapter 8 quotes supporting arguments from his own *Christian Meditations*.

Chapter 9 takes up the claim that we see all things in God, and is principally directed against Arnauld's criticisms of this doctrine in Chapter 19 of *On True and False Ideas*. One thing that Arnauld had maintained there was that 'even if we depended on God for the representations of material things we need for perception, this dependence is not so considerable that we need to make so much fuss about it,' because we are already so completely dependent upon God that He must continually recreate us at each instant if we are to persist through time. Malebranche points out that he himself has only devoted a small part of his book to this question, whereas Arnauld devotes a sizeable portion of his to denying the doctrine, so if anyone is making a fuss it is surely Arnauld. The reply to Arnauld's next objection – that Malebranche's doctrine, far from encouraging spirituality, does more harm than good – is again *ad hominem*. Arnauld himself had maintained that, when a vain woman looks in a mirror, on Malebranche's account what she sees is not her own face but part of an infinite intelligible extension which is contained in God, whereas our soul, although it is created in the image of God, can never see itself in God. Malebranche does not so much deny this as show that Arnauld has similar problems. For when one sees the woman, it is the colour of her face that is visible, and Arnauld himself argues that the colour is not in the face itself but is a modification of the mind of the perceiver. So if Arnauld is to be consistent, he must also maintain that men never see women, but only a coloured expanse, which is a mode of the soul and not something external. Here again, Malebranche uses Arnauld's acceptance of a representational account of colour to try to push him into full representationalism.

Malebranche turns next to a related argument in Chapter 17, where Arnauld presents the following 'formal demonstration':

Major premiss: Strictly speaking, what we see is the immediate object of our mind.

Minor premiss: When we see creatures, the immediate object of our mind is God, who is ultimately united to our soul.

Conclusion: In seeing creatures, it is strictly speaking God that we see and not His creatures.

Malebranche points out that the same argument can be turned on Arnauld himself, if we take as our minor premiss the statement that 'When we see a woman, colour is the immediate object of our mind', for what we see is strictly speaking only colour. Thus the soul would only be able ever to see itself. But Arnauld of course maintains that it sees external objects. As a consequence, he is caught in the same contradiction that he imputes to Malebranche. In fact, Malebranche argues, the crucial difference is that Arnauld wants us to see everything in ourselves, whereas *he* wants us to see everything in God, for the intelligible extension in which we see things is contained in God. Arnauld criticises Malebranche for 'spiritualising' and 'divinising' everything: Malebranche replies that Arnauld wants to humanise everything. The general polemical thrust of the argument is that one must choose between seeing everything in oneself and seeing everything in God – solipsism or a theologically inspired conception of reality. Malebranche is not prepared to allow Arnauld the thesis that we see external objects in an independent external world, and his refusal to allow Arnauld this turns on the latter's advocacy of the theory that colours are merely modifications of the mind, and the idea that when we see an external object the immediate object of our mind is a coloured expanse.

In Chapter 10, Malebranche examines the definitions put forward in Chapter 5 of *On True and False Ideas*, and argues that they are question-begging. In the third definition, for example, Arnauld says he takes 'the *idea* of an object and the *perception* of that object to be the same thing'. But this presupposes that our mind, in knowing external objects, does not need representations distinct from perceptions, which is what he is supposed to be demonstrating on the basis of the definitions. What he needs to show, Malebranche points out, is that one can have a *perception* of an object without having an *idea* of that object, i.e. without also having something over and above a modification of the soul. Moreover, Arnauld says in the same definition that, leaving to one side whether there are other things that one can call ideas, 'it is certain that there are ideas in [Arnauld's] sense, and that they are attributes or modifications of the mind'. But since Malebranche is explictly denying that there are ideas in this sense, Arnauld cannot just say that it is certain that there are, as if this were beyond dispute.

Malebranche considers that the definitions from the fourth onwards are superfluous, since if we accept the first three, everything that Arnauld wants would follow. But in so far as they are contentious (and every one except the fifth is), they simply presuppose what needs to be shown. In the fourth, for example, Arnauld maintains that 'there can be no doubt that the sense in which I say an object is present to the mind, when the mind knows it, is one that cannot be questioned', but this is what he is trying to demonstrate. Similarly, the sixth definition, which Malebranche argues is just a combination of the third and the fourth, again presupposes what needs to be shown, namely that one can have a perception of something without having an idea of it (in Malebranche's sense).

Chapters 11 to 13 are devoted to the five 'demonstrations', which Arnauld presents in Chapters 7 to 11 of *On True and False Ideas*, designed to show that ideas cannot be representations distinct from perceptions. Chapter 11 deals exclusively with the first demonstration, which charges Malebranche with doing what Malebranche has just charged Arnauld with doing, namely taking something as certain, and using it as a first principle, when it is not certain at all. Malebranche agrees that he has claimed that 'everyone agreed that we do not perceive objects which are outside us by themselves', but he declares that he has neither simply taken this over from common sense, nor has he ever used it as a first principle on which to construct his philosophy of ideas, as Arnauld claims. In fact, he points out, if one looks at the chapters immediately preceding those in which he makes this claim, one will see that he does not use the principle at all in arguing against the scholastic theory of international species, for example. As for the remainder of the demonstration, Arnauld simply asserts that in thinking about geometrical objects such as cubes, for instance, I do not represent anything to myself, i.e. I am not conscious of any cognitive act over and above the perception of the cube. But in the absence of an independent argument, this appeal to what we might now term the phenomenology of the situation is unlikely to be conclusive, and Malebranche simply denies Arnauld's claim.

The second demonstration of Arnauld's (Chapter 8 of *On True and False Ideas*) rests on the claim that Malebranche denies that we can ever perceive anything which is at any distance from us. Malebranche categorically denies that he has ever held such a view and he maintains that it would be an obviously ridiculous view. His argument against Arnauld is somewhat disingenuous, however. He might never have explicitly maintained this, but it is clearly suggested by a great deal of what he says. He points out, in support of his denial, that he has explicitly stated in *The Search after Truth* that 'we often perceive things that do not exist, and even ones that have never existed' [ST, 217]. The point seems to be that, far from allowing that we see only those things we are in immediate contact with, we can even see nonexistent things, never mind distant ones. But of course this is to suggest that distant objects are some kind of intermediary case between present objects and nonexistent ones. But they are not. Arnauld's point is precisely that we only see the representations on Malebranche's account because only these are present to our mind; whether what the representations are representations *of* is close, distant or non-existent, is irrelevant. Malebranche is entitled to maintain that he does not invoke representations because of a concern about distant objects, but he cannot argue that, in allowing that we may perceive non-existent objects, he has thereby freed himself from any problems about the perception of distant ones.

In Chapter 13 Malebranche reiterates his argument that the perception of physical objects involve both a confused sensation and a clear idea. If I perceive a marble column, for example, I have a confused sensation of colour and a clear idea of extension. Now it is clear that colour is not essential to the column, and when I conceive the column independently of anything not essential to it I am conceiving it as an intelligible and not a sensible column. This much is reasonably straightforward Cartesianism, but then Malebranche makes a characteristic and most un-Cartesian move: the intelligible extension that I perceive is actually the archetype or idea by which God knows all material objects, and is indeed the archetype or idea on which He has created them. Sensation is quite different: this is a form of 'natural revelation' by which God makes His creation known to us through a combination of general laws (such as those linking mind and body) and occasional causes, and here I can be misled, e.g. into thinking that colours actually inhere in bodies.

In the second part of Chapter 13, Malebranche takes up Arnauld's criticism that he has maintained that the sun I look at and the sun I see are different. He denies this, holding that I see the sun that I look at, but not in itself – I only see it by means of a representation. This reduces the dispute to a semantic issue, whereas Arnauld's criticism surely has more substance.

From Chapter 14 onwards, Malebranche replies chapter by chapter to Arnauld, starting with Chapter 12 of *On True and False Ideas*.

In Chapter 12 of *On True and False Ideas*, Arnauld accuses Malebranche of constantly changing his mind, of saying on some occasions that we see everything in God, and on others that we see neither our own soul nor the souls of others there. Malebranche (Chapter 14) denies this, maintaining that it is clear from context that what we see in God is what we can know in the strict sense, and not what we are aware of only through consciousness or sensation. In the case of material bodies, for example, we see and know the nature or essence of these in an infinite intelligible extension which God contains, but we know of their existence only through consciousness and sensation (and, we should add, through faith). As for the soul, since we can only know this through sensation or consciousness, we cannot see or know it in God. Arnauld's general misunderstanding on these questions, Malebranche argues (Chapter 15), is due at least in part to his failure to distinguish between the fact of our seeing God in His works, and the way in which we see them. Because he does not distinguish the two questions, Arnauld takes the earlier chapters of *The Search after Truth* to be devoted to both of them, whereas they in fact only deal with the first question. The account in the *Elucidations*, on the other hand, which Arnauld thinks contradicts the earlier account, does not deal with the same question but is devoted to explaining *how* we see all things in God.

In Chapter 16 of his *Reply*, Malebranche turns to the doctrine that we see material objects in an infinite intelligible extension, a doctrine which Arnauld has criticised in detail in Chapter 14 of *On True and False Ideas*. Malebranche's reply is short, and in essence turns on the fact that if one understands ideas as Arnauld does, which Malebranche says he has already shown to be mistaken, then the need for an infinite intelligible extension is indeed hard to grasp. But when ideas are understood properly, as archetypes on which God modelled His creation, and when it is understood that what one sees in the infinite intelligible extension contained in God is only the natures or essences of things, and not their existence, then the doctrine shows itself to be a perfectly natural one. Malebranche is certainly right here to stress that the doctrine that we see things in an infinite intelligible extension contained in God is something that depends crucially on our accepting his doctrine of ideas, and that there is little to be gained from discussing it in isolation from the latter. But this is a two-edged sword, for the sheer intuitive implausibility of the intelligible extension theory may drive us to question the doctrine of ideas that gives rise to it, and this is surely part of the thrust of Arnauld's argument.

The next chapter deals with Arnauld's elaborate story of the sculptor who, in asking what St Augustine looked like, is presented with a block of marble and told that the exact shape of the head is contained therein, and that all he has to do is to chisel away the extraneous marble. Malebranche replies that, once again, the objection rests on a misunderstanding. The objection deals with a point about the *origin* of material things, whereas the passage Arnauld is criticising says nothing whatever about origins, but only about the *nature* of material things. The point was not to look at how the mind can know bodies in intelligible extension, but only to show that intelligible extension is fully able to represent bodies.

The central part of Chapter 18 focuses on Malebranche's statement, at the beginning of the *Second Elucidation*, that 'the soul's desire is a natural prayer that never goes ungranted, for it is a law of nature that ideas are all the more present to the mind as the will desires them more fervently' (ST, 559). Arnauld takes this statement quite literally, and maintains that it effectively means that my degree of knowledge of something is directedly proportional to the degree of my desire to know that thing. Malebranche maintains that this is a ridiculous interpretation to place on the statement, and by extensive quotation puts it in context to show how it is quite innocuous.

The next three chapters are directed against chapters 16–20 of *On True and False Ideas*. The central thesis of the first two is the apparent discrepancy in Malebranche's account, between the statement that we see all things in God and the statement that we do not see the soul in God. Both this apparent discrepancy, and the general doctrine that we see all things in God, have been dealt with earlier in the *Reply* and little new is added in these chapters. The theme of Chapter 21 is the doctrine that God is our source of intellectual illumination, and again little is added to what Malebranche has already said earlier in the *Reply*.

Chapter 22 deals with the question of our knowledge of the soul. One of Malebranche's most radical and contentious claims was that we can know extended substances but not our own souls. This was anathema to more orthodox Cartesians, and indeed it strikes right at the heart of Cartesianism, for which it is virtually axiomatic that our soul/mind/self be something which is quite transparent to us, and many crucial epistemological, psychological, moral and other questions hinge on this. Arnauld's response, in Chapter 22 of *On True and False Ideas*, is to argue that, if we accept Malebranche's doctrine that we see the ideas of things in God, then there is as much if not more reason to suppose that we see there the idea of our soul (and the souls of others) as there is to suppose that we see the ideas of external things. He replies by repeating his distinction between the kind of representational knowledge we have of geometrical figures, and the sensation or consciousness which provides us with access to our own soul. The point seems to rest on an appeal to the different phenomenologies of geometrical reflection and self-consciousness, as much as on an appeal to the degree of knowledge that we can attain to in the two cases. As for Arnauld's argument that, if God has willed that extended body be represented to us, then there is no reason why He should not also have represented our soul to us, Malebranche replies that this is just question-begging: his own arguments are designed precisely to show what the reason is. On the question of whether, on his account, the activity of God always 'conforms to order', he slips into an Augustinian mode, saying that we are sinners and that ignorance is the price of sin, so we are not in a position to say that the account of God's activity he has given does not conform to order. But what underlies the difference here is a difference in how God's relation to His creation is conceived: on Malebranche's account, God is completely aloof from His creation, and He is not specifically concerned with human welfare, whereas for Arnauld the qualities of order and uniformity must be manifested in creation in a clear and recognisable way.

Chapter 23 briefly summarises Malebranche's doctrines that we have no clear idea of our soul, that we do have a clear idea of extension, and that our idea of our body is sufficient to show that the soul must be immortal. He does not reply to Arnauld's detailed arguments against the first of these doctrines in Chapters 22–24 of *On True and False Ideas*, saying that they consist of misinterpretations and sophisms which are easy to detect, and he ignores Chapter 25.

Chapter 24 deals with the question of our knowledge of God, and is a direct response to Chapter 26 of *On True and False Ideas*. Malebranche's view is that we do not know God by means of an idea that we have of Him because there is no such idea: there is no archetype on which God has been modelled. Moreover, an idea represents a thing's nature to us and nothing could do that in the case of God except God Himself, if only because He is infinite. Nor could we know God by inner sensation or consciousness, or by conjecture, and the only other way of knowing things is directly. Such direct knowledge is not clear, however, for we only know God in an imperfect and confused way. Arnauld has quite formidable objections to this account. Amongst other things, in knowing things in God our mind must, on Malebranche's construal, be united to certain portions of God, where the archetypes of those things are, but it can never be united to the whole of Him for, if it were, our knowledge of Him would presumably be perfect. But, Arnauld points out, it is impossible to understand how there could be portions of a simple and non-composite God. Malebranche does not satisfactorily address these issues, preferring to repeat what he has said elsewhere.

The *Reply* finishes with replies to Arnauld's objections to the idea that the soul is passive, and to his argument that Malebranche's arguments from faith are circular. The responses are perfunctory, doing little more than reiterating what Malebranche has already said in *The Search after Truth*.

Bibliography

This is a listing of selected secondary works having a bearing on the dispute between Malebranche and Arnauld. For a list of the exchanges themselves, see the Appendix.

Alquié, Ferdinand, *Le Cartésianisme de Malebranche*, Paris, 1974.

Arbini, Ronald, 'Did Descartes have a philosophical theory of sense perception?', *Journal of the History of Philosophy*, 21 (1983), 317–38.

Ayers, Michael, 'Are Locke's "ideas" images, intentional objects, or natural signs?', *Locke Newsletter*, 17 (1986), 3–36.

Balz, Albert G. A., *Cartesian Studies*, New York, 1951.

Bouillier, Francisque, *Histoire de la philosophie Cartésienne*, 2 vols., Paris, 1868.

Bracken, Harry, 'Berkeley and Malebranche on ideas', *The Modern Schoolman*, 41 (1963), 1–15.

Butler P. J. (ed.), *Cartesian Studies*, New York, 1972.

Church, Ralph W., *A Study in the Philosophy of Malebranche*, London, 1931.

Cooke, Monte, 'Arnauld's alleged representationalism', *Journal of the History of Philosophy* 12 (1974), 53–64.

——, 'The alleged ambiguity of "idea" in Descartes' philosophy', *South-Western Journal of Philosophy* 6 (1975), 87–103.

——, 'Descartes' alleged representationalism', *History of Philosophy Quarterly*, 4 (1987), 87–103.

Costa, Michael J., 'What Cartesian ideas are not', *Journal of the History of Ideas* 21 (1983), 537–50.

Cronin, Timothy J., *Objective Being in Descartes and Suarez*, Rome, 1966.

Dalbiez, Roland, 'Les sources scolastiques de la théorie Cartésienne de l'être objectif', *Revue d'histoire de la philosophie* 3 (1929), 464–72.

Dijksterhuis, E. J. (ed.), *Descartes et le Cartésianisme Hollandais*, Paris, 1950.

Doney, Willis (ed.), *Descartes: a Collection of Critical Essays*, London,

1967.

Duhem, Pierre, 'L'optique de Malebranche', *Revue de métaphysique et de morale* 45 (1938), 411–35.

Garin, Pierre, *La Theorie de l'idée suivant l'école thomiste*, 2 vols., Paris, 1932.

Gaukroger, Stephen (ed.), *Descartes: Philosophy, Mathematics and Physics*, Sussex, 1980.

Gouhier, Henri, *La Pensée religieuse de Descartes*, Paris, 1970.

——, *Cartésianisme et Augustinisme aux XVIIe siècle*, Paris, 1978.

Grene, Marjorie, *Descartes*, Sussex, 1985.

Gueroult, Martial, *Descartes' Philosophy Interpreted According to the Order of Reasons*, 2 vols., Minneapolis, 1984.

——. *Malebranche*, 3 vols., Paris, 1955.

Hessen, J., 'Malebranches Verhältnis zu Augustin', *Philosophisches Jahrbuch* 33 (1920), 52–62.

Hooker, Michael (ed.), *Descartes: Critical and Interpretive Essays*, Baltimore, 1978.

Imlay, Robert A., 'Arnauld on Descartes' essence: a misunderstanding', *Studia Leibnitiana* 11 (1979), 134–45.

Kremer, Elmer J., 'Malebranche and Arnauld: The Controversy Over the Nature of Ideas', Ph.D. diss., Yale University, 1961.

Laird, John, 'The legend of Arnauld's realism', *Mind* 33 (1924), 176–9.

Lennon, Thomas M., 'The inherence pattern and Descartes' ideas', *Journal of the History of Ideas* 12 (1974), 43–52.

——, 'Philosophical commentary', in ST, 755–848.

Lennon, Thomas, M.; Nicholas, J. M. and Davis, J. W. (eds.), *Problems of Cartesianism*, Kingston and Montreal, 1982.

Loeb, Louis E., *From Descartes to Hume*, Ithaca, 1981.

Lovejoy, Arthur O., 'Representative ideas in Malebranche and Arnauld', *Mind* 32 (1923), 449–61.

——, 'Reply to Professor Laird', *Mind* 33 (1924), 180–1.

——, *The Revolt Against Dualism*, LaSalle, 1930.

McCracken, Charles, J., *Malebranche and British Philosophy*, Oxford, 1983.

McRae, Robert, ' "Idea" as a philosophical term in the 17th century', *Journal of the History of Ideas* 26 (1965), 175–84.

Moreau, Joseph, 'Le réalisme de Malebranche et la fonction de l'idée', *Revue de métaphysique et de morale*, 56 (1946), 97–141.

Nadler, Steven, *Arnauld and the Cartesian Philosophy of Ideas*, Manchester, 1989.

O'Neil, Brian E., *Epistemological Direct Realism in Descartes' Philosophy*, Albuquerque, 1974.

Popkin, Richard H., *The History of Skepticism from Erasmus to Spinoza*, Berkeley, 1979.

Radner, Daisie, 'Representationalism in Arnauld's act of perception', *Journal of the History of Philosophy* 14 (1976), 96–8.
——, *Malebranche*, Amsterdam, 1978.
Robinet, André, *Système et existence dans l'oeuvre de Malebranche*, Paris, 1965.
Rodis-Lewis, Geneviève, *Nicholas Malebranche*, Paris, 1963.
Rorty, Amelié (ed.), *Essays on Descartes' Meditations*, Berkeley, 1986.
Schulthess, Daniel, 'Antoine Arnauld et Thomas Reid, défenseurs des certitudes perceptives communes et critiques des entités représentatives', *Revue Internationale de Philosophie* 40 (1986), 276–91.
Smith, Norman Kemp, *Studies in the Cartesian Philosophy*, London, 1902.
Tipton, Ian C. (ed.), *Locke on Human Understanding*, Oxford, 1977.
Watson, Richard A., *The Downfall of Cartesianism, 1673–1712*, The Hague, 1966.
Wells, Norman J., 'Material falsity in Descartes, Arnauld, and Suarez', *Journal of the History of Philosophy* 22 (1984), 25–50.
Yolton, John, *Perceptual Acquaintance from Descartes to Reid*, Oxford, 1984.
Zimmerman, C., 'Arnaulds Kritik der Ideenlehre Malebranches', *Philosophisches Jahrbuch* 24 (1911), 3–47.

Index